Preface Books

A series of scholarly a
for those needing mo
characteristic difficultie
standing and enjoyme

General Editor: JOHN
Founding Editor: MAI

A Preface to Wordswo
A Preface to Donne (*F*
A Preface to Jane Aus

A Preface to Lawrence
A Preface to Forster

A Preface to Dickens
A Preface to Shelley

A Preface to Keats
A Preface to Orwell   DAVID WYKES
A Preface to Milton (*Revised edn*)   LOIS POTTER
A Preface to the Brontës   FELICIA GORDON
A Preface to T.S. Eliot   RON TAMPLIN
A Preface to Shakespeare's Tragedies   MICHAEL MANGAN
A Preface to Hopkins (*Second edn*)   GRAHAM STOREY
A Preface to James Joyce (*Second edn*)   SYDNEY BOLT
A Preface to Hardy (*Second edn*)   MERRYN WILLIAMS
A Preface to Conrad (*Second edn*)   CEDRIC WATTS
A Preface to Samuel Johnson   THOMAS
                                WOODMAN
A Preface to Pope (*Second edn*)   I. R. F. GORDON
A Preface to Yeats (*Second edn*)   EDWARD MALINS
                                with JOHN PURKIS
A Preface to Shakespeare's   MICHAEL MANGAN
   Comedies: 1594–1603
A Preface to Ezra Pound   PETER WILSON
A Preface to Greene   CEDRIC WATTS
A Preface to Oscar Wilde   ANNE VARTY

Oscar Wilde in March 1892
Photograph by Ellis and Walery
By permission of the William Andrews Clark
Library UCLA (Ref BX-2N/1)

A Preface to Oscar Wilde

Anne Varty

LONGMAN
LONDON AND NEW YORK

Addison Wesley Longman Limited
Edinburgh Gate
Harlow
Essex CM20 2JE
United Kingdom
and Associated Companies throughout the world

*Published in the United States of America
by Addison Wesley Longman, New York*

First published 1998

ISBN 0 582-23483-2   CSD
ISBN 0 582-23482-4   PPR

British Library Cataloguing-in-Publication Data

A catalogue record for this book is available from the British Library

Library of Congress Cataloging-in-Publication Data

Varty, Anne.
    A preface to Oscar Wilde / Anne Varty.
        p.   cm. — (Preface books)
    Includes bibliographical references and index.
    ISBN 0–582–23483–2. — ISBN 0–582–23482–4 (pbk.)
    1. Wilde, Oscar, 1854–1900—Criticism and interpretation.
    2. Homosexuality and literature—Great Britain—History—19th
century.   I. Title.
    PR5824.V37   1998
    828'.809—dc21   97–27984
                                                              CIP

Set by 35 in 10½/11pt Mono Baskerville
Produced by Longman Singapore Publishers (Pte) Ltd.
Printed in Singapore

Contents

Contents

List of illustrations

Acknowledgements

I am grateful to the Departments of English and Drama at Royal Holloway College for granting me study leave to write this book. John Purkis has given generous help and encouragement throughout the project. Staff at the Bodleian Library, and at Royal Holloway Library, especially David Ward, have been an unfailing support. I am grateful to Merlin Holland for practical help and encouragement. Thanks to Ellie Roper for her keyboard virtuosity, to the production team at Addison Wesley Longman, and to Valerie Mendes for expert editing and advice. Special thanks to Danny and Joseph for tea, inspiration and the occasional distraction.

Anne Varty
Oxford

The publishers are grateful to Merlin Holland for permission to reproduce extracts from the *Letters* including *De Profundis* © Estate of Oscar Wilde 1962, 1979, 1985.

The publishers are also grateful to the following for permission to reproduce photographs or illustrations:

Frontispiece, by permission of the William Andrews Clark Library UCLA; *Front cover of Police News, 1895, Caricature of Wilde, Punch, 1881, Cover design by Charles Ricketts for A House of Pomegranates, 1891, The Dancer's Reward by Aubrey Beardsley in the first English edition of Salome, 1894, Costume sketches for An Ideal Husband reviewed in Queen, 1895,* and *Jack and Miss Prism in The Importance of Being Earnest, St James's Theatre, London, 1909* all by permission of the British Library; *Front Cover of Sale Catalogue, 1895* courtesy of the Bodleian Library: Shelf mark Ross d.216; *Helena in Troas, Hengler's Circus, London, 1886* by permission of the V & A Picture Library; *Oscar Wilde's tomb, Paris,* by permission of Merlin Holland.

Abbreviations

Works, *Complete Works of Oscar Wilde*, introduction by Merlin Holland (London: HarperCollins, 1994).

Letters, *The Letters of Oscar Wilde*, ed. Rupert Hart-Davis (London: Rupert Hart-Davis Ltd., 1963).

More Letters, *More Letters of Oscar Wilde*, ed. Rupert Hart-Davis (London: John Murray, 1985).

Critical Heritage, *Oscar Wilde. The Critical Heritage*, by Karl Beckson (London: Routledge and Kegan Paul, 1970).

Ellmann, *Oscar Wilde*, by Richard Ellmann (London: Hamish Hamilton, 1987).

Mikhail, *Oscar Wilde. Interviews and Recollections*, ed. E. H. Mikhail (London: Macmillan, 1979) 2 vols.

Introduction

Oscar Wilde liked secrets; he especially liked to keep them and to broadcast them at the same time. The first night audience of *Lady Windermere's Fan* was party to a typical display of such latent disclosures, not least of which was the show of green carnation buttonholes, worn by Cecil Graham on stage and by Wilde and his friends in the auditorium. 'And what does it mean?' 'Nothing whatever, but that is just what nobody will guess' (Ellmann, 345). This is sheer mischief, for the green carnation was the badge of homosexuality, but it is made by someone who takes calculated pleasure in exclusiveness and provocation, in self-advertisement, and in complicating the distinction between art and life. Subjected to this off-stage drama, the audience was also being teased by secrets kept and broken on stage.

These two examples of Wilde's use of secrets – the first mischievous and played out in the auditorium, the second aesthetic and a component of the plot on stage – illustrate the pleasure he took in generating an air of 'suspense and curiosity' around both his professional and private lives. Today, retrospective knowledge of Wilde's sexuality colours interpretation of his life and work. Wilde, like Mrs Erlynne in *Lady Windermere's Fan*, had a sexual identity of which the larger part of his contemporary public was unaware. Once revealed, Wilde was punished not just by his two-year prison sentence begun in 1895, but by the subsequent suppression of his work and, with it, his audience. It was not until the 1930s that his plays were regularly revived, or that Wilde could even be discussed in polite circles. This extraordinary reversal of fortunes tells more about social values than it does about either the man or his work, yet the two cannot be divorced. In 1995 Wilde was granted a place in Poet's Corner in Westminster Abbey. Welcomed therefore into the fold of cultural respectability his astonishing literary achievement is now given a measure of national recognition.

The celebrity status Wilde enjoyed at the peak of his career, a century earlier, is summarised by his friend Ada Leverson:

> It is difficult to convey in words the strange popularity, the craze there was at this moment [February 1895] . . . 'To meet Mr. Oscar Wilde' was put on the most exclusive of invitation cards, yet every omnibus conductor knew his latest jokes . . . His greatest pleasure was to amuse the mob, to frighten the burgess and to fascinate the aristocrat.
>
> (Mikhail, II, 268)

And what is the secret of this success? It is absurd even to frame the question, but it is hoped that this book will serve as an invitation to the reader to ponder the imponderable, to consider the sources of Wilde's extraordinary capacity to amuse, frighten and fascinate across a powerfully unified body of work. The achievements for which Wilde is best remembered today were written during a startlingly short five-year period from 1890 to 1895. This study focuses critical attention on the work from this period. But since Wilde's literary endeavours from 1881 contributed significantly to his mature success, work from this earlier period is also represented. During the 1880s Wilde worked as a poet, lecturer, journalist and short-story writer. All these aspects of his production are considered here. His ability to observe issues of the day and to comment obliquely on them – most important elements of his dramaturgical and critical power in the mature comedies – are evident as crafts learned early in his literary development, and during the 1890s he frequently returned to matters both of style and substance which he had treated earlier.

While the story of Wilde's life has sustained both scholarly and speculative investigation, his biography is not a major topic for this book. Students should consult Richard Ellmann's brilliant and compendious *Oscar Wilde* for biographical information, to which reference is made throughout this study. Instead, this 'preface' opens with a skeleton biography of Wilde in tabular form, and goes on to consider four major aspects of his life and afterlife: the two figures in his immediate family, his mother and his wife; the politics of the late-nineteenth century relating to Ireland and homosexuality; and, last, a glance at the legendary Wilde, as our culture has incorporated ghostly versions of the man in the visual arts, literature and film.

Part Two of this book surveys Wilde's philosophy through an analysis of his various non-fictional writings. The third section offers critical interpretations of his major works, arranged chronologically, and concludes with an account of his letters. Finally there is a reference section which both supports the preceding chapters and provides resources for further study.

For Hety and Kenneth

Part One
The Writer and His Setting

Chronology

	WILDE'S LIFE	OTHER EVENTS
1835		Théophile Gautier, *Mademoiselle de Maupin.*
1854	Oscar Wilde born in Dublin on 16 October, christened Oscar Fingal O'Flahertie Wills Wilde. (Elder brother, William, born 26 September 1852.)	
1855	Family move into the exclusive Georgian square, 1 Merrion Square North, Dublin.	
1857		First edition of *Les Fleurs du Mal* by Baudelaire.
1864	Father knighted for services to medicine.	Matthew Arnold (Oxford Professor of Poetry) lectures on 'The Function of Criticism at the Present Time'.
1864–71	Sent to board at Portora Royal School, Enniskillen, north west of Dublin.	
1867	Younger sister, Isola, dies, aged eight.	Zola, *Thérèse Raquin.*
1871–74	Reads Classics at Trinity College, Dublin.	
1873		Walter Pater's first edition of *Studies in the History of the Renaissance.*
1874	Graduates from Trinity College with a First Class	First Impressionist Exhibition in Paris.

3

Degree. Awarded Berkeley Gold Medal for Greek. Moves to England in October to matriculate, with a scholarship, at Oxford University.

Ruskin lectures on Florentine Art in Oxford. He encourages his students, Wilde included, to join him in a road-building project at nearby Ferry Hinksey.

1874–78 Reads 'Greats' (*Literae Humaniores*: Greek and Latin) at Magdalen College, Oxford.

1875 Visits Italy in June with his Dublin professor, J. P. Mahaffy.

1876 Father, Sir William Wilde, dies on 19 April. In July Wilde takes a First Class in Classical Moderations.

1877 Visits Greece with J. P. Mahaffy during March and April, returning to Oxford via Rome. Grosvenor Gallery opens in London: Wilde reviews the first exhibition of new work for the *Dublin University Magazine*.

Whistler sues Ruskin for the abusive review of his paintings exhibited in the Grosvenor Gallery.

1878 Wins the Newdigate Prize for poetry at Oxford University with his poem *Ravenna*. In July, finishes his studies with a First Class degree.

1879 Moves to London.

Punch launches its campaign of Wilde caricatures. Sarah Bernhardt and the Comédie Française perform *Phèdre* in London.

1881	*Poems* published at own expense in June. On 24 December, embarks for a lecture tour of America and Canada.	
1882	Tours America and Canada with a small repertoire of lectures on British aestheticism, sponsored by D'Oyly Carte to publicise Gilbert and Sullivan's comic opera *Patience*. Embarks for England on 27 December.	Married Woman's Property Act.
1883	Sets out for Paris in late January. Settles there for three months. Returns to London and, after visiting New York in August for the unsuccessful première of his play *Vera*, begins a lecture tour of Britain. Sells his blank verse tragedy, *The Duchess of Padua*, to the American actress, Mary Anderson.	
1884	Marries Constance Lloyd on 29 May in St James's Church, Sussex Gardens, London. Honeymoon in Paris and Dieppe. Returning to London, begins a six-year stint as a book reviewer for a variety of British journals.	*A Rebours*, by J.-K. Huysmans, published in Paris. E. W. Godwin and Lady Archibald Campbell collaborate to form 'The Pastoral Players' who produce *As You Like It* in Coombe Park, Surrey.
1885	Moves with Constance to 16 Tite Street, Chelsea. On 5 June their first son, Cyril, is born.	The German Duke of Saxe Meiningen brings his company to London to perform *Julius Caesar*. Whistler delivers his

'Ten O'Clock Lecture'. Pater publishes *Marius the Epicurean*. The Criminal Law Amendment Act passed: it prohibits 'gross indecency' between consenting males and sets out the terms under which Wilde will serve the maximum sentence.

1886	Wilde meets Robert Ross, said to have introduced him to the practice of homosexuality. On 3 November Wilde's second son, Vyvyan, is born.	Liberal Prime Minister Gladstone's first Home Rule Bill for Ireland is defeated in the House of Commons.
1887–89	Edits *Woman's World.*	
1888	*The Happy Prince and Other Tales* is published in May.	
1889	'The Portrait of Mr W. H.' is published in *Blackwood's Magazine* in July.	Maurice Maeterlinck's first play, *La Princesse Maleine*, published in Brussels.
1890	*The Picture of Dorian Gray* published in the American journal *Lippincott's Monthly Magazine* in June.	George Bernard Shaw lectures on 'The Quintessence of Ibsenism' at the Fabian Society.
1891	In June, introduced to Lord Alfred Douglas (1870–1945), youngest son of the Marquess of Queensberry. In January, second play, *The Duchess of Padua*, is produced unsuccessfully in New York as *Guido Ferranti*. Publications: 'The Soul of Man Under Socialism',	John Stuart Parnell, Irish political leader and advocate of Home Rule for Ireland, falls from public life through involvement in divorce proceedings. First English production of Ibsen's *Hedda Gabler* with Elizabeth Robins in the title role.

The Fortnightly Review, February; *The Picture of Dorian Gray*, in London, April; *Intentions*, May; *Lord Arthur Savile's Crime and Other Stories*, July; *A House of Pomegranates*, November. Wilde spends November and December in Paris, writing *Salome*.

1892   Lord Alfred Douglas and Wilde become lovers. In February, *Lady Windermere's Fan* produced in London by George Alexander at the St James's Theatre. In June, *Salome* banned by the Lord Chamberlain from a London production starring Sarah Bernhardt.

1893   The original French text of *Salome* published in Paris. In April, *A Woman of No Importance* is produced by Beerbohm Tree at the Haymarket Theatre, London. *Lady Windermere's Fan* published in November.

Gladstone's second Home Rule Bill is defeated by the House of Lords.

1894   *Salome*, translated into English by Lord Alfred Douglas and illustrated by Aubrey Beardsley, published in February. Wilde spends May in Florence with Douglas. Publications: *The Sphinx*, illustrated by Charles Ricketts, June; 'Poems in

Shaw's second play, *Mrs Warren's Profession*, published.

Prose' (five fables), *The
Fortnightly Review*, July; *A
Woman of No Importance*,
October; 'A Few Maxims
for the Instruction of the
Over-Educated', *Saturday
Review*, November;
'Phrases and Philosophies
for the Use of the
Young', *The Chameleon*,
December.

1895   *An Ideal Husband*,
produced by Lewis
Waller, opens in January
at the Haymarket
Theatre, London. In
February, *The Importance
of Being Earnest* opens at
the St James's Theatre,
London, produced by
George Alexander. After
visiting Algiers with
Douglas during January
and February, accused
of sodomy by the
Marquess of
Queensberry. Wilde
charges him with
criminal libel. On
3 April, the first of the
three trials in which
Wilde is involved opens
at the Old Bailey. The
Marquess of
Queensberry is acquitted
on 5 April. Wilde
immediately arrested for
'acts of gross indecency
with other male persons'.
Imprisoned in Holloway
6–26 April, awaiting
trial. Found guilty on 25
May. Judge Edward
Carson sentences Wilde

English translation of
Degeneration by Max
Nordau.

to imprisonment with two years hard labour. Constance withdraws divorce suit in October, but changes her name to Holland. In November Wilde declared bankrupt.

1896   His mother, Lady Wilde, dies 3 February. *Salome* produced by Lugné-Poë at the Theatre de l'Œuvre, Paris, in February.

1897   From January to March composes a long confessional and philosophical letter to Douglas, later known as 'De Profundis'. Released 19 May and immediately leaves Britain for the Continent, settling first at Berneval near Dieppe and later reuniting with Douglas in Italy. Adopts the pseudonym 'Sebastian Melmoth'. Publishes a letter in *The Daily Chronicle* about cruelty to children in British prisons.

1898   Moves to Paris. *The Ballad of Reading Gaol* published. A second letter of complaint about British prison conditions published in *The Daily Chronicle*. Constance dies in April and is buried in Genoa. Refused access to his two sons.

1899	*The Importance of Being Earnest* and *An Ideal Husband* published. Travels in France, Switzerland and Italy.
1900	Visits Rome. Returns to Paris, falls seriously ill in October. In last stages of illness baptised into the Roman Catholic Church. Dies 30 November in the Hotel d'Alsace, Paris. Requiem mass said for him at St Germain-des-Prés. Buried at Bagneux, 3 December.
1905	Robert Ross, literary executor, publishes extracts of 1897 letter to Douglas under the title 'De Profundis'. Richard Strauss composes the operatic setting for the French text of *Salome*. Sales of Wilde's work on the Continent, particularly in German translation, put his estate back into credit.
1908	Collected Edition of Wilde's work, edited by Ross.
1909	Wilde's remains are moved from Bagneux to Père Lachaise when the monument by Jacob Epstein is erected to mark the grave.
1962	Publication of *The Letters of Oscar Wilde*, edited by Rupert Hart-Davis,

including the first
complete uncensored
printing of
'De Profundis'.

1995   Memorial to Wilde
unveiled in Westminster
Abbey. A simple plate
'Oscar Wilde 1854–
1900' placed in the
window newly designed
by Graham Jones.

1 Biographical and historical context

Family life: Lady Wilde and Mrs Oscar Wilde

In Wilde's private life no woman was more honoured than his mother, 'La Madre Devotissima', and none was more betrayed than his wife, Constance. Oscillating between the poles of filial duty and adulterous neglect, Wilde's sexuality, from about 1886 (after two years of marriage), made orthodox family life an impossibility. Set, therefore, at a distance from the institution which had nurtured him as a child and which, at least as the publicly married and doting father of two sons, he continued to uphold, Wilde cultivated an intellectual notion of the ideal family. His most radical critique of the family is given in 'The Soul of Man Under Socialism', while the social comedies suggest that degrees of orthodoxy are appropriate according to the politics (radical or reactionary) of the partners involved. One of his earliest, and most conservative, pictures of the ideal family provides him with a model for the government of the State. Arguing for the involvement of women in politics, in an editorial for the *Woman's World*, he suggests:

> If something is right in a family, it is difficult to see why it is therefore, without any further reason, wrong in the State. If the participation of women in politics means that as a good family educates all its members so must a good State, what better issue could there be? The family ideal of the State may be difficult of attainment, but as an ideal it is better than the policeman theory. It would mean the moralisation of politics. The cultivation of separate sorts of virtues and separate ideals of duty in men and women has led to the whole social fabric being weaker and unhealthier than it need be.
>
> (*Woman's World*, May 1889)

A rejection of the 'policeman theory' of the State would turn out to be one of Wilde's greatest challenges to his contemporaries, but here, in 1889, it stands as a mildly voiced prelude to the creative fertility of the coming six years. His sense that a good family 'educates all its members', irrespective of sex, came from personal experience. Both his mother and his wife were educated (though not formally), and were unusually articulate. But it is his mother's voice which is heard loudest and longest among those of Wilde's women.

13

Lady Wilde

Jane Francesca Elgee was born on 27 December 1821 into a family of Conservative Protestants, recently moved from Wexford to Dublin. She was educated at home, and despite the potential political shelter of that environment, she became an ardent Irish Nationalist during the 1840s. Under the pseudonym 'Speranza' she began to contribute impassioning verse to the republican journal *Nation*, signing her first covering letter 'John Fanshaw Ellis'. She became a celebrated poet of the revolutionary 'Young Irelanders' in 1848. She married the distinguished doctor William Wilde in 1851, gave birth to her first son, William, in 1852 and to Oscar in 1854, by which time she had also published four prose translations from French and German. She continued to be a favourite of the nationalist movement, so that her first collection of *Poems* (1864) went to a second edition in 1871, a reissue in 1883, and a third, posthumous, edition in 1907. After the death of her husband in 1876 she turned to journalism to supplement her income (though not meagre, it never met her demands), and published five collections of essays between 1884 and 1893.

When her husband was knighted for his contributions to medicine in 1864 'Speranza' became Lady Wilde, and nothing could have better suited her flamboyance and grand social bearing. In 1870 she formalised the conviviality of their Georgian home in Merrion Square by founding the first Dublin *salon*. Her invitation cards read 'At Home, Saturday, 4pm to 7pm. *Conversazione*',[1] a practice she maintained until 1892 after moving to London in 1879. As a player in Society, hostess or guest, Lady Wilde is often remembered on the pages of memoirs written by fellow guests. The snapshot provided by the novelist, Marie Corelli, illustrates her extraordinary poise on such occasions: 'Lady Wilde was . . . in a train dress of silver grey satin, with a hat as large as a small parasol and long streamers of silver grey tulle all floating about her! She did look eccentric'.[2] But there was far more than cultivated eccentricity to Lady Wilde. Her own exercises in journalism portray the serious mind beneath the extraordinary appearance. Her rigorously worded response to the Married Woman's Property Act in 1882 illustrates this:

> Women have been so long politically non-existent that they almost tremble to assert they have any rights apart from their husbands. They require much training in habits of self-assertion and self-reliance, and full knowledge of their newly acquired legal rights, in order that they may become worthy of the nobler life of freedom . . . which they are destined henceforth to occupy and adorn.[3]

This kind of reasoned prose contrasts with the vigorous passion of her verse illustrated here by 'Attendite Popule':

> Oh! That I stood upon some lofty tower,
> Before the gathered people, face to face,
> That like God's Thunder, might my words of power
> Roll down the cry of Freedom to its base!
> Oh! that my voice, a storm above all storms,
> Could cleave earth, air, and ocean, rend the sky
> With the fierce earthquake shout: 'To arms! to arms!
> For Truth, Fame, Freedom, Vengeance, Victory!'[4]

A woman with a huge range of expression, politically ardent, socially knowing, compassionate and playful (Wilde once announced that she had founded a society for the suppression of virtue), she provided much inspiration and example for her son, Oscar. He gave her financial support in her old age, and he published two of her pieces in the *Woman's World* in 1888, a poem 'Historic Irish Women' in January, and an article, 'Irish Peasant Tales' in November, while her indirect appearances in his society comedies are manifold. She, in turn, was a devoted mother, proud of her son's manifold achievements. Like many Victorians, she kept a scrapbook of newspaper cuttings, but hers was filled exclusively with articles by and about the members of her immediate family. Lady Wilde died while Oscar was in prison, on 3 February 1896. The day before Constance visited to inform him of his bereavement he later claimed that his mother had appeared in his cell, dressed for walking, and would not stay.

Mrs Oscar Wilde

Wilde's last experience of his mother may have been of an apparition, but in life this became a characteristic more typical of his wife who remains even today a shadowy and enigmatic figure. A somewhat overstated article by Lady Wilde on 'Genius and Marriage' sounds an ironic caution to her daughter-in-law:

> The daughters of men who wed with the sons of the gods should have courage to face the lightnings and the thunders, if they dare to stand on the mountain heights with an immortal husband. For such a man, and to insure his happiness, a woman should be ready to give her life with sublime self-immolation. At once an angel and a victim, sensitive to every chord of his nature, yet with a smile for ever on the lip, no matter what anxieties may corrode the heart.[5]

Too late to sound a warning for Constance Wilde who, after only five years of marriage, endured increasing absences of her husband with precisely the poise Lady Wilde recommends. A rare glimpse of Mrs Oscar Wilde waiting for her husband is recorded by the actress Elizabeth Robins who called unexpectedly on Wilde to deliver a manuscript she wanted him to read:

> Mr Wilde was not at home. But Mrs Wilde was – in white muslin with a blue sash round her waist, insisting that I should come in. She was like a grave, beautiful school girl, dressed for an Occasion, ready to welcome distraction till the party should begin. It was one of those bitter days that I thought only the vaunted English spring can provide. In my outdoor wraps I sat in the fireless drawing room and shivered, while Mrs Wilde . . . told me that if I had brought something for her husband, she would see that it was given to him . . . She apologized for having no fire. 'We never have a fire after 1st May', she said. Perhaps I had stared at her midsummer frock. 'My husband likes me to wear white', she said gravely . . . 'How long did she imagine he would be?' She couldn't be sure. 'He *is* in London, I suppose?' No. I opened my eyes. She thought he was in Paris . . . and there she sat in white muslin, without a fire, waiting . . . I left my manuscript behind.[6]

The juxtaposition is bleak between this and Wilde's complaint, during his bachelor days, about the false terms of aesthetic judgement. 'At present the newspapers are trying hard to influence the public to judge a sculptor, for instance, never by his statues but by the way he treats his wife.'[7] Yet he was not above playing to the same gallery. A century on, and Constance Wilde – as she became on 29 May 1884 (Constance Holland in October 1895) – seems to play a costumed but largely silent role. We see her posed in a variety of extraordinary dresses, a living sculpture, a model partner, extravagant or reformist, but always an accessory to Wilde's heterosexual identity.

The show begins when the couple were married at St James's Church in London. The *New York Times* describes the wedding gown which Wilde is said to have designed himself:

> The dress was made from 'rich creamy satin' with 'a delicate cowslip tint; the bodice, cut square and somewhat low in front, was finished with a high Medici collar; the ample sleeves were puffed; the skirt, made plain, was gathered by a silver girdle of beautiful workmanship, the gift of Mr Oscar Wilde; the veil of

saffron-coloured Indian gauze was embroidered with pearls and worn in Marie Stuart fashion; a thick wreath of myrtle leaves, through which gleamed a few white blossoms, crowned her fair frizzed hair; the dress was ornamented with clusters of myrtle leaves; the large bouquet had as much green in it as white.'

(Ellmann, 235)

From this description one might assume that Wilde was actually marrying a dress. The woman's identity is subsumed by her costume, and by the role she performs in it. It was an identity that would cling to 'Mrs Oscar Wilde' whether she was acting in a play or in exile on the Continent. And it seems that it was not just the gossip columnists who transfigured Constance in this way. Wilde himself, according to Frank Harris, had made the same mistake. 'When I married, my wife was a beautiful girl, white and slim as a lily, with dancing eyes and gay rippling laughter. In a year or so the flowerlike grace had all vanished; she became heavy, shapeless, deformed . . .' (Ellmann, 250). Acceptable as long as her sexual identity was unconfirmed, this 'girl' is aestheticised according to *fin de siècle* convention, a 'lily', with 'dancing' eyes and 'rippling' laughter, nothing more than a diverting ornament. Once pregnant, the formerly unsexed object admonishes the beholder with unequivocal life, and is perceived as profoundly unattractive.

Four months pregnant with their second son, Constance, at her husband's behest, took to the stage in the role of handmaiden to Helena, in a Greek revivalist play by John Todhunter, designed and directed by William Godwin. *Helena in Troas* was performed in Hengler's Circus (then Argyll Street, now Great Pulteney Street) in May 1886, and again the press turned attention to the way Mrs Wilde was dressed: '[Helen's] two handmaidens (Mrs Oscar Wilde) in sea-green woollen chiton, edged with gold, her hair gathered in a knot, filletted with sea-green ribbon; and (Miss Hare), in white, were graceful attendant figures'.[8] While the chitons worn here by the choric figures were motivated by attempts at historical accuracy by the design of the play, it was also a garment championed by the Rational Dress movement of the period as more comfortable than the heavy constrictions of corset and tailored suit – and Constance Wilde was coincidentally modelling it on stage as maternity wear.

Constance Wilde campaigned for the Rational Dress movement in Britain, which sought to liberate women from more than their corsets by promoting issues of health and mobility in relation to dress codes. The title of her lecture to the Rational Dress Society on 6 November 1888 was 'Clothed In Our Right Minds'; she also edited the first eight issues of the Society's *Gazette* from 1888 to

17

1889. Her husband added his voice to the debate from time to time, but he was as eloquent on the subject of dress for men as for women. In the *Woman's World* for November 1887 – the month in which Wilde began to edit the journal – he wrote an editorial attacking slavish adherence to fashion, and justifying the relegation of the now shortened fashion pages to the back of the journal:

> And, after all, what is fashion? From the artistic point of view, it is usually a form of ugliness so intolerable that we have to alter it every six months. From the point of view of science, it not infrequently violates every law of health, every principle of hygiene.

This attitude contrasts with the superior tone of a notice about the Rational Dress Movement carried by the same journal (but called *Lady's World*) in February 1887, before Wilde took office:

> In the opinion of the majority of Englishwomen, Fashion is a ruler whose laws may not be disobeyed or even disregarded with impunity . . . dress reformers . . . have a weary task to perform, and they may look forward to a long period of crying in the wilderness.

This 'majority' would find itself at the receiving end of much of Wilde's satire, but for the next two years his approach was gentle, and he was content for 'Mrs Oscar Wilde' to contribute to the cause with two articles on fashion for the *Woman's World*. In July 1888 she published 'Children's Dress this Century' and in February 1889 she wrote about 'Muffs', an historical survey of their use which turns to the 'rational' movement in the closing paragraph.

Whatever the politics of her appearances as Mrs Oscar Wilde, they were always notable. Marie Belloc Lowndes (sister of Hilaire Belloc) remembers:

> when she accompanied her husband to functions such as private views . . . she would appear in what were regarded as very peculiar and eccentric clothes. She did this to please Oscar not herself . . . I recall seeing her at a private view at the Grosvenor Galleries when she wore a green and black costume reminiscent of an eighteenth-century highwayman. It made a considerable sensation, and instead of looking at the pictures on the walls, a great many people were asking each other if they had seen Mrs Oscar Wilde.[9]

It seems that the political activities of Mrs Oscar Wilde simply added a tang of the radical to a thoroughly picturesque marriage. Constance was not just active in the Rational Dress movement, but also in the Women's Liberal Association, founded in 1886. She was a speaker in this movement which opposed Gladstone in 1892 by supporting the campaign for women's suffrage. In 1888 she was actively campaigning for her friend Lady Margaret Sandhurst to be elected as the Liberal candidate (termed 'Progressive' in local politics) for Brixton to the London County Council. Lady Sandhurst was successfully elected, but failed to take her seat because of her sex. The only representative of the Women's Liberal Association in Wilde's fiction is Lady Chiltern in *An Ideal Husband* (1895), a role model who attracted only the distaste of the theatre critics of the day: 'stupidly good'; 'rather trying'; 'abnormally moral' and 'unwomanly' in her condemnation of her husband.[10] The text itself links feminist politics with dress, and *Queen* declared that the character was a 'paragon of correct principles [who] nevertheless dresses enchantingly'.[11] The moral thrust of the play is to temper her puritanism, and her public activism is portrayed as sadly disjointed from her private life. Returning from a Women's Liberal Association meeting wearing a white satin walking dress, it seems that Lady Chiltern's role in public life provides her merely with a decorative diversion in her leisure hours.

Was Wilde simply ruthless, using Constance as his passport to money and respectable society, a constant alibi? He certainly contemplates such a role in his drama, explicitly in *Lady Windermere's Fan*: 'I might serve as a blind to whatever relations exist between you and him,' says Lady Windermere to Mrs Erlynne; or 'You would have to be to him the mask of his real life, the cloak to hide his secret,' Darlington warns Lady Windermere (Works, 445, 438), and implicitly in the *alter ego* disguises established by *The Importance of Being Earnest*. The view of the street balladeers after Wilde's condemnation in 1895 was unequivocal:

> You've been 'An Ideal Husband,' in your
> tin pot way no doubt,
> Though 'A Woman of No Importance,'
> was your wife, when you were out,
> At least that's what the papers say, of
> course they can't be wrong;[12]

Preparing to leave prison in April 1897, Wilde wrote to Robert Ross about his attitude to his divorce from Constance.

> Whether I am married or not is a matter that does not concern me. For years I disregarded the tie. But I really think that it is very hard on my wife to be tied to me. I always thought so. And,

19

though it may surprise some of my friends, I am really very fond of my wife and very sorry for her . . . She could not understand me, and I was bored to death with the married life.

(Letters, 516)

Lord Alfred Douglas' comment in 1940 was typically fatuous: 'Honesty compels me to say that Oscar during the time I knew him was not always very kind to his wife'.[13]

The situation of the Wildes' marriage represents a broader set of social problems. The undoubted painfulness of Constance's life, and Wilde's periodic insensitivity to it, bluntly illustrate the appalling double-bind of Victorian mores on necessarily dysfunctional marriages. Whether this alone calls Wilde's 'feminism' into question is a moot point. Yet it suggests that his articulation of social inequities suffered by women are more obliquely linked to the restrictions placed on his own sexual and social freedoms than with an uncomplicated concern for women's rights. Mrs Oscar Wilde, tricked out to play a number of roles for the public while enduring private distress, was neither more nor less compromised than was her husband. Her parts in his costume drama invite critical attention to the strategies of subterfuge in Wilde's plays, where female characters can be seen to act out the dilemmas of male homosexual accommodation with a heterosexual establishment.

The last time the couple saw each other was in February 1896 when Constance brought the news of his mother's death to Reading Gaol. Constance died, 40 years old, on 7 April 1898. Wilde visited her grave in Genoa in 1899. In later years, when it was easy to be wise with hindsight, W. B. Yeats recorded his impressions of Wilde's family life from his first visit to their home on Christmas Day 1888: 'I remember thinking that the perfect harmony of his life there, with his beautiful wife and his two young children, suggested some deliberate artistic composition.'[14]

In terms of sexual politics, a profoundly ironic postscript to Wilde's sentencing for homosexual practice was the concluding response voiced by the *Chronicle* (6 April 1895):

The unspeakable disclosures of the last few days will convert many an enemy of the woman's plea for social equality, for an opportunity of taking her place in the modern State as the helper, the fellow-worker, and the friend of man.

Faced with two evils – male homosexuality and female emancipation – conservative opinion hopes, vainly and illogically, that promotion of the latter will contain the former. This can hardly have been a motivating factor for Wilde's sense of the injustice of 'having one law for men and another for women'. The social roles which Wilde saw both his mother and his wife adopt anticipate the number of startling, innovatory female roles he created in his plays, while they also show the elements of social inflexibility or rigorous propriety which he ridiculed in figures such as Lady Hunstanton or Lady Bracknell.

Ireland

> They may laugh till they're ill, but the fact remains still,
> A fact I've proclaimed since a child.
> That it's taken, my dears, nearly two thousand years
> To make neighbour O'Flaherty's child![15]

> I am not English. I am Irish which is quite another thing.
> (Wilde, *Pall Mall Budget*, 30 June 1892)

Born into a famous Dublin family in 1854, educated at Portora Royal School and then at Trinity College Dublin, before leaving Ireland for good in 1874, Wilde's Irish colours were asserted at key moments in the changing fortunes of his homeland, and his own life, while the inflexions of the language stayed with him to the end of his career. Correcting the proofs of *A Woman of No Importance* in 1894 he asked that the publisher's reader 'go through the play once and correct any slips in the use of "will" and "shall" – my use of the words is Celtic not Saxon' (More Letters, 124). His father's passion for Ireland's past, and his mother's campaigns for the future of a nation (which did not come to fruition until 1922 when Ireland gained independence from colonial rule of Great Britain), assured a political awareness for Oscar Fingal O'Flahertie Wills Wilde from birth. Christened after an ancient Irish hero, Wilde had a book of revolutionary poems dedicated jointly to himself and his brother by the time he was ten years old. 'I made them indeed, speak plain the word Country. I taught them, no doubt, that a country's a thing man should die for at need!', 'Speranza' wrote on the title page of her *Poems* in 1864.

Wilde's espousal of the Irish cause was not just inherited but actively cultivated in adult life. In London it made him an outsider, and technically homeless (since the campaign for Irish Home Rule was then, as now, a matter of contentious debate and electioneering). His eventual exile on the Continent during the last three years of his life, when he adopted the name Sebastian Melmoth after the hero of an Irish novel *Melmoth the Wanderer*, seemed to confirm his own and his country's fate. 'I am a wanderer by nature,' he had told *The Atlantic Constitution* on 5 July 1882. But Wilde was never sentimental about Home Rule politics, nor about the oblique view of Anglo-Saxon life which his perspective from the colonies gave him. He also saw his self-imposed exile from his native land as a deliberate choice about where to concentrate his effort, as he explained to an interviewer for the San Francisco *Daily Examiner*:

> I live in London for its artistic life and opportunities . . . There is no lack of culture in Ireland, but it is nearly all absorbed in politics. Had I remained there my career would have been a political one.
>
> (27 March 1882)

In America Wilde was welcomed by the Irish immigrant population, swollen since the potato famines. He was invited to the St Patrick's Day Celebrations at St Paul's, where he then chanced to be. The local paper, one *Daily Globe*, reported the speech he gave on the occasion:

> The generous response you have given to the mention of the efforts of my mother in Ireland's cause has filled me with pleasure and a pride that I cannot properly acknowledge . . . There was a time, before the time of Henry the Second, when Ireland stood at the front of all the nations of Europe in the arts, the sciences, and general intellectuality . . . But with the coming of the English, art in Ireland came to an end, and it has had no existence for over seven hundred years. And he was glad it had not, for Art could not flourish under a tyrant.
>
> (18 March 1882)

The article concluded with the announcement, 'Mr. Wilde declared himself a Home Ruler'.

This was not just a pose which Wilde adopted on foreign shores. Back in London he made no disguise of his allegiance. Working as a journalist reviewer, he was quick to admonish any publication which came his way that seemed to trivialise the Irish cause. This included a hostile review of *Greek Life and Thought: From the Age of Alexander to the Roman Conquest* by Mr Mahaffy, his former tutor at Trinity College Dublin, with whom he had travelled to Italy and Greece in 1877.

> Mr Mahaffy's new book will be a great disappointment to everybody except the Paper-Unionists and the members of the Primrose

League . . . How can there be anything more depressing than Mr Mahaffy's continual efforts to degrade history to the level of the ordinary political pamphlet of contemporary party warfare? There is . . . no reason why Mr Mahaffy should be called upon to express any sympathy with the aspirations of the old Greek critics for freedom and autonomy . . . But in his attempts to treat the Hellenic world as 'Tipperary writ large,' to use Alexander the Great as a means of whitewashing Lord Salisbury, and to finish the battle of Chaeronea on the plains of Mitchelstown, Mr Mahaffy shows an amount of political bias and literary blindness that is quite extraordinary.

(Pall Mall Budget, 17 November 1887)

Mahaffy had assaulted two worlds which Wilde cherished: Ancient Greece and Modern Ireland. After pointing out scholarly defects of the work, ridiculing Mahaffy's efforts to draw contemporary parallels, the review ends with a personal attack on the man who was once a friend and teacher. Wilde declares that there is something 'if not parochial, at least provincial' about the author's 'passion for imperialism', and that Mahaffy has added nothing to 'his reputation . . . as a historian, a critic, or a man of taste'. Behind Mahaffy's apparently localised suspicions of autonomy and democracy lurked offensives against large principles which Wilde consistently held to: those of freedom and individualism.

On 18 April 1889 Wilde again used his review column in the *Pall Mall Budget* to defend his country. The distinguished historian J. A. Froude (Professor of Modern History at Oxford University) had been rash enough to offer the public an historical romance set in eighteenth-century Ireland, called *The Two Chiefs of Dunday*. Wilde calls his review 'Mr Froude's Blue Book' as though the novel were the consequence of a government commission. He begins:

Blue Books are generally dull reading but Blue Books on Ireland have always been interesting. They form the record of one of the greatest tragedies of modern Europe. In them England has written down her indictment against herself, and has given to the world the history of her shame. If in the last century she tried to govern Ireland with an insolence that was intensified by race-hatred and religious prejudice, she has sought to rule her this century with a stupidity that is aggravated by good intentions.

He concludes with a warning:

There are some who will welcome with delight the idea of solving the Irish question by doing away with the Irish people.

There are others who will remember that Ireland has extended her boundaries and that we have now to reckon with her not merely in the Old World but also in the New.

By the end of the review neither Froude's fiction, nor British Government policy on Ireland, is left with a shred of integrity, and Wilde's rage at the double insult to aesthetics and politics represented by the novel is unambiguous.

The 'Irish Question' had been a matter of urgency at Westminster and beyond from the 1870s onwards, with the Liberal Leader Gladstone favouring Home Rule for Ireland. Returned to power at the general election of 1885, Gladstone introduced the first Home Rule Bill to the House of Commons in April 1886. After 14 nights of bitter debate it was defeated by 30 votes. Gladstone's Party had divided over the issue, with 93 Liberals voting against him. Shocked by the collapse of both Bill and Party, Gladstone dissolved Parliament to seek reindorsement from the Country. Badly underestimating British strength of feeling on the issue, the result of the July election was a Conservative majority supported by the rebel Liberals, while the Liberal Party was weakened and dependent on Parnell's Irish Party to defeat Government Bills. The new Prime Minister was Lord Salisbury who appointed his nephew, Arthur Balfour, as Chief Secretary for Ireland in March 1887. Balfour announced that with regard to Ireland his policy was for 'repression as stern as Cromwell; reform as thorough as Mr Parnell can desire'.[16] This was Wilde's most immediate target when he referred to 'stupidity' and 'good intentions'. Under Lord Salisbury's government, Irish tenant farmers found themselves hard hit by rent increases and low prices for agricultural produce. In Ireland the years 1886 to 1888 saw increasing evictions, and emigrations to America. When the Liberal Party won a majority in the election of 1892 Gladstone presented his second Bill for Irish Home Rule to the Commons in February 1893. It met an astonishing, though narrow, victory – only to be quashed by the Lords, 419 votes to 41. Gladstone retired in 1894, aged 85. Wilde had regarded him as an ally, writing to him in 1888 of

the deep admiration that I along with my countrymen feel for the one English statesman who has understood us, who has sympathised with us, whom we claim now as our leader, and who, we know well, will lead us to the grandest and justest political victory of this age.

(Letters, 231)

Wilde allowed the controversy over Irish Home Rule to be aired in the pages of the *Woman's World*. In January 1889 he published a political address given by Margaret Sandhurst in Cambridge, 'On Women's Work in Politics'. (This was the Lady Sandhurst for whose election, on 17 January 1889, to the London County Council, Constance Wilde had campaigned.) She was forthright on the topic:

> Have we, from first to last, ever made a persistent effort to govern Ireland for her Good? Have we given up anything for her? . . . Has not precisely the reverse been the case? Has not Ireland with her true interests been sacrificed to a false, short-sighted expediency; to English prejudices, to narrow, ignorant ideas of English material prosperity? . . . Can it be right to tyrannise over any nation committed to our charge? Can robbery, oppression, unequal laws, with administration of them miscalled justice, be worthy of England's rule?

The hare was running, and when Mrs Fawcett, a nominal Liberal and distinguished campaigner for Women's Rights, was interviewed for the *Woman's World* in October 1890, she announced an opposite view: 'I am a decided Unionist . . . I hardly know any highly educated Irishman or woman residing in Ireland who is not in favour of the Union.' Her words are chosen carefully (although Wilde left Cassells in November 1889) to exclude the former Editor from her frame of reference. This was a move typical of the selective blindness with which the British public viewed Wilde's nationality. When *Salome* was censored by the Lord Chamberlain in 1892 Wilde was so incensed that he threatened to adopt French nationality. But first he had to remind the British public that, 'I am not English. I am Irish which is quite another thing.' Reporting this controversy in the colonies, the *South African Empire* also had to conclude its article, 'By the way, Oscar Wilde is not an Englishman, he is Irish' (9 July 1892).

When his work became too controversial, discussion was deflected by mention of Ireland. In 1890 Wilde responded to jibes published in the *Scots Observer* by clarifying the false logic. His critics, he claimed, 'proposed that the test of art should be the political opinions of the artist, and that if one differed from the artist on the question of the best way of misgoverning Ireland, one should always abuse his work' (*Scots Observer*, 16 August 1890). Inevitably, Wilde's Irish identity came to the fore when he was in the dock. Rather than trying one of their own, the British establishment could purge themselves of a foreigner spreading 'deadly infection' (*Chronicle*, 6 April 1895) in order to assert its own health. Or, as the *Daily Telegraph* responded, 'every . . . wholesome-minded Englishman must grieve to notice how largely this French and Pagan plague has filtered into the healthy fields of British life' (6 April 1895). For the first time since his student days in the 1870s, the public heard the culprit's unassimilated Irish name 'Oscar Fingal O'Flahertie Willes (*sic*) Wilde'.[17]

Beyond the party politics of the Irish question lay a celebration of his race, and Wilde loved to pit the imaginative Celt against the dullard Anglo-Saxon. Romantic as it is, there was cultural precedent for this use of the term 'Celtic': Matthew Arnold had coined it as a way of challenging the dominant ethics of Puritanism and Philistinism in English society in his essay 'On The Study of Celtic Literature' (1867). Wilde formed ready alliances with other Irishmen in exile, with Shaw, and Yeats; he generously baptised others 'Celtic' if he admired them. When Grant Allen's essay 'The Celt in English Art' was published in tandem with the 'Soul of Man Under Socialism' in the *Fortnightly Review* (February 1891), Wilde wrote enthusiastically to Allen: 'You are, of course, a Celt. You must be' (Letters, 287). He proposed to 'inaugurate a Celtic dinner, and assert ourselves, and show these tedious Angles or Teutons what a race we are, and how proud we are to belong to that race.' To Shaw he confided that 'England is the land of intellectual fogs but you have done much to clear the air: we are both Celtic, and I like to think that we are friends' (Letters, 332). When Shaw sent Wilde a copy of his first play, *Widowers' Houses*, in May 1893, he received thanks for 'Op. 2 of the great Celtic School' (Letters, 339), while Shaw's copy of *Lady Windermere's Fan* was a gift inscribed by Wilde: 'Op. 1 of the Hibernian School, London '93'. These two satirical Celts were attacking the enemy from within. But Wilde uses the term without irony in the last years of his life when his efforts to reform English society were more direct. Campaigning for change in the penal system he wrote to a friend: 'It is the lack of imagination in the Anglo-Saxon race that makes the race so stupidly, harshly cruel. Those who are bringing about Prison Reform in Parliament are Celtic to a man. For every Celt has inborn imagination' (Letters, 751).

Even setting aside his mature sexual orientation, Wilde's sensitivity to the figure of the social outsider, as to the double life, was conditioned by his awareness of the political circumstances of the age. It is no accident that Mrs Erlynne, in *Lady Windermere's Fan*, one of his many fictional outsiders, finally abandons her quest for a place in Society with a rejection that echoes Wilde's words of confraternity with Shaw: 'Whether the fogs produce the serious people or whether the serious people produce the fogs, I don't know, but the whole thing rather gets on my nerves, and so I'm leaving' (Works, 457).

Front cover of the Police News, *4 May 1895*
By permission of the British Library (shelfmark: 182B)

Homosexuality

While it was not possible to imprison somebody for being Irish, after Gladstone's Government passed the Criminal Law Amendment Act in 1885 it was possible to imprison somebody for practising homosexuality:

> Any male person who, in public or private, commits, or is party to the commission of, or procures or attempts to procure the commission by any male person of, any act of gross indecency with another male person, shall be guilty of a misdemeanour, and, being convicted thereof, shall be liable, at the discretion of the Court, to be imprisoned for any term not exceeding two years with or without hard labour.
>
> (Ellmann, 386)

This was the law which criminalised Wilde, and under which he received the severest possible sentence.

The iconic overlap between green, the national colour of Ireland, and the green carnation, the badge of aestheticism and homosexuality, allowed Wilde to wear both his nationalism and his sexuality on his lapel. But few saw it, and fewer saw both. Unlike his political sentiments about Ireland, Wilde was not able to openly articulate his feelings about the analogous imperialism which criminalised his sexuality. But the means by which he queried the heterosexual politics of the day afford, in retrospect, a challenge to the legislation which restricted his own freedom of expression and identity. The way in which any reader after 1895 responds to Wilde's work is radically altered by knowledge of his homosexuality. For some, his writing became eclipsed by his life, and both became unmentionable; for later generations, more open sexual politics have brought the work back into view, but have changed its frame of reference.

After Wilde lost his libel suit against the Marquis of Queensberry, father of Lord Alfred Douglas, who goaded Wilde into legal action by leaving his card with the words 'To Oscar Wilde posing Somdomite' [sic] at the Albemarle Club on 18 February 1895, Wilde wrote to Douglas: 'Our love was always beautiful and noble, and if I have been the butt of a terrible tragedy, it is because the nature of that love has not been understood' (Letters, 393). This private expression of consolation followed Wilde's public eloquence about the nobility of homosexual love, delivered in the courtroom on 26 April 1895:

> The 'Love that dare not speak its name' in this century is such a great affection of an elder for a younger man as there was between

David and Jonathan, such as Plato made the very basis of his philosophy, and such as you find in the sonnets of Michelangelo and Shakespeare. It is that deep, spiritual affection that is as pure as it is perfect. It dictates and pervades great works of art like those of Shakespeare and Michelangelo . . . . It is in this century misunderstood, so much misunderstood that it may be described as the 'Love that dare not speak its name,' and on account of it I am placed where I am now. It is beautiful, it is fine, it is the noblest form of affection. There is nothing unnatural about it. It is intellectual, and it repeatedly exists between an elder and a younger man, when the elder man has intellect, and the younger man has all the joy, hope and glamour of life before him. That it should be so the world does not understand. The world mocks at it and sometimes puts one in the pillory for it.

(Ellmann, 435)

The speech (anticipated in *The Picture of Dorian Gray* by Dorian's interior monologue about Basil's love for him (Works, 92)) met with applause (according to Max Beerbohm) and, though too late for Wilde himself, it marks a turning point in the cultural representation of same-sex passion, and the social understanding of it, as Alan Sinfield has argued recently.[18]

Wilde's public emphasis on the cultural misunderstanding that surrounded homosexual love was quite different from Douglas' expression of the social embarrassment that incumbered it. The refrain 'the Love that dare not speak its name' which Wilde uses in this speech comes from one of Douglas' poems, 'Two Loves', published in *The Chameleon*, the single issue of a homosexual journal circulated among his coterie but still manifestly inhibited by a certain coy and covert form of expression. Much of the contents of *The Chameleon*, to which Wilde had contributed the sequence of maxims, 'Phrases and Philosophies for the Use of the Young' was used as evidence against him in the libel suit. The short story, 'The Priest and the Acolyte', published there anonymously but thought to be by Wilde (actually by Jack Bloxam) was also used against him. Wilde described the story as 'disgusting twaddle',[19] and objected to its poor literary taste. It, even more than Douglas' poem, is a distressed apologia for homosexual love. The melodrama of the scenario, the extreme aestheticism of vision and the clumsiness of discourse, are all products of a desire struggling to find acceptable expression. A 28-year-old priest is in love with a 14-year-old acolyte. Their guilty love, discovered by the priest's superior, is defended:

You do not understand me: I have never been attracted by a woman in my life. Can you not see that people are different, totally different, from one another? To think we are all the same

29

is impossible; our natures, our temperaments, are utterly unlike. But this is what people will never see; they found all their opinions on a wrong basis. How can the deductions be just if their premises are wrong? One law laid down by the majority, who happen to be of one disposition, is only binding on the minority *legally*, not *morally*. What right have you, or any one, to tell me that such-and-such a thing is sinful for me?

In God's eyes we are martyrs, and we shall not shrink even from death in this struggle against the idolatrous worship of convention.

(*The Chameleon*, 42, 44)

More accomplished in expression and designed for wider circulation was Robert Hichens' novel *The Green Carnation* (1894). It parodies the open secret of Wilde's relationship with Lord Alfred Douglas through the leading characters Mr Esme Amarinth (Wilde) and Lord Reggie (Douglas). Amarinth announces:

A child is unnatural if it hates its mother. A mother is unnatural if she does not wish to have children. A man is unnatural if he never falls in love with a woman. A boy is unnatural if he prefers looking at pictures to playing cricket, or dreaming over the white naked beauty of a Greek statue to a game of football under Rugby rules ... If our vices are not according to rule, they are unnatural.[20]

When Lord Alfred Douglas returned to the subject of Wilde's homosexuality in 1940 with his book *Oscar Wilde. A Summing Up*, he surveyed the hysteria, and also the courage with which Wilde met it, with dismissive distance: 'Wilde was never in the least degree ashamed of his homosexuality. On the contrary he gloried in it and was not above attributing the same tastes to Shakespeare ... and even to Plato.'[21]

Douglas announced that

the exaggerated horror [of homosexuality] which prevailed in Wilde's time and in my youth was mainly hypocritical and squared very imperfectly with the private lives of a large proportion of those people who most loudly condemned it.[22]

While he may have had in mind his own elder brother's suicide in 1894 as a consequence of the threatened revelation of his affair with the then Foreign Minister, Lord Rosebury, as a tragic result of this hypocrisy, Douglas failed to admit Wilde's remarkable part in dismantling the double standards of the era and clearing the way for the more 'open atmosphere' Douglas observes between 1914 and 1940.[23]

BY ORDER OF THE SHERIFF.

A.D. 1895.   No. 6907

16, Tite Street, Chelsea.

Catalogue of the Library of

Valuable Books,

Pictures, Portraits of Celebrities, Arundel Society Prints,

HOUSEHOLD FURNITURE

CARLYLE'S WRITING TABLE,

Chippendale and Italian Chairs, Old Persian Carpets
and Rugs, Brass Fenders,

Moorish and Oriental Curiosities,

Embroideries, Silver and Plated Articles,

OLD BLUE AND WHITE CHINA,

Moorish Pottery, Handsome Ormolu Clock,
and numerous Effects :

Which will be Sold by Auction,

By Mr. BULLOCK,

ON THE PREMISES,

On Wednesday, April 24th, 1895,

AT ONE O'CLOCK.

May be Viewed the day prior, and Catalogues had of Messrs. CLARKE & Co.
16, Portugal Street, Lincoln's Inn; and of the Auctioneer,

211 HIGH HOLBORN, W.C.

Front cover of the bailiff's Sale Catalogue *for Wilde's family home,*
24 April 1895
By permission of the Bodleian Library, University of Oxford.
Shelfmark: Ross d.216

Wilde lost his libel suit against Lord Queensberry on 5 April 1895.
On 6 April he was immediately arrested, accused of practising 'gross
indecency', and prosecuted by the Crown. He had to endure two
further trials: the jury which met 26 April 1895 was unable to reach
a unanimous verdict at the end of the trial on 1 May. The second
trial opened on 20 May 1895 and five days later Wilde's fate was
sealed. Public outrage, registered by the press, at how the darling of
the aristocracy and prince of aesthetes had conned their admiration
and respect, was astonishing. Journalists reported every detail of the
libel case as it was tried and on 6 April 1895 Wilde's name, 'The

31

Man Wilde', was emblazoned in headlines and dragged through leader columns in zealous acts of public purification. Vilification did not stop at Wilde ('pestiferous *poseur*'); the entire literary school with which he was associated fell instantly into the same disrepute ('"Decadence" among us has received a death-blow'). 'Great names' had to be rescued from contamination: Keats, Ruskin, Dante Gabriel Rossetti, and the figure 'as pure and high as the name of CHRISTINA ROSSETTI' were dragged from the mire (*Chronicle*, 6 April 1895). The *Daily Telegraph* was typical in its method of attack:

> The pranks of POSTLETHWAITE . . . were innocent so long as they were merely aesthetic. But, in spasmodic search for ancient graces . . . the worst and boldest of these innovators set themselves to import into the healthy and honest English art and life the pagan side of bygone times, with all its cynicism, scepticism and animalism. Everybody can see and read for himself, and every wholesome-minded Englishman must grieve to notice how largely this French and Pagan plague has filtered into the healthy fields of British life.
>
> The superfine 'Art' which admits no moral duty and laughs at the established phrases of right and wrong is the visible enemy of those ties and bonds of society – the natural affections, the domestic joys, the sanctity and sweetness of the home.
>
> (6 April 1895)

English culture is pictured as innately and essentially 'wholesome', only temporarily corrupted by the plague-ridden foreigner, whose vices are exposed by the native individual (Lord Queensberry) and punished by native justice. The suggestion which even the conservative critic Matthew Arnold made – that the role of literature is to 'teach us how to live' – is forgotten in the rush to claim the moral high ground. 'Postlethwaite's' pranks were 'innocent' as long as merely 'aesthetic': that is, without bearing on conduct. But Wilde's enterprise had been to force the link which Arnold observed between literature and life. As the playwright Howard Brenton has argued more recently, Wilde fell because he wanted to breach the gap between aesthetics and politics.[24]

The *Morning* was a lonely voice expressing a sense of the loss to cultural life which would result from Wilde's fall:

> Yet, with the contempt that one feels for such a person as Wilde, taking him only at his own estimate, there necessarily mingles an element of sadness. Let the result of the criminal proceedings now taken against him by the police be what they may, the world already sees in him a man who was writing his way to an assured literary position, who held a conspicuous place in the better sort

of Bohemian society, who, both in a social and literary sense, had the ball at his foot, and who has flung all his chances away. It is inexplicable. For its own sake the stage may well regret this turn of events.

People laughed at, as well as with, him, but they crowded to see his plays. And now the farce has turned to tragedy.

(6 April 1895)

Wise after the event, the *Chronicle* announced that '[e]verybody has suspected and feared: nobody – no decent person – has known' (6 April 1895). Wilde's arrest forced the visibility of his sexual practice, and homosexuality in general, into the public arena. And the public was shocked, as much at being forced to acknowledge what it chose to disregard as at the revelations about the private life of a prominent cultural player. But Wilde had been skilful in concealing the nature of his conduct from friends to whom his private sexuality was irrelevant. One of his oldest friends and earliest biographers, R. H. Sherard, had failed to see this aspect of Wilde's life until the trials and later adopted a number of strategies to explain away Wilde's homosexuality. Lord Alfred Douglas, self-appointed guardian of Wilde's posthumous reputation, wrote to him on 17 October 1929:

> You are not and never have been competent to write about Oscar, because obviously you never knew what his real life and character were ... Oscar knew you well and at one time liked you very much, *but he carefully concealed from you the side of his life and character which governed his conduct.*[25]

Sherard published this letter, together with his own extraordinary defence of Wilde in 1933, in a pamphlet, Sherard is fighting several enemies at once, including the interpretation *Oscar Wilde*, offered by the French psychologist, Renier, in 1933:

> Renier ... disregards the fact that when by the hideous alchemy of *psychopathia sexualis* the benign Jekyll in Wilde was transmuted into the depraved Mrs Hyde, his acts were manifestly Masochist and feminine and in no wise the virile and sadist performances of a Sodomite.
>
> The squalid details of Wilde's offences are available to all and the perusal of them establishes as clear a case of feminine masochism as is any where recorded ... And as Renier ought to know, no offences other than these were charged or proven against Mrs Wilde-Hyde. Wilde was homosexual and irresponsible. Gide and Renier wish to send him down to posterity as a sodomite and a criminal.[26]

In grasping at the explanations offered by a prejudiced 'psychology' about homosexuality, Sherard seeks to restore the honourable

reputation of his friend. Although his account now sounds so bizarre
as to be laughable, Sherard was building on a branch of serious psychological discipline which circulated during the latter decades of the
nineteenth century. Wilde had mocked related disciplines in 'Lord
Arthur Savile's Crime', while he availed himself of it in his desperate
plea to the Home Secretary in 1896 for early release from prison:

> the petitioner is fully conscious now . . . that his whole life, for the
> two years preceding his ruin, was the prey of absolute madness –
> the insanity of perverted sensual instinct is the one most dominant
> in its action on the brain.
>
> (Letters, 411)

In an earlier petition to the Home Secretary for release, Wilde had
named the sources of the discipline which called him mad and diseased:

> The petition of the above-named prisoner humbly sheweth that
> he does not desire to palliate in any way the terrible offences of
> which he was rightly found guilty, but to point out that such
> offences are forms of sexual madness and are recognised as such
> not merely by modern pathological science but by much modern
> legislation, notably in France, Austria, and Italy, where the laws
> affecting these misdemeanours have been repealed, on the ground
> that they are diseases to be cured by a physician, rather than crimes
> to be punished by a judge. In the works of eminent men of science,
> such as Lombroso and Nordau, to take merely two instances out
> of many, this is specially insisted on with reference to the intimate
> connection between madness and the literary and artistic tempera-
> ment, Professor Nordau in his book 'Degenerescence' published
> in 1894 having devoted an entire chapter to the petitioner as a
> specially typical example of this fatal law.
>
> (Letters, 401)

Logically persuasive in the argument that his punishment was
inappropriate, Wilde was accurate in every detail save the date and
title of Nordau's work. *Degeneration* (1895), the English title of *Entartung*
(1893), contained a chapter called 'Decadents and Aesthetes', which
discussed Wilde at length as an example of the neurotic whose diseased art was provoked by too fine a sensitivity to the stressful urban
environment of modern Europe. Nordau responded wholeheartedly
to the evidence supplied in support of his theories by Wilde's trials,
and updated his study accordingly for the third edition in 1896.
There were many sceptical responses, most distinguished among
which in Britain was Shaw's 'A Degenerate's View of Nordau' (July
1895), revised as *The Sanity of Art* in 1908.

The myth of Wilde

> To be suggestive for fiction is to be of more importance than a
> fact.
>
> ('Pen, Pencil and Poison. A Study in Green', *Works*, 1107)

Wilde's powers of self-dramatisation were met during his lifetime by
multiple dramatisations of his persona in the public domain. Cartoons, plays, spoof biographies, poems, songs and dances were all
composed in response to the elaborately constructed 'self' which
Wilde put on display. When Walter Hamilton wrote to him in 1889
collecting parodies for what would become his six-volume anthology
Parodies of English and American Authors (1884–89), Wilde replied:

> I have never collected the parodies of my poetry. Collecting
> contemporaneous things is like trying to hold froth in a sieve . . .
> Parody, which is the Muse with her tongue in her cheek, has
> always amused me; but it requires a light touch, . . . and, oddly
> enough, a love of the poet whom it caricatures. One's disciples
> can parody one – nobody else.
>
> (*Letters*, 239)

After his fall in 1895, and death in 1900, literary responses to Wilde
continued to be written, but their tone changed radically. Parody
was inappropriate. Serious plays, taking as their subject the tragic
demise of an heroic figure, or comedies, overlooking the politics of
his biography and celebrating instead the achievements of his work,
became the fashion.

The first sustained appearance of a Wilde figure was in the shape
of the poet Postlethwaite, George du Maurier's cartoons for *Punch*
drawn during the early 1880s. Postlethwaite is always accompanied
by Maudle, a parody of Whistler, and they circulate among a coterie
of effete aesthetic admirers among whom Mrs Cimabue-Brown
(a version of Lady Archibald Campbell) is a prominent hostess.
The intellectual attitudes of the young Wilde are physicalised in a
sequence of absurd postures. His social poise is mocked as a preten-
tious pose, and the tenets of the aesthetic movement are ridiculed
into the bargain. Despite du Maurier's youthful friendship with both
Wilde and Whistler, the 'love' of the subject which Wilde holds as
paramount for successful parody is not dominant. This duo gave
way to Bunthorne and Grosvenor in Gilbert and Sullivan's comic
operetta *Patience, or Bunthorne's Bride* which opened at the London
Opera Comique on 23 April 1881. The divided self of the interchangeable protagonists points towards Wilde's use of pairing in *The
Importance of Being Earnest*. Bunthorne was modelled on Wilde:

PUNCH'S FANCY PORTRAITS.—No. 37.

"O. W."

" O, I eel just as happy as a bright Sunflower
Lays of Christy Minstrelsy

Æsthete of Æsthetes !
What 's in a name ?
The poet is WILDE,
But his poetry 's tame.

Caricature of Wilde, taken from a page in Punch, *25 June 1881*
By permission of the British Library (shelfmark: PP5270)

> Though the Philistines may jostle, you will rank
>   as an apostle in the high aesthetic band,
> If you walk down Piccadilly with a poppy or a lily
>   in your medieval hand.[27]

Three dramatic parodies of the figures of the aesthetic movement
had enjoyed previous success. In December 1877 a play called *The*

Grasshopper had satirised the opening of The Grosvenor Gallery earlier that year: the event which sparked Wilde's first published review essay and initiated his friendship with Pater. The play contains a dance by three characters, supposed to represent Wilde, Whistler and Miles. James Albery burlesqued the aesthetes again with *Where's the Cat?* It opened at the Criterion Theatre in London on 20 November 1880 with Herbert Beerbohm Tree imitating Wilde's mannerisms in the role of the writer Scott Ramsay. In February 1881, F. C. Burnand, the editor of *Punch*, enjoyed commercial success at the Prince of Wales Theatre with his comedy, *The Colonel*, mocking aesthetes and aestheticism alike. The character Lambert Stryke was modelled on Wilde.

When Wilde toured America in 1882 – ostensibly to promote *Patience* – a new sequence of parodies was generated. 'Oscar Dear!', a comic song by M. H. Rosenfeld, was written for performance by the celebrated comedian Solsmith Russell. This was accompanied by the 'Oscar Polka Mazurka', a song and dance piece, with the waltz refrain 'Oscar dear, Oscar dear, How flutterly, utterly *flutter* you are, Oscar dear, Oscar dear, I think you are awfully "Wild", ta! ta!', and the choral refrain 'Oscar dear! Oscar dear! take your hand away sir; someone might be looking, love, Take your hand away sir'. The music was set for female voices, but another arrangement was set for male voices and designed for performance by the 'favourite motto singer and character artist, Tony Pastor'. A further series of dances was composed and published by Oliver Dickson in Boston in 1882: 'Jolly Utter Galop'; 'Too All But, Waltz'; 'Dream of the Lily, Waltz'; 'Sunflower, Polka'; 'Too Utterly Utter, March'; 'Oscar's Schottische'. These were performed at popular entertainments and the 'Sunflower Dances' which sprang up in the wake of Wilde's lecture tour. Chas Kendrick published and illustrated a parodic biography, *Ye Soul Agonies In Ye Life of Oscar Wilde* (1882) to cash in on the Oscar fever sweeping the country.

Wilde's return to England was celebrated with the poem 'The Returning of Oscar' in the *Whitehall Review* on 11 January 1883. The last stanza of six reads:

> Rejoice, O Mother England! and rejoice,
> Ye dear disciples of the Pagan creeds,
> To hear again the music of my voice,
> That is more tuneful than the captured reeds
> Of Menelaus. Prepare the goodly feast
> For him who long has named himself as Beauty's
>   chosen priest.

Punch, that 'perfectly adjusted barometer of celebrity',[28] maintained its satirical attention to Wilde during the 1880s, but his persona had altered on his return from America. Aestheticism was moving into a new phase, and Wilde himself was heavily involved in journalism. It was not until *Lady Windermere's Fan* revivified his celebrity status in 1892 that fresh parodic responses were provoked. A musical travesty, *The Poet and the Puppets*, making fun of Wilde and his new play, opened at the Comedy Theatre on 19 May 1892 and ran, at a small loss, until the end of July. Incensed at the licensed vulgarisation of his person at the very time when his own play *Salome* was refused a performance licence, Wilde wrote to his friend Will Rothenstein about the dismal artistic standards maintained by the office of the Lord Chamberlain:

> a Mr Pigott, who panders to the vulgarity and hypocrisy of the English people, by licensing every low farce and vulgar melodrama. He even allows the stage to be used for the purpose of the caricaturing of the personalities of artists, and at the same moment when he prohibited *Salome*, he licensed a burlesque of *Lady Windermere's Fan* in which an actor dressed up like me and imitated my voice and manner!!!
>
> (Letters, 316)

The actor to whom Wilde refers was Charles Hawtrey, co-author of the piece, together with Charles Brookfield who made a living as the writer and performer of burlesques. The music was composed by Jimmy Glover. Wilde was acquainted with all of them, and Hawtrey and Brookfield both performed roles in the first production of *An Ideal Husband* at the Haymarket Theatre in 1895. During this time they were in the pay of Lord Queensberry, who was secretly collecting evidence against Wilde for use in the trial which acquitted Queensberry of libel on 5 April 1895. A more friendly dramatic lampoon, *Aristophanes at Oxford*, by Y. T. O. was published anonymously in 1894. This was a play for eight characters centring on versions of Lord Alfred Douglas and Wilde (including the representation of Lewis Carroll) and chorus.

The most affectionate but least amusing parodies of Wilde's work during his lifetime were published by his close friend Ada Leverson whom he nicknamed 'The Sphinx'. Her own parody of Wilde's poem *The Sphinx* was entitled 'The Minx – a Poem in Prose' (*Punch*, 21 July 1894) and Wilde thought it 'delightful' (Letters, 357). She followed this with a skit on *An Ideal Husband*, 'Overheard Fragment of a Dialogue' (*Punch*, 12 January 1895) and another, three weeks later, on *The Importance of Being Earnest*, 'The Advisability of not being brought up in a handbag. A Trivial Tragedy for Wonderful People (Fragment found between the St James's and Haymarket Theatres)'.

Leverson's friendship with Wilde was loyal and lasting; she and her husband Ernest received him at their home on his release from gaol in 1897 and assisted his departure to France.

In *The Importance of Being Earnest* Wilde turns the joke back on two of the principal progenitors of Wildean parody. When Jack and Algernon enter the final Act, 'they whistle some dreadful popular air from a British Opera' (Works, 405). Alexander's stage directions add to this that they enter 'arm in arm' and 'whistle out of tune'. In one typescript of the play, 'Home Sweet Home' is named as the dreadful tune, but other versions give no specific reference.[29] *Patience*, with its dual heroes, Bunthorne and Grosvenor, may stand as the obvious target. In an early draft of the play's conclusion, when the race is on to discover the Christian name of Jack's military father, reference books are distributed among the characters and Lady Bracknell is given a copy of Robert Hichens' novel, *The Green Carnation* (1894). She glances at it and announces that it 'seems to be a book about the culture of exotics. It contains no reference to Generals in it. It seems a morbid and middle-class affair' (Works, 418). *The Green Carnation*, a novel whose setting is a Surrey country-house party reflecting the context of *A Woman of No Importance*, satirised Wilde's life and work in general and focused specifically on the affair between Douglas and Wilde. Among the characters of the novel is one particularly incompetent rural vicar, a Mr Smith, who may well be enjoying an afterlife in the shape of Canon Chasuble.

Wilde's conviction in 1895 and death in 1900 banished this form of personal parody. The rehabilitation of his reputation followed slowly. In 1928 the German playwright, Carl Sternheim, who learned much craft from Wilde's plays, wrote *Oskar Wilde*. This three-act play for an exclusively male cast confronts and defends Wilde's homosexuality, representing his transition from celebrity playwright to the director of his personal tragedy. The protagonist is seen as a courageous victim of English hypocrisy; his fall indicts the social forces which destroy him, and his decision to stand and fight flags the triumph of Wildean 'individualism', linking it with the first signs of a political campaign against sexual discrimination. In Britain Wilde's rehabilitation has not been so candid. John Betjeman's poem 'The Arrest of Wilde at the Cadogan Hotel' (1937) continues to mock Wilde's extravagant habits; while *The Importance of Being Oscar*, a one-man play written and performed by Michael Mac Liammoir, first performed at the Gate Theatre in Dublin (which he co-founded) in 1960, glosses over Wilde's sexuality. He is represented as exclusively heterosexual, in his youth infatuated with Lily Langtry and in his maturity grief-stricken at his wife's death, rushing to Genoa to fall on her grave. The play was published in 1963, having enjoyed a successful world tour and having been televised by Granada. *Travesties* (1974), by Tom Stoppard, shifts the focus away from the biography of Wilde and celebrates the achievement of *The Importance of Being Earnest* by centring its astonishingly complicated farce on the performance of that play in Zurich in 1918.

Like Peter Ackroyd's novel, *The Last Testament of Oscar Wilde* (1983), Terry Eagleton's *Saint Oscar* (1989), directed by Trevor Griffiths and designed by Bob Crowley for the Irish Field Day Company, returns to the sphere of fictionalised biography. Eagleton plays up to the received picture of Wilde as a martyr of gay rights (a latter-day St Sebastian) only to parody that view. Instead he presents the incarceration and ruin of the chameleon protagonist as a moment in the history of colonial oppression of the Irish by the British. 'You subjugate whole races, you condemn the mass of your people to wretched toil, you have reduced my nation to despair, and all you can think about is which sexual organ goes in where' accuses Wilde from the dock. The British resistance to this portrayal of Wilde was conspicuous in the reviews the production received when it was performed in London in 1990. Almost unanimously, theatre critics declared that the historical Wilde had turned his back on the 'Irish Question', and the use of his biography to participate in Anglo–Irish polemics was inappropriate on the part of the playwright.[30] Apart from the ill-informed nature of such opinion, Eagleton can simply be seen to further the kind of criticism meted out to the British Establishment of the 1890s which the Continental playwright, Carl Sternheim, had been able to voice without incurring censure. *Saint Oscar* updates the theatre of ideas which Wilde's biography can sustain, to focus on colonial rather than on sexual politics.

The examples named here are complemented by the editions and translations of Wilde's work, film versions of his plays, stories and biography, and adaptations of his stories for performance on the amateur stage. All these have generated a kind of industry in themselves to create Wilde's legendary reputation.

Notes

1 Joy Melville, *Mother of Oscar. The Life of Jane Francesca Wilde* (London: John Murray, 1994) 115.
2 Ibid., 203.
3 *Gentlewoman*, 13 January 1883.
4 Speranza (Lady Wilde), 'Attendite Popule', *Poems* (Dublin: James Duffy, 1864) 34, ll.1–8.
5 *Social Studies* (London: Ward and Downey, 1893) 31.
6 Kerry Powell, 'Wilde & Two Women: Unpublished Accounts by Elizabeth Robins & Blanche Crackenthorpe', *Rediscovering*

Oscar Wilde, ed. C. G. Sandalescu (Gerrards Cross: Colin Smythe, 1994) 316.

7   'Art and the Handicraftsman', *Essays and Lectures*, ed. Robert Ross (London: Methuen, 1909) 191.

8   *Queen*, 22 May 1886.

9   *Diaries and Letters of Marie Belloc Lowndes 1911–1947*, ed. Susan Lowndes (London: Chatto & Windus, 1971) 13–14.

10 G. B. Shaw, *Saturday Review*, 12 January 1895; William Archer, *Theatrical World*, 19 January 1895; Clement Scott, *Daily Telegraph*, 4 January 1895.

11 Cited in J. H. Kaplan and S. Stowell, *Theatre and Fashion. Oscar Wilde to the Suffragettes* (Cambridge: Cambridge University Press, 1994) 28.

12 'OH! OSCAR WILDE, WE NEVER THOUGHT That You Was Built That Way', facsimile in John Stokes, *In The Nineties* (London: Harvester Wheatsheaf, 1989) 4.

13 Lord Alfred Douglas, *Oscar Wilde. A Summing Up* (London: Duckworth, 1940) 97.

14 W. B. Yeats, *Autobiographies* (London: Macmillan, 1955) 135.

15 Charles Brookfield, *The Poet and the Puppets*, The Ross Collection, Bodleian Library Oxford, Ross d.95, 5.

16 Cited in Grenfell Morton, *Home Rule and the Irish Question* (London: Longman, 1980) 43.

17 Unidentified newspaper cutting, The Ross Collection, Bodleian Library Oxford, Ross d.212, 89.

18 Alan Sinfield, *The Wilde Century. Effeminacy, Oscar Wilde and the Queer Moment* (London: Cassell, 1994).

19 Cited in Jonathan Goodman, *The Oscar Wilde File* (London: Allison & Busby, 1988) 53.

20 Robert Hichens, *The Green Carnation* (London: Heinemann, 1894) 108.

21 Douglas, *Oscar Wilde. A Summing Up*, 9.

22 Ibid., 14.

23 Ibid., 17.

24 Howard Brenton, 'The Unbearable Heaviness of Being English', *Hot Irons. Diaries. Essays. Journalism* (London: Nick Hern Books, 1995) 57–62.

25 Cited in R. H. Sherard, *A Letter from Lord Alfred Douglas on André Gide's Lies about Himself and Oscar Wilde. Set forth with comments by Robert Harborough Sherard* (Calvi (Corsica): The Vindex Publishing Co., 1933) 7.

26 Ibid., 4.

27 W. S. Gilbert, *Patience, The Complete Annotated Gilbert and Sullivan*, ed. Ian Bradley (Oxford: Oxford University Press, 1996) Act I, ll. 415–16, 293.

28 L. C. Ingleby, *Oscar Wilde* (London: T. Werner Laurie, n.d.) 22.
29 *The Importance of Being Earnest. The First Production*, ed. Joseph Donohue (Gerrards Cross: Colin Smythe, 1995) 304.
30 *London Theatre Record*, 26 February–11 March 1990.

Part Two
Aesthetic and Political Philosophy

2 Critical writings

Wilde was fluent in non-fiction. His flamboyant personality generated a public to be addressed face to face in the lecture hall, or more indirectly through the persona of journalist and editor. The carefully structured prose of 'The Soul of Man Under Socialism' and the eventual collection of criticism, *Intentions* (1891), formalises the immediate style of public speaking he had practised a decade earlier. The essays collected in this volume are 'The Decay of Lying', which first appeared in *The Nineteenth Century* in January 1889; 'Pen, Pencil, and Poison' from *The Fortnightly Review*, January 1889; 'The Critic as Artist', Parts I and II, from *The Nineteenth Century* in July and September 1890; and 'The Truth of Masks', an essay on the production methods for Shakespeare's plays, revised from *The Nineteenth Century*, May 1885. Some commentators contend that all of Wilde's work, whether ostensibly fiction or non-fiction, is fired by critical response to the aesthetic fashions of his era. Richard Le Gallienne, reviewing *Intentions*, was one of the first to suggest that Wilde's work transgressed the boundaries between criticism and creation, fiction and non-fiction:

> Mr. Wilde, in speaking of the methods open to the critic, well says that Mr. Pater's narrative is, of course, only criticism in disguise: his figures are but personifications of certain moods of mind, in which he is for the time interested, and which he desires to express. Now I have been wondering whether one should not, similarly, regard Mr. Wilde essentially as a humorist who has taken art-criticism for his medium.
>
> (Critical Heritage, 97)

Lectures

Wilde's lecturing career took off with meteoric energy during his tour of America in 1882, when from January to December he delivered at least 140 lectures at as many different locations, and was constantly engaged in the business of 'interviews' for an American press eager for closer acquaintance with the curiosity of this Irish aesthete. If it did nothing else, this punishing regime of travel, lecture and interview honed Wilde's skills in the construction of a compelling public presence and performance. That there was something to be honed is indicated by the measured appraisal of his second lecture to New York on 11 May 1882:

> Mr Wilde has much improved in his delivery, hardly looked at his notes, talked much less above the heads of his audience than on his first appearance, and, though he used again a number of his pet phrases, said a number of sensible and interesting things, which were, however, somewhat lost in picturesque verbiage.[1]

The American audience had been prepared for his arrival by the publication of his *Poems* in 1881 and by the fact that his tour was sponsored by D'Oyly Carte to promote the production of Gilbert and Sullivan's comic opera *Patience*. The audience in New York was particularly primed by the fashion in the music halls for *tableaux vivants* based on 'the Society drawings in *Punch* by Du Maurier and the late John Leech'.[2] Wilde, therefore, had a difficult job on his hands. *Poems* had prepared the Americans to be shocked, *Punch* and *Patience* raised the expectation of a laugh. Wine had been turned into water and Wilde had to reverse the miracle: 'Satire, always as sterile as it is shameful and as impotent as it is insolent, paid [the Pre-Raphaelites] that usual homage which mediocrity pays to genius'.

> You have listened to *Patience* for a hundred nights and you have heard me for one only. It will make, no doubt, that satire more piquant by knowing something about the subject of it, but you must not judge of aestheticism by the satire of Mr. Gilbert. As little should you judge of the strength and splendour of sun or sea by the dust that dances in the beam, or the bubble that breaks on the wave.[3]

Wilde's subject was serious, if not original. He was informing the New World about contemporary developments in the arts back in the Old World. 'The English Renaissance of Art', the first lecture he used (beginning in New York on 9 January 1882) was about the Pre-Raphaelite Movement in Britain and an *avant-garde* in France in the work of Gautier and Baudelaire. Wilde built on the critical opinions of his two Oxford mentors, Ruskin and Pater, and wore his erudition on his sleeve, referring comfortably across a breathtaking cultural range from the Ancient Greeks, the German Romantics, to his friends and contemporaries.

The second lecture in his repertoire was called 'The Practical Application of the Principles of the Aesthetic Theory to Exterior and Interior House Decoration, with Observations upon Dress and Personal Ornaments'. The first known date of its delivery was 11 May 1882, when he came back to New York and could hardly deliver the same material again. As we have seen, it fell on more receptive ears. This lecture was particularly indebted to Ruskin's social aestheticism contained in *The Stones of Venice*, and to the 'Arts and Crafts' movement this helped to inspire. By now Wilde had learned enough about American culture to weave homely examples into his material. 'The old furniture brought over by the Pilgrims, two hundred years ago, which I saw in New England, is just as good and as beautiful today as it was when it first came here.' Or 'You have too many white walls. More colour is wanted. You should have such men as Whistler among you to teach you the beauty and joy of colour.'[4] 'Art and the Handicraftsman' is the title Wilde's literary executor and editor Robert Ross gave to what seems to have been another lecture delivered in America, and written there, in Philadelphia, at the start of his tour. This too is heavily dependent on Ruskin. It contains the anecdote of how Ruskin rallied a group of young students, Wilde included, to go road-building in a swamp in South Oxford as a gesture 'by which we might show that in all labour there was something noble'. Wilde, exaggerating his importance in the group at that time, turns this episode into a moment of personal conversion. This 'is how it first came to me at all to create an artistic movement in England, a movement to show the rich what beautiful things they might enjoy and the poor what beautiful things they might create.'[5] The opportunity for self-creation was there and Wilde took it. 'Our Aesthetic Visitor' manifested himself not just as a speaker for a movement, but as its founder and leading exponent.

The *Daily Graphic* describes how his audience remained divided:

> They had been induced to come to hear Wilde just as they might have been induced to go to see a five-legged monkey – that is, out of sheer curiosity. Their curiosity was quickly satisfied. They had seen the man dressed as a guy: they had heard him speak, and they had learned that he had nothing to tell them.

The other part of the audience

> fancied themselves to have been enthused and captivated by a love for the beautiful, and . . . prostrated themselves at the feet of Wilde as its embodiment.

(10 January 1882)

On his return to Britain in 1883, Wilde continued to make regular public appearances as a lecturer. In this there was nothing unusual. Ruskin and William Morris, among others, lectured routinely up and down the country promoting their socialist and aesthetic doctrines. In the days before television or radio it was the only way to reach a public beyond the less animated form of print. Wilde combined his elegant, arrogant style of address with the performance qualities of a stand-up comedian – a less normal feature of this form of communication. He also fed his extensive acquaintance with American culture into the material of his talks: 'Personal Impressions of America' became a number in his repertoire back home. A newspaper report of this lecture indicates the punctuating laughter of the audience, and with it the form of dialogue that evolved from Wilde's lecturing style:

> The American girl being one of the most charming despots that it would be thought possible to find living in a country with free republican institutions. (Laughter) She was often a most delightful oasis of unreasonableness in the desert of common sense.
>
> (Laughter)[6]

Journalism

In Wilde's career the decade of the 1880s is marked by enormous industry as a journalist. His regular review columns (often weekly) in the *Pall Mall Gazette* during 1885 to 1887 gave him ample opportunity to sharpen his critical wit, and to keep abreast of the divergent achievements of both popular and serious literary endeavour. It provided him with a space in which to refine his powers of succinct critical expression, and to meet the challenge Gilbert sets to Ernest in 'The Critic as Artist':

> from subjects of little or no importance . . . the true critic can, if it be his pleasure so to direct or waste his faculty of contemplation, produce work that will be flawless in beauty and instinct with intellectual subtlety . . . Treatment is the test.
>
> (Works, 1124–5)

Divergent topics met with urbane generosity if approved, mild or fierce ridicule if found wanting. Of the book *Dinners and Dishes*, Wilde asked:

> Who, indeed, in these degenerate days would hesitate between an ode and an omelette, a sonnet and a salamis? . . . we strongly recommend *Dinners and Dishes* to every one: it is brief and concise and makes no attempts at eloquence, which is extremely fortunate. For even on ortolans who could endure oratory?
>
> (Works, 950)

Wilde's advice about the use of Mahaffy's *The Principles of the Art of Conversation* was less generous to its author. Under the headline 'Aristotle at Afternoon Tea' he wrote:

> In discussing this important question of conversation, he has not merely followed the scientific method of Aristotle which is, perhaps, excusable, but he has adopted the literary style of Aristotle for which no excuse is possible . . . [T]he book can be warmly recommended to all who propose to substitute the vice of verbosity for the stupidity of silence.
>
> (Works, 970)

Wilde's review columns are a treasure house of wit which he was careful not to waste amid the ephemera of journalism: many of his most polished utterances are recycled in the critical dialogues he would later write. The cultural ground Wilde covered as a journalist was vast. It gave the strength of encyclopaedical authority to his work in aesthetic criticism, and provided precise targets for his work in social satire.

The Woman's World

Wilde's editorship of the monthly journal the *Woman's World* from 1887 to 1889 gave him the opportunity for direct, unified engagement in the arena of sexual politics. He began by changing the name of Cassell's fashion pages, which up to November 1887 had been called the *Lady's World*, to the *Woman's World* (no doubt enjoying privately the Latin pun on *mundus muliebris* – 'the woman's world' – while publicly professing to depart from it). Wilde stated his aims for the paper to Wemyss Reid, the Manager of Cassell's publishing house:

> It seems to me that at present it is too feminine, and not sufficiently womanly . . . it seems to me that the field of the *mundus muliebris*, the field of mere millinery and trimmings, is to some extent already occupied by such papers as *Queen* and the *Lady's Pictorial*, and that we should take a wider range, as well as a high standpoint, and deal not merely with what women wear, but with what they think, and what they feel. The *Lady's World* should be made the recognised organ for the expression of women's opinions on all subjects of literature, art, and modern life, and yet it should be a magazine that men could read with pleasure, and consider it a privilege to contribute to.

Wilde went on to list a host of distinguished women, some aristocratic, others not, some English, others American or South African, who might be asked to contribute to the journal under his editorship. He acknowledges that 'though many of our charming women have not had much literary experience' they could be encouraged to begin writing, in the clear hope that once a vehicle for women's writing had been established, more adventurous work would follow. This made good commercial sense, as well as holding out an idealism about sexual politics. Even so, he never abandons his aesthetic principles in the fervour of reform: 'But we should not rely exclusively on women, even for signed articles; artists have sex but art has none, and now and then an article by some man of letters would be of service.'

Wilde had plans for the layout as well as the contents of the new journal. 'Literary criticism I think might be done in the form of paragraphs; that is to say, not from the standpoint of the scholar or the pedant, but from the standpoint of what is pleasant to read.' He objects to the disguised form of advertising which some of the illustrations promulgate:

> at present there is too much money spent on illustrations, particularly illustrations of dress. They are also extremely unequal; many are charming . . . but many look like advertisements and give an air to the magazine that one wants to avoid, the air of directly puffing some firm or *modiste*.

Wilde wants 'news from Girton and Newnham Colleges at Cambridge, and from the Oxford colleges for women'. He proposes an article 'on the attitude of Universities towards women from the earliest times down to the present – a subject never fully treated of'. He suggests that 'a children's column' would be more popular than a section on music, and asserts that 'a popular serial story is absolutely necessary for the start', with a keen sense of how to catch and sustain a new readership. 'In conclusion let me say that I will be very happy indeed to give any assistance I can in reconstructing the *Lady's World*, and making it the first woman's paper in England' (Letters, 194–6).

Wilde was exceptionally well-connected to put such ambitious plans into action. He turned his 'At Homes' into editorial meetings: 'My wife is at home the first and third Thursdays in each month. Do come next Thursday and talk over the matter' he wrote to Helena Sickert, soliciting an article on Political Economy (Letters, 197–8). He asked for work from his friends in America, visited others for this purpose in London and in Paris. Contributions from his wife and mother were commissioned successfully, while his unanswered request to Queen Victoria for her poetry shows the uninhibited nature of his ambition for the paper. For two brief years, journalism for women and by women flourished as the *Woman's World* became exactly what Wilde had hoped. The abbreviated fashion pages were relegated to the end of the journal. In January 1888 they were completely eclipsed by five pictures of Sarah Bernhardt's dresses for her appearance in Paris in *La Tosca*, emphasising the theatricality of dress (which did have real commercial impact) and following the fate of one of Wilde's especial favourites. Matters of serious literary and political concern dominated the contents and new writers were encouraged.

The first issue with Wilde in charge, in November 1887, was a model of new woman's new journalism. It contained an article on 'The Position of Woman' by Eveline Portsmouth, heralding 'some new spring of feeling' that 'attracts women of all classes to each other' as a political force for the future. This was followed by a more light-hearted piece on 'The Oxford Ladies' College' by 'a member of one of them'. Wilde's editorial column, 'Literary and Other Notes' reviewed Princess Christian's translation of 'The Memoirs of Wilhelmina, Margravine of Bayreuth' and Mrs Sharp's anthology of women's writing, 'Women's Voices' which was praised as an endeavour, but criticised for its omission of many women writers, particularly those from earlier periods. Wilde went on to comment on the recent Church Congress at which women had been 'amongst the prominent speakers', and he argued that this in itself was 'a very remarkable proof of the growing influence of women's opinions on all matters connected with the elevation of our national life, and the amelioration of our social conditions'. He compared Britain and America, attributing the 'remarkable intellectual progress' of the United States to the significant participation of women in matters of public interest, made possible in part by 'American women, who edit many of the most powerful magazines and newspapers'. He explained his relegation of the fashion pages, and launched into discussion of 'rational dress', recapitulating views which he had aired elsewhere in 1884 and 1885. 'It is more probable that the dress of the twentieth century will emphasise distinctions of occupation, not distinctions of sex' he prophesied. But the editor himself soon lost interest in the scheme, and within a year 'Literary and Other Notes' featured rarely. He had become so lax by November 1889 when he officially left the editor's desk at Cassell's that his departure was only noticeable by the rapid degeneration of the journal into its previous commercial orientation. The conjunction of feminism and journalism begun by Wilde was taken forward by other papers emerging during the next decade such as *Woman's Life*, or *The Woman's Signal*.

'The Soul of Man Under Socialism'

The only other overtly political work which Wilde published was 'The Soul of Man Under Socialism' in *The Fortnightly Review* of 1891. With this essay he was participating in the national polemic about the values of socialism, promoted by George Bernard Shaw and the Fabian Society on one hand, and F. D. Maurice and the Christian Socialists on the other. William Morris had just published his noble Utopian romance, *News From Nowhere* (1890), and Annie Besant was pamphleteering with *Modern Socialism* (1886). Public debates such as 'Socialism versus Individualism' between Annie Besant representing the Fabians, and Frederick Miller representing the Liberty and Property Defence League, which took place in Nottingham Mechanics' Hall on 25 October 1890, represented the polarisation of opinion between radicals and conservatives. Like so many serious movements in Victorian politics, the polemic descended into parody, with such contributions as Robert Blatchford's 'Socialism: A Reply to the Encyclical of the Pope', reprinted from the *Clarion* in 1893, and 'A Litany for the use of the Respectable Classes' edited by Edward Carpenter, also in 1893:

> *Good Lord, deliver us,*
> From all loss of our position in society, and taint of vulgarity in our manners or connections, from poor relations, and from being mistaken for the butler or the lady's maid in our own houses.

> *Good Lord, deliver us,*
> From manual labour and the necessity of working for a living.[7]

Wilde's essay is not a parody – but he certainly means mischief, establishing his own orthodoxy in the face of raging socialist factions. He set out to dismantle the dichotomy between 'socialism' and 'individualism'; he emphasised the spiritual gains of socialism, relegating as an incidental advantage the material gain associated with the redistribution of wealth; he characterised Christ as a subversive, asocial agent, and grants Christianity a relative position in the march of progress rather than one of absolute authority. Even when his message resembles that of orthodox Fabianism, his aphoristic manner removes him from their pulpit. A comparison between Annie Besant's depiction of legislation in an ideal future state, and Wilde's, serves to illustrate the difference in tone. Besant writes:

> It may be that at some future time humanity shall have evolved to a point which shall render communism the only rational system; when every man is eager to do his share of work; anxious not to make too much for his own enjoyment; holding the scales of justice with a perfectly even hand; his one aim the general good, and his one effort the service of his brethren; when each individual is thus developed, law will become unnecessary, and communism will be the natural expression of social life; perfect freedom will be the lot of each, because each will have become a law unto himself.[8]

Wilde writes:

> a community is infinitely more brutalized by the habitual employment of punishment, than it is by the occasional occurrence of crime . . . The less punishment, the less crime . . . Starvation, and not sin, is the parent of modern crime . . . When private property is abolished there will be no necessity for crime, no demand for it; it will cease to exist . . . When each member of the community has sufficient for his wants, and is not interfered with by his neighbour, it will not be an object of any interest to him to interfere with any one else.

> (Works, 1182–3)

The style of Wilde's argument is supremely poised. He deploys structural balance and antithesis to posit a view which shows an ideal future in relation to a corrupt present. The tone is witty, the matter put succinctly. He is disingenuous, and uses surprise as a way of disarming opposition. The ideas that crime is necessary (for the starving), and that it is nurtured by the very establishment that punishes it, that crime is simply a matter of 'interference', are highly contentious. But the clarity of the phrasing, the simple-seeming authority of the voice, make the logic sound incontrovertible. This is all quite different from Besant's method of argument, which here makes no attempt to suggest evolutionary links between present and future, and which rests on the hardly credible belief that man is innately good and flourishes on altruism. The high moral ground which Besant occupies makes her position hard to accept, the leap between present and future impossible to imagine.

'The Soul of Man Under Socialism' turns aestheticism into a subversive political force, anarchic in function and aim. 'We are all of us more or less Socialists now-a-days . . . I think I am rather more than a Socialist. I am something of an Anarchist, I believe; but, of course, the dynamite policy is very absurd indeed,' Wilde announced in 1894 (Mikhail, I, 232). His ideology is only superficially linked with the Utopian vision of William Morris expressed in *News from Nowhere*, the literary culmination of the practical Arts and Crafts movement which Morris supported. Whereas Morris focuses on man as a social animal, and postulates ideal forms of action in which man can engage to promote the health of his society, balancing productive labour with creative work and turning creativity into a means to produce wealth and health, Wilde focuses on ideal man as supremely antisocial. He dismisses action as a lower form of existence than inaction, and prizes contemplation, 'being' rather than 'doing' as the end to which man should strive and which the ideal State should facilitate. 'The true perfection of man lies, not in what man has, but in what man is' (Works, 1178). 'Socialism', for Wilde, is a means to this end, not an end in itself: 'Socialism itself will be of value simply because it will lead to Individualism' (Works, 1175).

Paradoxically, this equips Wilde with a vocabulary and a strategy to counter fierce opponents of Socialism. These were the Liberals, who viewed the idea of the conversion of 'private property into public wealth', and the substitution of 'co-operation for competition' (Works, 1175) as gross interference by the State into the favourite British occupation of 'doing as one likes', that tolerant liberalism which John Stuart Mill had outlined so eloquently and persuasively in *On Liberty* (1859). From the start Wilde makes 'Individualism' into the keystone of his argument. But he takes the vocabulary of the opposition in order to redefine it, discriminating a 'true Individualism' from 'an Individualism that is false' (Works, 1178).

Wilde begins where Besant, in *Modern Socialism*, had left off. Her conclusion was defensive; Wilde starts, and continues, on the offensive. Besant states:

> It remains, in conclusion, to note the chief objections raised to Socialism by its opponents. Of these the most generally urged are three: that it will check individual initiative and energy; that it will destroy individuality; that it will unduly restrict personal liberty.

She controverts these 'three' objections by flat denial: 'instead of destroying individuality [socialism] will cultivate and accentuate it, and indeed will make it possible for the first time in civilisation for the vast majority'. Her very last gesture is to let the argument degenerate into emotional song:

> O nations undivided,
> O single People, and free;
> We dreamers, we derided,
> We mad blind men that see,
> We bear you witness ere ye come that ye shall be.[9]

Wilde operates at a consistently intellectual level, never appealing to the emotions, never appealing to the moral conscience. Indeed, these are both cheap strategies which he recognises and scorns. 'All sympathy is fine, but sympathy with suffering is the least fine mode. It is tainted with egotism' (Works, 1195). His argument begins with this point: 'it is much more easy to have sympathy with suffering than it is to have sympathy with thought' (Works, 1174). He rejects sympathy as a motive for political action, castigates altruism and its practical social corollary under capitalism, acts of charity. Charity, he argues, in line with Fabians such as Shaw, is iniquitous because it simply prolongs the degradation of the poor under an unjust political regime. The first principle he establishes is that 'The proper aim is to try and reconstruct society on such a basis that poverty will be impossible' (Works, 1174). He has managed to erect a standard tenet of socialism on what looks like the ideology of the opposition. He drives this method home by looking at charity from the point of view of the supposed beneficiary who then emerges as the victim of precisely that kind of interference which the Liberals purport to resent. 'Charity they feel to be a ridiculously inadequate mode of partial restitution, or sentimental dole, usually accompanied by some impertinent attempt on the part of the sentimentalist to tyrannize over their private lives.' He regards the ungrateful, rebellious poor, and criminals, as positive agents of change: forces to overthrow the various tyrannies which restrict personal freedom. 'Disobedience, in the eyes of any one who has read history, is man's original virtue' (Works, 1176).

Wilde is then free to consider what benefits will accrue to the individual in such a system, and to outline a cult of self-development, open to every individual only when freed from the constraints of material poverty or concern:

> With the abolition of private property, then, we shall have true, beautiful, healthy Individualism. Nobody will waste his life in accumulating things and the symbols for things. One will live. To live is the rarest thing in the world. Most people exist, that is all.
>
> (Works, 1178)

The arrogance of tone here permitted reviewers to take exception to Wilde's definition of 'individualism': 'The sort of individuality to which Oscar attaches great moment is that which recognises no law or authority. He wants the world to be all Oscar Wilde.'[10]

For Wilde, the highest expression of individualism, and of life, is art. 'Art is the most intense mode of Individualism that the world has known': a principle reached by careful economic argument and not vague or idealistic aestheticism (Works, 1184). The rest of the essay is devoted to an exploration of the relationship between the artist and the State. Wilde considers the real terms of late nineteenth-century Britain, where intolerant, ignorant 'Public Opinion' expressed through journalism exercises tyranny over the artist, and compels degenerative art forms to dominate a false cultural life. He contrasts this with the ideal terms of his revisioned Utopia. 'The form of government that is most suitable to the artist is no government at all' (Works, 1192). This is the most radical expression of his anarchism, given that he envisions a classless society in which every member is an artist devoted to the development of their 'personality'.

Throughout the essay Wilde uses a rhetorical technique which he learned from Matthew Arnold, whose *Culture and Anarchy* (1869) he is implicitly criticising. Arnold, neglecting economics, had addressed exclusively the middle class, and promoted 'culture' as a means of elevating its spiritual life; his argument proceeds by repetition and refrain. 'Sweetness and Light' is pitted against 'Barbarians' and 'Anarchy'. Wilde too uses repetition, setting the prized term 'personality' against the 'demoralizing' factors that inhibit its development. Both these terms acquire a resonance in the course of the essay. The distance at which Wilde situates himself from Arnold, even while deploying his rhetorical tactics, can be seen in his rejection of all external forms of authority, and his promotion of anarchy as the only form of government which will allow the individual to develop fully. A concrete example of Wilde's rejection of Arnold's vision is given by their opposed attitudes to the 'classics' of literature. For

Arnold these provided the ultimate resource of 'sweetness and light' available to all who could read; for Wilde they are simply another form of iniquitous authority, inhibiting spiritual growth. 'The fact is, the public make use of the classics of a country as a means of checking the progress of Art' (Works, 1186). 'Progress,' he argues, 'is the realization of Utopias' (Works, 1184). This perpetual state of departure for undiscovered terrain is made possible by an attitude of dynamic criticism, not complacent or fearful obedience.

Critical dialogues

The realms into which the spirit of criticism can take humanity are described in the two-part dialogue 'The Critic as Artist': a further revision of Matthew Arnold's dogmatism:

> [T]here has never been a creative age that has not been critical also. For it is the critical faculty that invents fresh forms. The tendency of creation is to repeat itself.
>
> (Works, 1119)

The first title Wilde gave to these dialogues for publication in *The Nineteenth Century* signalled his engagement with Arnold more emphatically: 'The True Function and Value of Criticism: with some Remarks on the Importance of Doing Nothing'. Wilde was responding to Arnold's essay 'The Function of Criticism at the Present Time' (1865). In that essay Arnold had announced that criticism is 'the endeavour . . . to see the object as in itself it really is'.[11] Wilde notoriously states: 'the primary aim of the critic is to see the object as in itself it really is not' (Works, 1128), establishing an apparent anarchy in the sphere of criticism to match that in the social sphere set out by 'The Soul of Man Under Socialism'. The root of each is the same: a privileging of 'individualism'. He does not arrive at this aphorism without the aid of Pater, whose Preface to *The Renaissance* outlined the aims of the 'aesthetic critic' in cautious terms which prize the subjective view more highly than Arnold's professed objectivity:

> 'To see the object as in itself it really is,' has been justly said to be the aim of all true criticism whatever; and in aesthetic criticism the first step towards seeing one's object as it really is, is to know one's own impression as it really is, to discriminate it, to realise it distinctly.[12]

So fundamental was the intrusion of the relative spirit, or subjectivity of knowledge, into the domain of criticism that it dictates even the dialogue form in which Wilde chose to cast his aesthetic philosophy. His choice of form constitutes a statement of the matter expressed within the dialogue. 'For what is Truth?' asks Gilbert. 'In matters of religion, it is simply the opinion that has survived. In matters of science, it is the ultimate sensation. In matters of art, it is one's last mood' (Works, 1143). Dialogue, in homage to Plato as the father of dialectic, permits a multiplicity of perspective, and evades the falsifying objectivity of Arnold's stance. 'By its means [the thinker] can both reveal and conceal himself, and give form to every fancy, and reality to every mood. By its means he can exhibit the object from each point of view, and show it in the round, as a sculptor . . .' (Works, 1143). So Wilde permits his leading partner of the dialogue, Gilbert, the leisure to reflect on the activity in which he is engaged. This act of literary self-reflexivity mirrors the refined self-consciousness that Wilde's critical spirit inculcates: 'self-consciousness and the critical spirit are one' (Works, 1118). The critical dialogue is a method of seeking 'truth' in 'endless dialogue with one's self',[13] when 'truth itself is but a possibility, realisable not as a general conclusion, but rather as the elusive effect of a particular personal experience'.[14]

The subjects discussed by Ernest and Gilbert range widely over contemporary polemics. The most radical proposition of the first part of the dialogue, and that which has been taken forward by literary theory in the twentieth century, is that the 'highest criticism' (examples of which Gilbert offers from the work of Ruskin and Pater) 'treats the work of art simply as a starting-point for a new creation':

> It does not confine itself – let us at least suppose so for the moment – to discovering the real intention of the artist and accepting that as final. And in this it is right, for the meaning of any beautiful created thing is, at least, as much in the soul of him who looks at it, as it was in his soul who wrought it. Nay, it is rather the beholder who lends to the beautiful thing its myriad meanings, and makes it marvellous for us, and sets it in some new relation to the age, so that it becomes a vital portion of our lives, and a symbol of what we pray for, or perhaps of what, having prayed for, we fear that we may receive.
>
> (Works, 1127)

Wilde establishes a dynamic relationship between the work of art and its spectator, reader or audience. The individual is responsible for the construction of meaning or mystery generated by a work of art. The originator of the work lays no greater claim to its signification than its receptive public. Meaning is not single, static or authorised, but multiple, changeful and relative. A work of art cannot be explained; an author's 'intention' cannot be recovered and is anyway of no consequence. The 'beautiful created thing' acquires its own plural life with the beholder and relative to the era of the beholder. A host of theoretical disciplines this century find inspiration here, from Wimsatt's argument about the 'intentional fallacy' and the importance of this for the principles of 'practical criticism' developed by I. A. Richards, to Barthes' account of 'the death of the author' and the significance of this argument for the schools of deconstruction and post-structuralism.

The second part of the dialogue concerns the liberating and spiritualising benefits that accrue to the individual who practises this method of critical response. Although Wilde rejects all forms of authority that do not come from within the individual, the critic is nevertheless paradoxically liberated from the constraints of personality. 'There is no passion that we cannot feel, no pleasure that we may not gratify, and we can choose the time of our initiation and the time of our freedom also' (Works, 1135). By engaging with the artistic work of others, 'the imagination . . . enables us to live . . . countless lives' (Works, 1138). The experiential and emotional range of the individual is extended by art, as the critic is led further and further into the realm of contemplation and removed from the sphere of action. It is because the experience of art is inward and contemplative that Wilde prizes it so highly: 'the contemplative life, the life that has for its aim not *doing* but *being*, and not *being* merely, but *becoming*' permits us to 'make ourselves spiritual by detaching ourselves from action, and become perfect by the rejection of energy' (Works, 1138–9). Because art can engender a critical spirit that leads away from external action and towards internal experience, Wilde announces that 'all art is immoral'. His choice of vocabulary is deliberately provocative, but he permits Gilbert to justify the use of the term 'immoral' to the puzzled Ernest. 'Yes. For emotion for the sake of emotion is the aim of art, and emotion for the sake of action is the aim of life, and of that practical organization of life we call society' (Works, 1136). Art generates 'sterile' emotions, those which do not lead to action and so inevitably into the sphere of behaviour susceptible of moral judgement. He does not mean that art is culpable in any sense, but rather that it permits the critic experience that operates outside the parameters of ethically evaluated behaviour. There is much overlap between the aesthetic philosophy of this dialogue and the political philosophy of 'The Soul of Man Under Socialism'. The same vision of human perfection or ideality is posited by each.

The subject of 'The Decay of Lying', Wilde's first critical dialogue, picks up on Plato's famous dismissal (in Book 10 of *The Republic*) of poetry from his ideal State on the grounds that it celebrated illusion or 'lying'. Wilde's contention in the dialogue is to defend literature from the taint of corruption, and to argue that art only has a degenerative effect when it seeks to imitate life. When the 'art of lying' decays, when the imagination is atrophied, and takes to 'a morbid and unhealthy faculty of truth-telling' (Works, 1074), fiction takes its inspiration from the environment inhabited by the artist and a 'realist' school develops. This, Vivian explains, is 'the true decadence' (Works, 1078) both for artist and public. In place of realism, Vivian celebrates romance:

> The only beautiful things . . . are the things that do not concern us. As long as a thing is useful or necessary to us, or affects us in any way, either for pain or pleasure, or appeals strongly to our sympathies, or is a vital part of the environment in which we live, it is outside the proper sphere of art. To art's subject matter we should be more or less indifferent.
>
> (Works, 1077)

When the *Newcastle Chronicle* came to summarise the contents of the essay, the reviewer announced that Vivian's complaint against realism and contemporary culture was that:

> there is too much calling a spade a spade instead of glorifying it by imaginative powers into something beautiful and less practical. In fact in reading him one almost wonders whether he takes such mundane things as meals as ordinary mortals do, or has them conveyed to his inward parts by some novel aerial arrangement of his own subtle invention.
>
> (22 September 1891)

Unlike 'The Critic as Artist', which was set in London and in which two fictional aesthetes discuss the metropolitan topics of the day, 'The Decay of Lying' is set in Nottinghamshire, in the provinces, and the characters' names are Cyril and Vivian: the names of Wilde's sons who at the time of writing were aged three and two. Vivian (the name of the younger son) is the leading partner in the dialogue. His insights have the uninhibited confidence of one who has not learned to be cowed by received wisdom, but who looks at art, and its relationships with life, with unclouded eyes that see keenly according to his own authority. The partners in the dialogue observe the fashions of the day from a geographical and intellectual distance that permits discriminating perspective – so obvious to the clear-sighted as to be 'child's play' – and also, Wilde implies, necessary for proper education. 'The proper school to learn art in is not Life but Art,' Vivian announces (Works, 1080). But, as we have seen, the appeal to the provinces was in vain, at least in Newcastle. The dialogue becomes more radical still, reversing the traditional metaphor of mimesis that art holds the mirror up to nature. Instead Vivian argues that Life imitates Art. The anecdotal evidence for this is amusing but not compelling, while the illustration Vivian picks from Impressionist painting to further the argument that 'Nature, no less than Life, is an imitation of Art' carries persuasion into the heart of the discussion:

> Where, if not from the Impressionists, do we get those wonderful brown fogs that come creeping down our streets, blurring the gas-lamps and changing the houses into monstrous shadows? . . . Nature is no great mother who has borne us. She is our creation. It is our brain that she quickens to life. Things are because we see them, and what we see, and how we see it, depends on the Arts that have influenced us.
>
> (Works, 1086)

The argument anticipates that developed in 'The Critic as Artist. Part II' in so far as art not only extends, but actually determines, the experiential or perceptual range of the spectator. Wilde replaces naturalist determinism with aesthetic determinism. It is art that provides the categories which make experience meaningful, which imposes an order on natural chaos to make knowledge possible and interpretation accessible. The illustration Wilde offers from the visual arts provides a pictorial version of the linguistic argument in 'The Critic as Artist', that 'language . . . is the parent, and not the child, of thought' (Works, 1121). The 'brown fogs' are facetiously chosen since fog would normally be held to obscure vision rather than to enhance it, and it is normally taken as something to look through rather than to look at. It is a judiciously selected illustration of the principle that the subject matter of art is secondary to the style in which it is executed. 'Art begins with abstract decoration with purely imaginative and pleasurable work dealing with what is unreal and non-existent,' Vivian declares (Works, 1078). Fog could hardly be more apposite.

Taking these two dialogues together, a complex interrelationship between the spectator and the work of art, between art and life, is established. Fundamental to Wilde's critical enterprise is the notion that vision, truth and insight are constructed by human intelligence and are relative to the individual's experience. There is no authority external to humanity or the individual. There is nothing of value except what man has made.

But Wilde's contemporaries were distracted from the philosophical import of the message by his outspoken impatience with middle-class values. The bourgeoisie found their spokesman in one 'John Middleman' who wrote an angry letter about 'The Decay of Lying' to the *London Figaro* complaining about 'our sage-green friend, Oscar' (10 October 1891). Others, less class-bound in their response, were still distracted by the style of Wilde's address:

To call Mr. Wilde's favourite rhetorical figure by the name of paradox is really too complimentary; he carries his joke too far, and makes paradox ridiculous. The form of language in which he chooses to conceal his thoughts is easily described. His method is this: he takes some well-established truth, something in which the wisdom of centuries and the wit of the greatest men have concurred, and asserts the contrary; he then whittles his assertion down, and when at his best arrives at the point which might have been reached by starting at the other end.

(Critical Heritage, 92)

Arthur Symons, in his review of *Intentions*, notices the link between Wilde's contempt for middle-class values, and his choice of paradoxical expression:

A passion for caprice, a whimsical Irish temperament, a love of art for art's sake – it is in qualities such as these that we find the origin of the beautiful farce of aestheticism, the exquisite echoes of the *Poems*, the subtle decadence of *Dorian Gray*, and the paradoxical truths, the perverted common sense, of the *Intentions*. Mr. Wilde, with a most reasonable hatred of the *bourgeois* seriousness of dull people, has always taken refuge from the commonplace in irony.

(Critical Heritage, 94)

Even Richard Le Gallienne recommends *Intentions* as 'delightful reading, especially . . . for their humour' (Critical Heritage, 102). It remained for theorists of the twentieth century to take Wilde's incisive criticism forward.

The ultimate distillations of Wilde's criticism are, as the early reviewers of *Intentions* signal, the two sequences of paradoxes which he published in 1894: 'A Few Maxims for the Instruction of the Over-Educated' (*Saturday Review*, 17 November 1894) and 'Phrases and Philosophies for the Use of the Young' (*The Chameleon*, 1894). These draw together the range of subjects, social, political and aesthetic, which he explored at length in his essays in criticism, and voice his insights in the most contentious style possible. 'A truth ceases to be true when more than one person believes in it' (Works, 1245).

Notes

1 *New York Herald*, 12 May 1882.
2 *Pan*, 8 January 1881.
3 'The English Renaissance of Art', *Essays and Lectures*, ed. Ross, 120, 136.
4 'The Practical Application . . .', *Essays and Lectures*, 161, 166.

5 'Art and the Handicraftsman', *Essays and Lectures*, 193, 192.
6 Unidentified newspaper article, The Ross Collection, Bodleian Library Oxford, Ross d.211, 88–9.
7 *A Socialist Ritual*. Reprinted from *Justice* (London: Twentieth Century Press, 1893) 11.
8 *Modern Socialism* (London: Freethought Publishing Company, 1886) 10.
9 *Modern Socialism*, 49–50.
10 *Weekly Dispatch*, 8 February 1891.
11 Matthew Arnold, *Complete Prose Works*, ed. R. H. Super (Ann Arbor: University of Michigan Press, 1962) III, 258.
12 Walter Pater, *The Renaissance. Studies in Art and Poetry*, ed. D. L. Hill (Berkeley: University of California Press, 1980) xix.
13 Walter Pater, *Plato and Platonism* ([1893] London: Macmillan, 1895) 177.
14 Ibid., 175.

3   Theatre practice and innovation

In England during the 1880s and 1890s there were repeated calls among the generation of playwrights that included Pinero, Jones, Shaw and Wilde, and theatre critics such as William Archer and Max Beerbohm, for new theatre writing to be 'literary'. They wanted a British *avant garde* to match the exciting experiments on the Continent, where the Naturalism practised by Zola, Ibsen and Strindberg was challenging audiences with socially and scientifically based issue plays, as well as innovative stage craft. There was no State subsidy for theatre in Britain at that time, and commercial interests dominated the stage. Spectacular melodrama, music hall, long-running revivals of Shakespeare plays, and adaptations of French well-made-plays filled the theatres with popular successes but apparently failed to use the stage as an instrument of literary expression or political change. During the 1860s the actor turned playwright, T. W. Robertson, had begun to write 'problem plays', to confront social issues, but their success was short lived and little work was done in this area for the next 20 years. In this context the plays Wilde wrote during the 1890s appeared extraordinary. On the first production of *A Woman of No Importance* in 1893, William Archer hailed Wilde as unique:

> the one essential fact about Mr Oscar Wilde's dramatic work is that it must be taken on the very highest plane of modern English drama, and furthermore, that it stands alone on that plane. In intellectual calibre, artistic competence – ay, and in dramatic instinct to boot – Mr Wilde has no rival among his fellow-workers for the stage. He is a thinker and a writer; they are more or less able, thoughtful, original playwrights.
>
> (Critical Heritage, 144)

Wilde's ambition as a playwright coupled with an immensely practical concern for stage craft and a fascination with the art of acting. There is a 12-year gap between his first efforts to write for the stage, with *Vera; or, The Nihilists* (1880) and *The Duchess of Padua* (1883) and the large artistic or commercial successes of *Salome* and the society comedies that began in 1892. Writing to Richard D'Oyly Carte about *Vera*, Wilde claimed that 'the play is as good an acting play as it is [because] I took every actor's suggestion I could get' (Letters, 104). During the period which followed he learned much about the practicalities of the theatre from his work as a reviewer for the

63

journals *Theatre* and the *Dramatic Review*, from his involvement in the
rational dress movement, and with E. W. Godwin, the designer and
theatre archaeologist. He made friends with theatre critics William
Archer and George Bernard Shaw, and with many actors, not least
among whom were Lily Langtree, Sarah Bernhardt, Elizabeth Robins,
Ellen Terry and Henry Irving. He also cultivated the actor-managers
who produced his plays: George Alexander at the St James's Theatre
and Herbert Beerbohm Tree at the Haymarket. Even when not
engaged in professional reviewing Wilde was an ardent visitor to the
theatre, familiar with the classical revivals of the period and with
fashions in new writing.

Wilde's letters throughout the decade of the 1880s show him to
be a regular theatre-goer ('Will you come to my wife's box at *The
Hunchback*, Lyceum, on Saturday evening,' he wrote to E. W. Godwin
in early 1885 (Letters, 172)) and embroiled in all sorts of plans to
make and break the careers of theatre workers. His support of friends
whom he respected was both unstinting and professionally helpful.
Elizabeth Robins recorded how, on her arrival in London from
America in 1888, Wilde 'did . . . everything for me':

> He warned me against a shady theatre manager, advised me about
> a reliable agent and solicitor, when I needed their help, and sug-
> gested plays for matinée production to introduce the unknown
> actress to London managers and public.
>
> He was generous, too, in coming to see me act; and in sending
> or giving me afterwards his valuable opinion on play, production
> and acting. Busy as he then was with his own creative work and
> social engagements, he even came to see me in plays that were
> not at all in his line, such as the sugar-coated *Little Lord Fauntleroy*
> in which I played Dearest under Mrs Kendall's direction.
>
> (Letters, 222)

Wilde's knowledge of how commercial success was to be achieved in
the theatre is evident as early as 1882. Preparing for the unrealised
production of his *Duchess of Padua* in New York, he wrote to Mary
Anderson who was to play the lead, indicating that he was well
aware that a good script was only half the battle for success:

> I am very anxious to learn what decision you have come to as
> regards the production of my play. It is in our power to procure
> all the conditions of success by the beauty of costume, the dignity
> of scenery, the perfection of detail and dramatic order, without
> which, in England at any rate, you could not get your right position
> as an artist.
>
> (Letters, 126)

Three years later, back in England, Wilde devoted considerable critical attention to the methods of production used for Shakespeare's plays. He began with a short article for the *Dramatic Review*, 'Shakespeare on Scenery', looking at the internal evidence of Shakespeare's plays for authorial concerns with the practical constraints on staging, before turning to the contemporary situation:

> It is impossible to read him without seeing that he is constantly protesting against the two special limitations of the Elizabethan stage – the lack of suitable scenery, and the fashion of men playing women's parts – just as he protests against other difficulties with which the managers of theatres still have to contend, such as actors who do not understand their words; actors who miss their cues; actors who overact their parts; actors who mouth; actors who gag; actors who play to the gallery, and amateur actors.
>
> (14 March 1885)

Wilde saw theatre as a collaborative art, which incurred impediments as great as its opportunities. And he wished, in this article, to draw attention away from the star-centred glamour of the actor, which dominated practical theatre, in order to dignify the participation of others. He recognised early that theatre was pre-eminently a form of visual art, rather than literary art, declaring: 'theatrical audiences are far more impressed by what they look at than by what they listen to'.[1] For this reason Wilde wished to promote the art of the 'scene-painter' or set-designer:

> It were better for the critics to exert whatever influence they may possess towards restoring the scene-painter to his proper position as an artist, and not allowing him to be built over by the property man, or hammered to death by the carpenter. I have never seen any reason myself why such artists as Mr. Beverley, Mr. Walter Hann, and Mr. Telbin should not be entitled to become academicians.[2]

When Wilde wrote this, Walter Hann had designed all Bancroft's productions at the Haymarket Theatre for the previous five years (1880–85). Hann went on to contribute designs to all four productions of Wilde's comedies, and to be the set-designer, together with H. P. Hall, of *The Importance of Being Earnest* at the St James's Theatre in 1895.

Wilde's interest in the visual dimension of performance was stimulated by his acquaintance with Edward William Godwin (1833–1886) who, during 1884 and 1885, was designing the interior of the Wildes' 'House Beautiful' at 16 Tite Street in Chelsea, and who was also an experimental set-designer. Godwin's partner from 1865 to 1875 had been the star actress Ellen Terry. Their daughter, Edith,

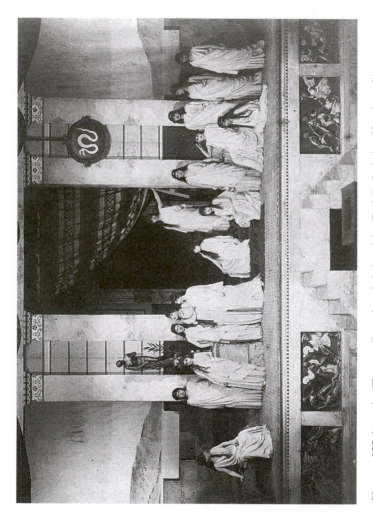

Chorus of Helena in Troas, *directed and designed by E. W. Godwin, Hengler's Circus, London, May 1886*
V & A Picture Library (Neg. No. BW 44931)

became an actress – less successful than Ellen – while their son, Edward Gordon Craig, went on to make a much more distinguished name for himself as a theatre designer than Godwin, but not without deploying many of his father's ideas. In 1882 Godwin founded the 'Costume Society' which, as stated in the title of the Society's manifesto, existed for 'Promoting the Knowledge of Costume by Copying and Publishing Historical Costume from Contemporary Sources Only'. Godwin was joined in this project by Whistler, Beerbohm Tree, and Wilde, among others, and he used the Costume Society to promote his archaeological interest in theatre design:

> I maintain that we do not go to a theatre simply to hear passionate recitations and funny speeches, but to witness such a performance as will place us as nearly as possible as spectators of the original scene or the thing represented, and so gain information of man, manners, customs, costumes, and countries – and this result is obtainable where accuracy in every particular is secured.[3]

In fact, for Godwin, the educational benefits of this approach to theatre design were secondary to the aesthetic effect produced, which was to unify the visual mood in harmony with the action represented. In 1884 he collaborated with Lady Archibald Campbell and her company of 'Pastoral Players' to produce an outdoor *As You Like It* in Coombe Park in Surrey. The production was revived in 1885 when it was seen by the influential experimenter in ensemble playing and archaeological production, the Duke of Saxe Meiningen, and reviewed by Wilde in the *Dramatic Review* (6 June 1885). Lady Archibald explained Godwin's direction of the play in an article, 'The Woodland Gods', for the *Woman's World* in November 1888:

> The composition of stage effect and the art of acting generally, whether indoors or outdoors, meant for his wonderful genius what the art of musical composition meant for . . . Wagner – it meant growth, originality, freedom from tradition. As art-director of our natural stage, he urged more than ever on the actor (whether the actor occupied the principle *role*, or that of the silent super) the necessity that the ordinary *technique* of the stage must be held by him subordinate, and sacrificed to pictorial and realistic effect.

In May 1886 Godwin collaborated with the playwright John Todhunter to produce the Greek revivalist play *Helena in Troas* at Hengler's Circus in Argyll Street (Great Pulteney Street). This was the only London venue large enough to hold Godwin's ambitiously 'authentic' ancient Greek set and design. Constance Wilde participated as a chiton-wearing handmaiden to Helena. She also reviewed the production for the *Lady*, while Wilde himself reviewed it for the *Dramatic Review* on 22 May 1886.

This is the context in which Wilde put his radical call for the renewal of theatre practice into the lengthy article 'Shakespeare and Stage Costume' for *The Nineteenth Century* in May 1885. It eventually found its way into *Intentions*, under the new title 'The Truth of Masks. A Note on Illusion'. The essay joins the chorus of complaints and calls for the renewal of the contemporary theatre by other playwrights and critics of the period. But what distinguishes Wilde's contribution to the debate is the fact that he focuses on the practical methods of production, and not, like his colleagues, on the literary quality of plays written for production. The essay is an elaborate defence of Godwin's archaeological staging methods and his pictorial vision for the design of the theatre set. But whereas Godwin sought to promote theatrical realism, Wilde emphasised dramatic illusion:

> Art, and art only, can make archaeology beautiful; and the theatric art can use it most directly and most vividly, for it can combine in one exquisite presentation the illusion of actual life with the wonder of the unreal world.
>
> (Works, 1163)

Wilde represents Godwin ('one of the most artistic spirits of this century in England') as a visionary designer, gifted with the ability to let an audience experience 'the rules of lofty composition and the unity of artistic effect' (Works, 1163). Wilde wished to alter the hierarchical method of communication which ruled the stage in his time; he was dissatisfied with the predominance of the star actor, and the subordination of all forms of dramatic communication to performance by this one figure. He also recognised that naturalism in the theatre had arrived to stay, but he would still plead for this style to be yoked in the service of 'illusion' or romance, and not to serve as an end in itself. 'The background should always be kept as a background, and colour subordinated to effect.' He argued that such aesthetic integrity could only be maintained 'when there is one single mind directing the whole production . . . a theatre should be in the power of a cultured despot. There may be division of labour, but there must be no division of mind' (Works, 1172). This may seem commonplace to us now, but in Wilde's period it was far from the norm. Actor-manager establishments, developing house styles and controlling the productions which took place at certain theatres were in their infancy.

On the very practical matter of 'dress rehearsals', Wilde argued these should be practised more frequently because they would explain to actors that 'there is a form of gesture and movement that is not merely appropriate to each style of dress, but really conditioned by it', and 'until an actor is at home in his dress, he is not at home in his part' (Works, 1172–3). Wilde's quest for a unity of aesthetic effect on stage extended to the actor's meaningful use of the body, which was determined as much by the internal emotions to be represented in the role, as by its external apparel. His first mention of George Alexander, playing Laertes in Henry Irving's fabled 1885 production of *Hamlet*, was to admire the actor's ability to be 'at home' in his costume, as in his role: Alexander was 'a most effective presence' with a 'charming voice, and . . . capacity for wearing costumes with ease and elegance' (Works, 953). Godwin's archaeological method of production and design offered Wilde a form of 'mask'. It permitted playwright and company to step outside themselves, to impersonate through the impersonality of a unified aesthetic effect. 'Man is least himself when he speaks in his own person. Give him a mask, and he will tell you the truth,' Wilde announced in 'The Critic as Artist' (Works, 1142).

In that dialogue Wilde also offers a radical appraisal of the art of acting: 'The actor is a critic of the drama. He shows the poet's work under new conditions, and by a method special to himself. He takes the written word, and action, gesture and voice become the media of revelation' (Works, 1131). In the context of the developing argument, this position anticipates twentieth-century notions of the theatre as a place of intellectual arousal to be achieved in part by the precision of an actor who shows that he is acting. In Wilde's vocabulary, the actor assumes a mask at the same time as he shows that this is what he has done. Wilde's mask in the critical dialogue, Gilbert, continues:

> there is no such thing as Shakespeare's Hamlet. If Hamlet has something of the definiteness of a work of art, he also has all the obscurity that belongs to life. There are as many Hamlets as there are melancholies . . . Yes: and as art springs from personality, so it is only to personality that it can be revealed, and from the meeting of the two comes right interpretative criticism . . . The critic . . . will always be showing us the work of art in some new relation to our age.
>
> (Works, 1131–2)

Wilde's use of epigram within the dialogue of his plays can be seen as just as effective a means of breaking dramatic illusion as of sustaining the fictional world of debonair society. The aphorisms are gifts to the actor who, as critic of the drama in which he performs, can use them to reveal his mask in the process of impersonating it. The early reviewer who declared of *Lady Windermere's Fan*, for instance, that 'paradox is the thing, not the play' (Critical Heritage, 127), noticed this effect without having a dramatic theory in which to place it. Equally disruptive of the suspension of belief for an audience of Wilde's plays is his deployment of the conventions of melodrama, and his scripting of grand emotional tableaux, which can seem at aesthetic odds with the intellectual play of dialogue. These features can be observed in all Wilde's plays, but are particularly conspicuous in *A Woman of No Importance* where so much of the aphoristic dialogue is lifted from *The Picture of Dorian Gray* and the overt melodrama is deployed self-consciously.

In representing the actor as 'critic of the drama', and in writing plays for such a breed of actors, Wilde was addressing an ideal state of affairs. There were frustrating times, such as the censorship of *Salome* in June 1892, when Wilde held the actor in nothing but contempt:

> The curious thing is this: all the arts are free in England, except the actor's art; it is held by the Censor that the stage degrades and that actors desecrate fine subjects, so the Censor prohibits not the publication of *Salome* but its production. Yet not one single actor has protested against this insult to the stage – not even Irving, who is always prating about the Art of the Actor. This shows how few actors are artists.
>
> (Letters, 317)

Wilde's calmer views about the ideal actor's art, and about the simultaneity of the playwright's criticism and creation, are well ahead of the conventions of his era. In 'The Soul of Man Under Socialism' he elevates 'even Irving' to exactly this *avant-garde* stature, and analyses the causes of his success:

> With his marvellous and vivid personality . . . with his extraordinary power, not over mere mimicry but over imaginative and intellectual creation, Mr Irving . . . could have . . . made as much success and money as a man could possibly desire. But his object was not that. His object was to realize his own perfection as an artist, under certain conditions, and in certain forms of Art. At first he appealed to the few: now he has educated the many. He has created in the public both taste and temperament . . . that success is entirely due to the fact that he did not accept their standard, but realized his own.
>
> (Works, 1190)

The ideal actor's blend of mimicry and intellectual creation corresponds with the way Wilde wanted his society plays to be mounted on stage. He was scrupulous about how the illusion of contemporaneous Society settings was to be achieved (they are all set 'in the present'). This was to establish a dynamic critical relationship between the work of art and the age in which it is performed – and to lace it with satire. Advising Grace Hawthorne who wished to produce *Lady Windermere's Fan* in Boston in 1894, Wilde wrote:

My plays are difficult plays to produce well: they require artistic setting on the stage, a good company that knows something of the style essential to high comedy, beautiful dresses, a sense of the luxury of modern life, and unless you are going out with a management that is able to pay well for things that are worth paying for, and to spend money in suitable presentation, it would be much better for you not to think of producing my plays.

(Letters, 374)

This represented not simply the desire for a composed artistic effect of the kind for which Godwin had campaigned, but also Wilde's understanding of the only terms in which the mechanism of his comedy could work properly. This was by problematising the relationship between the world on stage and the world off stage, by transgressing the boundaries between fiction and reality. Only under these conditions would the actor have the opportunity to be a 'critic of the drama', and the playwright a critic of his age.

Wilde was fortunate with the managements in London who took on his work. Not only did George Alexander at the St James's Theatre who produced *Lady Windermere's Fan* in 1892, hold to ensemble-playing as house policy, believing in 'the proper balance of the play and not the predominance of the leading part',[4] but he was also as lavish in his attention to scenic detail as Wilde could wish. This too was policy at St James's, as Alexander's wife Florence recalled. 'I arranged the flowers, in those days we had so much detail, and I loved to make things look real. I ordered the gowns to suit the decorations of the scene so that nothing clashed or was ugly'.[5] When the play toured the provinces later in 1892 these methods of production were maintained and admired:

> Mr. Alexander toured the play with *all* the London props, scenery and costume. And the trouble was well worth taking; for half the effect of a play like *Lady Windermere's Fan* lies in its 'society' atmosphere. The exquisite taste and suitability of the dresses, the care with which the minor parts are performed, are essential to the success of the production.[6]

It was, of course, possible for the Society audience of these plays to miss the critical point. As Florence Alexander stated, 'I was rather "extreme" with clothes on stage, for in those days people went to see the St James's plays *before* ordering a new gown'.[7] Joel H. Kaplan and Sheila Stowell have shown how these production methods acted as advertisements for the commercial costumiers and milliners employed by the Theatre to devise costume. Mesdames Savage and Purdue designed the clothes for *Lady Windermere's Fan*, and found themselves highlighted by every fashionable lady's paper reviewing the play. But this does not detract from Wilde's artistic and critical enterprise, just as Caryl Churchill's stockbroking satire *Serious Money* (1987) stands undiminished by its commercial success as the financiers themselves flocked to see their world on stage.

Wilde honoured with reluctance his call for the theatre to be in the charge of a 'cultured despot'. He found it difficult to relinquish control of his plays to their producers: George Alexander in the case of *Lady Windermere's Fan* and *The Importance of Being Earnest*, Herbert Beerbohm Tree for *A Woman of No Importance*, and Lewis Waller for *An Ideal Husband*. He attended rehearsals regularly: an activity which seems to have played on his nerves as much as it did on the directors and actors concerned. He missed a crucial two days of rehearsal for *Lady Windermere's Fan* 'through illness caused by the worry and anxiety I have gone through at the theatre' in February 1892 (Letters, 308), and returned upset to find that stage business had been altered and new dialogue was needed. Beerbohm Tree claimed to have been so irritated by Wilde's constant interference in the rehearsal process that he banned the author from the Haymarket for the last week before opening *A Woman of No Importance* in 1893.[8] Julia Neilson, who played Lady Chiltern in *An Ideal Husband* at the Haymarket in 1895, remembers that at rehearsal she 'took Oscar very much for granted; his tall, heavy figure was always about the theatre' and she 'enjoyed his monologues, but didn't like his handshake' (Mikhail, I, 244). Scholarly examination of the manuscripts and typescripts of the plays, of the kind undertaken by Ian Small, Russell Jackson and Sos Eltis, shows the extent to which Wilde's writing benefited from collaboration, however fraught, with the companies that first produced the work. It also banishes the idea that he ever arrived at the theatre with a 'finished' script, ready simply to be put into action.

Notes

1 'Shakespeare on Scenery', *Dramatic Review*, 14 March 1885.
2 Ibid.
3 Cited in John Stokes, *Resistible Theatres*, 37.
4 A. E. W. Mason, *Sir George Alexander and the St James's Theatre* (London: Macmillan & Co., 1935) 3.
5 Ibid., 227–8.
6 Review in the *Era*, 22 October 1892, of the performance at the Grand Theatre, Leeds, on 17 October 1892.
7 Mason, 233.
8 Hesketh Pearson, *Beerbohm Tree. His Life and Laughter* (London: Methuen, 1956) 68–9.

Part Three
Critical Survey

4 Poetry

Poems *(1881)*

The Ballad of Reading Gaol *(1898)*

Wilde launched his literary career when he won the Newdigate Prize at Oxford University for his long poem 'Ravenna' in 1878 and read it publicly in the Sheldonian Theatre in Oxford. He completed the same career 20 years later as the anonymous and outcast author of *The Ballad of Reading Gaol.* This chapter looks at the poetry with which Wilde's corpus opens and closes.

Ambition and serious intent mark the collection of *Poems* in 1881. Wilde presented his first volume of work at his own expense; within a year *Poems* had run to five separate editions in England, and three in America. Admittedly the English editions each had a print run of only 250 copies – but public interest was intense and the first American edition is said to have sold out within days of its appearance.

Most of the poems collected had been published before, in journals and magazines. But the way in which Wilde arranged their sequence in book form lent better-known and occasional poems the novelty and weight of becoming part of a remarkably coherent whole. Between the bookends of prelude ('Hélas!') and envoi ('Flowers of Love') are six arrangements of short poems grouped thematically, interspersed by five longer poems. The first section is called 'Eleutheria' (meaning 'Freedom') and it contains political verse, critical of the British Empire and what became of the democracy for which Cromwell had fought in the Civil War. The second section, 'Rosa Mystica', considers the attractions of Catholicism for the author and draws on his visits to Italy and Greece in 1870s. These poems deliberately confuse ostensible autobiography with a purely literary ancestry. 'Wild Flowers' and 'Flowers of Gold', the third and fourth groups, are aesthetic lyrics of love and nature. 'Impressions de Théâtre' address sonnets to performers: Sarah Bernhardt, Ellen Terry and Henry Irving. Finally, 'The Fourth Movement' (actually the sixth, but the title asserts a musical analogy) holds a more diverse group of lyrics that pick up the themes of preceding sequences. The longer narrative and contemplative poems, all written in the same metre and stanza form, explore the conflicting claims of sensuous experience and spiritual awakening.

The collection announces the hurry of the young Wilde. Fluent in the contemporary Pre-Raphaelite style, immensely learned in the

Classical tradition, his voice speaks of admiration for the older generation of English poets such as Keats, Tennyson, William Morris,
Burne-Jones, Rossetti and Swinburne. It asks to be measured against
their achievements. He has also learned from the French poets,
Gautier and Baudelaire, and puts their symbolist vision into practice. *Poems* reads like an anthology of the fashionable *avant-garde*. The
derivative quality of his verse is unquestionable, but there is also
nothing inept about it. At 27, Wilde was showing off his command
of the contemporary and sorting through a wardrobe of available
styles. He was as willing to plunder his own writing as that of other
people: the sonnet 'At Verona', 'How steep the stairs within Kings'
houses are' (Works, 777) marks the beginning of his most characteristic of literary misdemeanours – self-plagiarism – for this is lifted from
'Ravenna'. The repeated references within the poems to personal
journeys suggest a hunger for literary adventure and quest. Skill in
craft must satisfy both author and reader for the moment, since
Wilde was not yet distinguishing himself. But the start is more than
promising, and as a diary of his apprentice years *Poems* repays careful
reading.

Different poems have caught the public imagination at different
times. Two contrasting examples can be found in 'Ave Imperatrix'
from 'Eleutheria', and 'Requiescat' from 'Rosa Mystica'. In 1882
the Americans lavished admiration on 'Ave Imperatrix' which they
took as Wilde's expression of Republican sympathy. The poem begins
with a question:

> Set in this stormy Northern sea,
> Queen of these restless fields of tide,
> England! what shall men say of thee,
> Before whose feet the worlds divide?

A catalogue of wars serves as answer. Wilde indulges his love of
sonorous and exotic words, naming places that have fallen to imper-
ialist powers:

> The almond-groves of Samarcand,
> Bokhara, where red lilies blow,
> And Oxus, by whose yellow sand
> The grave white-turbaned merchants go.

Is this nothing more than aesthetic self-indulgence, naming victims
of colonialism in terms that render them colourfully pleasant to the
reader, plundering them for the senses as England plundered her
Empire in an expansion of power? Or can Wilde claim a moral
achievement by this stylistic treatment of the subject? By investing
each place with a unique beauty and worth that is stolen from it by
the invading force, by pointing to strange names, the more exotic

and unassimilated by familiar English, the more invasive imperialism is shown to be. The poem goes on to consider human suffering inflicted by war, on both victim and aggressor:

> In vain the laughing girl will lean
> To greet her love with love-lit eyes:
> Down in some treacherous black ravine,
> Clutching his flag, the dead boy lies.

The terms are conventional, even stereotypical – but that is the point. Imperialism is shown to destroy the most ordinary of life's pleasures and conventions, and powermongering rather than the poem is seen as no respecter of persons. The last stanza is one of hope, explaining the American preference for this poem. After the excesses of colonisation, a new order is prophesied:

> Yet when this fiery web is spun,
> Her watchmen shall descry from far
> The young Republic like a sun
> Rise from these crimson seas of war.
>
> (Works, 851–4)

Here is the young Irishman, sharing his mother's hopes for her country, looking for hard-won independence from English rule. However, when the poem was anthologised in the American *Golden Treasury of Irish Songs and Lyrics* in 1907, a New York reviewer described it, bizarrely, as 'a whole-hearted panegyric to England, a false note in pages so full of the grief of the exile and the patriot',[1] suggesting that the Republican tide had turned.

The representation of Wilde as traitor to the Irish cause was likely to have been conditioned by the events of 1895, when he was sentenced to two years hard labour. At that time in England a very different kind of poem was brought back to public attention. This was 'Requiescat', from the 'Rosa Mystica' section of *Poems* which, from its first appearance, had been one of the most admired and quoted of Wilde's poems. It is thought to have been written in memory of his sister, Isola, who died at the age of eight in 1867, when Wilde was twelve.

> Tread lightly, she is near
> Under the snow,
> Speak gently, she can hear
> The daisies grow.
>
> All her bright golden hair
> Tarnished with rust,

She that was young and fair
Fallen to dust.

Lily-like, white as snow,
She hardly knew
She was a woman, so
Sweetly she grew.
Coffin-board, heavy stone,
Lie on her breast,
I vex my heart alone,
She is at rest.

Peace, Peace, she cannot hear
Lyre or sonnet,
All my life's buried here,
Heap earth upon it.

(Works, 748–9)

This was printed in full in the review of *Poems* which appeared in *The Ladies' Pictorial* (9 July 1881). Lamenting the loss of a young girl with the disingenuous rhymes and distracted logic of grief, this was deemed to appeal to Wilde's female readership. In April 1895 it was again printed in full for the first and second editions of the popular 16-page pamphlet published during his trials, *The Life of Oscar Wilde as Prosecutor and Prisoner*. There it was held up as the 'choicest specimen' of his poetical writing – and in that context it revealed both the innocence from which he had fallen and the duplicity of his public persona. While an event in Wilde's life is supposed to have occasioned the poem, here, as so often for his poetry, the literary progenitor is readily ostensible and at least as potent. Thomas Hood's lyric 'Take her up tenderly' anticipates 'Requiescat' while in turn it looks forward to Dowson's 'A Dead Child'. This should serve as a warning against reading other poems with an over-emphasis on Wilde's biography. The romance with Rome so passionately described in 'Rosa Mystica' and apparently linked with Wilde's tour of 1875 can be seen as another kind of tourism, through pre-Raphaelite verse. D. G. Rossetti's religious poem 'Ave' can serve as a particular example.

The section 'Wind Flowers' contains two love poems which are '*for music*', 'Serenade' and 'Endymion', and the 1911 setting for the former, by Jervis-Read who called it 'Ballad of the Greek Seas', indicates that the wish was taken seriously. Not only was Wilde already writing for performance, he was putting into practice major doctrines of *avant-garde* aesthetic theory, 'music being the typical, or ideally consummate art, the object of the great *Anders-streben* of all art, of all that is artistic' as Pater had written in 1877.[2] 'Serenade' sings of the quest to carry Helen from 'Grecian shores' and 'steer for

Troy'. But the 'Lady' is elusive: neither singer nor reader discern her clearly and she is never named.

> O noble pilot, tell me true,
> Is that the sheen of golden hair?
> Or is it but the tangled dew
> That binds the passion-flowers there?
> Good sailor come and tell me now
> Is that my Lady's lily hand?
> Or is it but the gleaming prow,
> Or is it but the silver sand?

(Works, 861)

The desired quarry is an aura rather than a woman, and Helen's physical absence from the poem represents a paradoxical fulfilment of the quest for 'the Queen of life and joy'. 'Serenade' invites reader or listener to glimpse ideal Beauty. The words seem to appeal particularly to the sense of sight, but no literal visual analogies link 'the sheen of golden hair' with 'dew that binds the passion-flowers', and the connection between 'lily hand', 'gleaming prow' and 'silver sand' is equally opaque to the eye. Instead, a symbolist sense of what Baudelaire termed 'correspondences' is invoked, lifting the reader/listener to a higher plane of vision where what is apprehended is infinitely evocative.

The poem, with or without its musical setting, is a perfect application of Pater's famous maxim: '*All art constantly aspires towards the condition of music.*' Explaining how this is to be understood, Pater comments 'the mere matter of a poem . . . its subject . . . should be nothing without the form, the spirit, of the handling . . . this mode of handling, should become an end in itself.'[3] This is what Wilde achieves in 'Serenade' where it is the adjectives that make the world cohere and the substantives that make it fall apart. The manner of the telling is more important than the matter told; 'lily', 'gleaming' and 'silver', positioned as adjectives, all describe qualities of light, whereas 'hand', 'prow' and 'sand' bear no literally meaningful connection with one another and the artificial link of rhyme simply adds to the spirit of the handling. The 'mere matter' of this poem, the Trojan snatch of Helen, is hardly present at all: the focus is on the perceptions and apprehensions of the voyager.

These features of aesthetic poetry are even more exaggerated in an example from the 'Flowers of Gold' section of the volume, 'In the Gold Room: A Harmony'. The homage in the title is to the work of Whistler, another exponent of musical analogue and symbolist synaesthesia, who was regularly exhibiting paintings called 'Symphony . . .', or 'Harmony . . .', and whose libel case against Ruskin for insulting the painting *Nocturne in Black and Gold: The Falling Rocket*

(1875) which took place in 1877 was still fresh in the memory. Wilde's poem, like Whistler's *Falling Rocket*, depicts energy both latent and spent. The three stanza 'harmony', 'In the Gold Room', offers a meditation on three colours, 'ivory', 'gold' and 'ruby', associating them initially with 'Her', a faceless and ultimately invisible woman. Each stanza follows the same pattern, naming a part of the woman's body, her 'ivory hands', her 'gold hair', and her 'red lips', announcing what the part does (the hands 'on the ivory keys/Strayed'; the hair 'fell on the wall of gold', and her lips 'on these lips of mine/ Burned'), and proceeding for four or five lines of each six-line stanza to associate similes with the colour and the action.

Most of the poem is therefore devoted to similes which disguise or even obliterate the woman with pictures of what she is 'like', masking her with the poet's apprehending imagination, substituting 'manner' for 'matter'. Apart from the violence done to the woman's body by anatomising it in this way (a metonymic analysis will not excuse this) – a view that contemporary feminists would be quicker to take than Wilde's first readers – the study in 'red' of the last stanza throws overtly violent and sexually resonant images to the fore:

> And her sweet red lips on these lips of mine
> Burned like the ruby fire set
> In the swinging lamp of a crimson shrine,
> Or the bleeding wounds of the pomegranate,
> Or the heart of the lotus drenched and wet
> With the spilt-out blood of the rose-red wine.
>
> (Works, 862)

Interweaving images of religiosity, captivity and sacrifice adumbrate and ultimately transform the initial picture of a kiss into something exotically dangerous and exquisitely threatening. Stylistic aestheticism tilts into moral decadence. The poem expresses desire for sensation and intense casual encounter without thought for a moral framework or a perceiving subject other than the lyrical 'I' behind 'these lips of mine'.

The five sonnets that comprise 'Impressions de Théâtre' pay direct compliments to prominent performers Wilde admired: Sarah Bernhardt, Ellen Terry and Henry Irving. They also follow in the tradition of Baudelaire who included a number of poems about theatre in *Les Fleurs du Mal* (1864) and anticipate the use of theatrical subject matter by later 'decadent' poets such as John Grey, John Davidson and Arthur Symons.

Two of the sonnets about contemporary plays indicate Wilde's dissatisfaction with the popular conventions of the stage. 'Fabien Dei

Franchi' is addressed to Henry Irving who played the parts of Louis and Fabien dei Franchi in Boucicault's *The Corsican Brothers* (1852). The octet offers an amused catalogue of the devices of melodrama, 'The silent room, the heavy creeping shade,/The dead that travel fast, the opening door . . .' only to dismiss them in the sestet ('these things are well enough') as unworthy of Irving's talents. These would be better served by the plays of Shakespeare, 'Thou trumpet set for Shakespeare's lips to blow!' (Works, 860). The sonnet 'Camma' is inspired by Ellen Terry's performance of that role in Tennyson's play *The Cup* which opened at the London Lyceum Theatre on 3 January 1881. While other poems in Wilde's collection proclaim a debt to the Laureate's poetry, his admiration clearly did not extend to his plays. The octet considers Terry's performance as Camma, and the sestet announces 'And yet – methinks I'd rather see thee play . . .' Again only Shakespeare can quicken and serve the talents of this actress, and the poet imagines her playing Cleopatra, 'great Egypt', only to dismiss this too as unsatisfying in comparison with a 'real' romance. 'Nay,/I am grown sick of unreal passions, make/The world thine Actium, me thine Antony!' This signals a reversal of the aesthetic hierarchy of art and life. On stage as Camma, Terry is all too easily distinguishable from the role she plays; off stage the poet's imagination invests her with a quasi-mythological status that would transfigure her lover into a tragic hero (Works, 861). Only Sarah Bernhardt, in the sonnet 'Phèdre', emerges as one of the immortals, indistinguishable from the role she plays, and walking on a different plane of reality from her audience and the poet. Wilde first published this sonnet in *The World* on 11 June 1879 to celebrate Bernhardt's performance of the role with the visiting Comédie Française at the London Gaiety Theatre. The sonnet entertains the Platonic myth of metempsychosis, suggesting that Bernhardt's consummate performances, her ability to 'become' the character, fulfil the shape-changing myths of the ancient world, doubly appropriate since she is performing the role of Phèdre in Racine's reworking of the ancient tragedy by Euripides (Works, 835).

The final arrangement of verses, 'The Fourth Movement', includes an example of the literary impressionism that would become stylistically dominant in the poetry of the British *fin de siècle*. Wilde's poem 'Impression: Le Reveillon', attempts to capture the moment of dawn. The rationale for this kind of writing had been provided by Pater in his notoriously famous 'Conclusion' to *The Renaissance*, in which he described a kind of existential flux affecting the whole of the natural world and the mind of man. Looking about himself, Pater saw that 'each object is loosed into a group of impressions – colour, odour, texture – in the mind of the observer'.[4] This dissolution of what had seemed fixed and certain required, Pater argued, a radical response: 'Not to discriminate every moment some passionate attitude in those about us ... is, on this short day of frost and sun, to sleep before evening'.[5] The aesthete is faced with a dilemma: because the world is in flux, either every moment is of value and must be captured and enjoyed for its uniqueness, or every moment is of no consequence whatsoever precisely because it is transient and will be gone before it can be apprehended. Wilde's poetic response to this, like that of many of his contemporaries, was to write about fleeting states of change, using the staying power of artifice to contain the momentary:

> The sky is laced with fitful red,
> The circling mists and shadows flee,
> The dawn is rising from the sea,
> Like a white lady from her bed.

> (Works, 864)

The 'impression' is told in the present tense and using present participles; a narrative unfolds, which takes time to tell, but it is constantly present time. The rhyme scheme, a b b a, compounds the sense that artifice can check flight: the two adjacently rhyming lines hurry the centre of each stanza along, but the last rhyme of the stanza sends us back to the start and seems to block the progress of the subject.

The publication of *Poems* in 1881 cannot be separated from their reception and place in the biographical context of the author. Wilde had been preparing for this moment ever since he left Oxford and he cannot have expected the derision, scorn, aesthetic and moral outrage that came his way, absolutely disproportionate to the quality of the verse. Wilde's cultivation of an extraordinary, novel and superior persona had built up expectations in his public that were bound to be disappointed, unless affected personal style was to be matched with verses 'straining for effect', as the reviewer for the Chicago-based journal, the *Dial*, declared (Critical Heritage, 42). The Oxford Union rejected its presentation copy on the grounds of redundancy, because the poems, 'for the most part, are not by their putative father at all, but by a number of better known and more deservedly reputed authors' already housed on the Library shelves (Ellmann, 140). The anonymous reviewer for the *Athenaeum* scorned the 'over-indulgence in metaphor, in affected neologisms, and in conceits behind which sense and reason are obscured' (Critical Heritage, 36). The American T. W. Higginson took moral offence, in an article called 'Unmanly Manhood' for the Boston *Woman's Journal*, announcing to his female readership that no man could read these poems aloud 'in the presence of women', typifying the moral prejudice and social stereotyping with which Wilde would repeatedly battle (Critical Heritage, 51). Even the friendly Oscar Browning, whose review Wilde himself had solicited, warned readers to be 'charitable and patient' (Critical Heritage, 39).

The Ballad of Reading Gaol is Wilde's most famous poem, and the only work he completed after his release from prison. He began its composition within days of his release on 19 May 1897, the compassion expressed within the poem for imprisonment quickened by his own freedom. Although Wilde claimed that 'the idea for *The Ballad* came to me while I was in the dock, waiting for my sentence to be pronounced' (More Letters, 171), the poem tells the story of a hanging which took place in Reading Gaol on 7 July 1896 which Wilde witnessed as an inmate. Like most ballads, it has a strong, simple narrative about how the soldier 'C. T. W.' (Charles Thomas Wooldridge) was hanged for murdering his wife. The poem departs from the narrative line to represent the responding emotions of the other prisoners. The subject matter opens out to consider the universality of guilt, moral weakness and the particular inhumanity of the prison system. As Arthur Symons noted in his favourable review, it 'is not really a ballad at all, but a sombre, angry, interrupted reverie; and it is the subcurrent of meditation, it is the asides, which count, not the story' (Critical Heritage, 220). Wilde was the first to admit the artistic deficiencies incurred by the broad ambitions of the piece: 'The poem suffers under the difficulty of a divided aim in style. Some is realistic, some is romantic: some poetry, some propaganda,' he wrote in 1897 before its completion (Letters, 654).

The form of *The Ballad of Reading Gaol* is reminiscent of several other ballads well known to Wilde's contemporaries: Coleridge's *Rime of the Ancient Mariner*, Thomas Hood's 'Dream of Eugene Aram', W. E. Henley's 'In Hospital', Kipling's *Barrack Room Ballads*, especially 'Danny Deever', and A. E. Housman's *A Shropshire Lad* (sent by Housman to Wilde on his release). All figure as precursors to the poem. But the particular metrical form which Wilde adopts repeats that which he would have heard at his mother's knee when she read the rebellious poems of the Young Ireland movement to her sons. *New Year's Song* (1844) by Denis Florence MacCarthy, published in one of 'Speranza's' favourite anthologies, *The Spirit of the Nation* (1845), calls Irish poets to protest at English domination in the identical rhythm which Wilde uses to describe the suffering of imprisonment:

> There's not a man of all our land
> Our country now can spare,
> The strong man with his sinewy hand,
> The weak man with his prayer!

> No whining tone of mere regret,
> Young Irish bards, for you;
> But let your songs teach Ireland yet
> What Irishmen should do![6]

This poem, like Wilde's, alternates lines of iambic tetrameter with lines of iambic trimeter.

Consider the metrical arrangement of the first of the 109 stanzas of *The Ballad of Reading Gaol*, which provides the exposition of the story to be told:

> He did not wear his scarlet coat,
> For blood and wine are red,
> And blood and wine were on his hands
> When they found him with the dead,
> The poor dead woman whom he loved,
> And murdered in her bed.

> (Works, 883)

Wilde's rhyme scheme, a b c b d b, for his six-line stanzas is more complicated than the a b a b c d c d scheme of MacCarthy's 'song', but *The Ballad*, like this metrical precursor, also uses the device of verbal repetition to create an incantatory, song-like effect. By its formal qualities alone *The Ballad* is drawn into a tradition of oral, spoken poetry, reinforced by the first-person narrative voice of the poem introduced in the second stanza, and developed in the third:

> I never saw a man who looked
> With such a wistful eye
> Upon that little tent of blue
> Which prisoners call the sky,
> And at every drifting cloud that went
> With sails of silver by.

As *The Ballad* unfolds this stanza is repeated (with minor variations) at line 103 (Works, 885), again to describe the condemned man; it recurs once more at line 415 (Works, 893), altered to describe the general mood among the prisoners once the hanging has taken place. The hanged man's sense of doom is transferred to the inmates, as his vision of captivity becomes a universalised condition.

Rhythm and repetition, unifying formal devices of the poem, themselves become important themes, particularly in their disruption by death. The rhythm or routine of the prison day is recreated by the verse. 'I walked, with other souls in pain,/Within another ring' (ll.19–20, Works, 883), the literal circularity of the prisoners' walk suggests its futility while also indicates at this early stage in the poem how the routine of the condemned murderer sets him apart from the others.

> I only knew what hunted thought
> Quickened his step, and why
> He looked upon the garish day
> With such a wistful eye;
> The man had killed the thing he loved,
> And so he had to die.
>
> (Works, 883)

The repetitious futility of their actions, which arrests time so that 'each day is like a year' (1.539, Works, 896), is paradoxically quickened by the narrator's imagination into a dance of death (like the one Wilde had represented in an earlier poem, 'The Harlot's House' (Works, 867)):

> It is sweet to dance to violins
> When Love and Life are fair:
> To dance to flutes, to dance to lutes,
> Is delicate and rare;
> But it is not sweet with nimble feet
> To dance upon the air!
>
> (ll.145–150, Works, 886)

This is the end to which the rhythm of the murderer's waiting hastens with terrible finality.

Already in the seventh stanza the narrative voice asserts, by a grimly distorted echo of *The Merchant of Venice*, the kinship between himself, the murderer, and humanity at large:

> Yet each man kills the thing he loves,
> By each let this be heard,
> Some do it with a bitter look,
> Some with a flattering word,
> The coward does it with a kiss,
> The brave man with a sword!
>
> (ll.37–42, Works, 884)

The reference is to the trial scene:

> *Bassanio*: Do all men kill the things they do not love?
> *Shylock*:   Hates any man the thing he would not kill?
> (*Merchant of Venice*, IV, i, 66–7)

Wilde's revision of these lines has become the most famous refrain of the poem and the one on which the poem concludes. In this final position the lines act as admonition, indicting narrator along with reader, appealing for clemency and withheld judgement.

In this poem, as so frequently in his work, Wilde has successfully married formula with authenticity. For him it contained a strong element of realism, as he described candidly in a letter:

> With regard to the adjectives, I admit there are too many 'dreadfuls' and 'fearfuls'. The difficulty is that the objects in prison have no shape or form. To take an example; the shed in which people are hanged is a little shed with a glass roof, like a photographer's studio . . . For eighteen months I thought it *was* the studio for photographing prisoners. There is no adjective to describe it. I call it 'hideous' because it became so to me after I knew its use. In itself it is a wooden, oblong, narrow shed with a glass roof.
>
> A cell again may be described *psychologically*, with reference to its effect on the soul; in itself it can only be described as 'whitewashed' or 'dimly-lit'. It has no shape, no contents. It does not exist from the point of view of form or colour.
>
> In point of fact, describing a prison is as difficult artistically as describing a water-closet would be . . . the horror of prison is that everything is so simple and commonplace in itself, and so degrading, and hideous, and revolting in its effect.

(Letters, 654–5)

It may seem strange to readers today that even the first hostile reviewers (of which there were many) valued the poem for its realism if nothing else. 'The document is authentic: hence its worth' (Critical Heritage, 211) is typical of its early reception. For us it may function as an epitaph for Wilde himself, and society's dealings with him, quoted aptly on his tomb. And as prison conditions and forms of punishment have changed over the century since its composition, so the meditative qualities of the poem are foregrounded. We respond to its statements of the burden of passion, frailty, fear and finitude, to the tensions generated between pleasure and remorse, mental freedom and physical captivity.

Notes

1. Stuart Mason, *Bibliography of Oscar Wilde* (London: T. Werner Laurie 1914; rpt. 1967) 291.
2. Pater, *Renaissance*, 106.
3. Ibid., 106.
4. Ibid., 187.
5. Ibid., 189.
6. Davis Coakley, 'The Neglected Years: Wilde in Dublin', *Rediscovering Oscar Wilde*, 52–3.

5   *Short fiction*

During the nineteenth century in Europe two very distinct kinds of fairy tale became fashionable. On the one hand there was the collection of folk material, transcribed from oral tradition in Germany by the Brothers Grimm, and from French oral culture by Perrault, versions of which began to appear in England during the latter half of the century. Constance Wilde herself contributed to this when she published *There Was Once! Grandma's Stories* in 1889. Mrs Wilde maintains a sense of *telling* stories and, indeed, of the specifically female domain of this activity, by writing in the Introduction:

> There was once, my children, a little girl who loved her grandmother to tell her stories . . . The little girl is grown up now, and the dear grandmother is gone, but there are still children who love the old fairy stories, so the little girl has written them out for you just as they were told to her.[1]

Mrs Wilde's collection contains a mixture of English nursery rhymes and European fairy stories from the folk anthologies. There is no sense in which she invented these tales and she claims that they have authority precisely because they are folk property. She is simply their spokeswoman.

The other kind of fairy story, overtly moralistic and sentimental, were those to which individual authors laid claim – and their invented, even contrived, qualities are their distinguishing feature. The most popular of these authors was the Danish writer Hans Christian Andersen (1805–1875) whose vogue in England during the 1840s coincided with his widespread European fame. It is to this school of fairy tales that Wilde's contribution to the genre belongs and, unlike the work of his wife, *The Happy Prince* and *The House of Pomegranates* are authoritatively his own. A bridge between them, however, is the two-volume collection of *Ancient Legends, Mystic Charms and Superstitions of Ireland*, published in 1887 by Lady Wilde who was raking through the antiquarian papers left by her husband. They were based on his field-work in Ireland. Her preface states that the material was 'obtained chiefly from oral communications made by the peasantry themselves',[2] a claim not for the credibility of the tales but for their accuracy in representing the culture of the Irish people. Some of the legends share tone and technique with the stories told in *The Happy Prince*. For example 'Shaun-Mor. A Legend of Innes-Sark' contains several talking creatures, a gander among which chides the anti-hero with 'what will your wife say when she hears of your being out so late at night wandering about in this way? It is very disreputable, and no well brought up gander would do the like, much less a man'.[3] She also presents a host of dangerous seducers among the Sidhe which anticipate features of *The House of Pomegranates*.

The Happy Prince

The Happy Prince was published in 1888 and contained five stories: 'The Happy Prince', 'The Nightingale and the Rose', 'The Selfish Giant', 'The Devoted Friend' and 'The Remarkable Rocket'. Wilde wrote to a friend that the tales were 'meant partly for children, and partly for those who have kept the childlike faculties of wonder and joy, and who find in simplicity a subtle strangeness' (Letters, 219). His readers could be naïve or sophisticated, young or old, their pleasures shaped by different features of the texts; but, in common with Wilde, they were to have an aesthetic sensibility, the capacity to experience 'wonder and joy' or to delight in strange 'simplicity'. Wilde had judged his readers correctly. He was immediately fêted as a writer for children: a new anthology of verse 'for Young People', *Jolts and Jingles*, was dedicated to him the following year. Equally, the grandfather of British aestheticism himself, Walter Pater, wrote gratefully for his copy of *The Happy Prince*, admiring the 'delicate touches and pure English' of the whole collection.[4]

To understand how Wilde envisaged the unlikely link between aesthete and child we have to go back to the lectures he gave in 1882 in America on the 'English Renaissance'. There the Platonism behind the socialist 'Arts and Crafts' movement propelled by Ruskin and championed by William Morris is spelled out. Wilde had lectured:

> in years to come there will be nothing in any man's house which has not given delight to its maker and does not give delight to its user. The children, like the children of Plato's perfect city, will grow up 'in a simple atmosphere of all fair things' – I quote from the passage in the *Republic* – 'a simple atmosphere of all fair things, where beauty, which is the spirit of art, will come on eye and ear like a fresh breath of wind that brings health from a clear upland, and insensibly and gradually draw the child's soul into harmony with all knowledge and all wisdom, so that he will love what is beautiful and good, and hate what is evil and ugly (for they always go together) long before he knows the reason why; and then when reason comes will kiss her on the cheek as a friend.
>
> That is what Plato thought decorative art could do for a nation, feeling that the secret not of philosophy merely but of all gracious

existence might be externally hidden from any one whose youth had been passed in uncomely and vulgar surroundings, and that the beauty of form and colour even, as he says, in the meanest vessels of the house, will find its way into the inmost places of the soul and lead the boy naturally to look for that divine harmony of spiritual life of which art was to him the material symbol and warrant.[5]

Six years after delivering this lecture Wilde found himself the father of two sons – the two-year-old Vyvyan and the three-year-old Cyril – in which position the teaching of Plato and the mission of William Morris would assume a practical urgency. The tales in *The Happy Prince* show Wilde appropriating these principles and using them to inform his work in an individual way. It is a species of Platonism that links the sensibility of the child with that of the aesthete. 'If children grow up among all fair and lovely things, they will grow to love beauty and detest ugliness before they know the reason why.'[6]

An analysis of the title story, 'The Happy Prince', illustrates how Wilde accommodated a seemingly diverse readership. The story itself, in terms of what happens next, what the Russian formalists call the *'fabula'*, offers the simplest level of enjoyment for the child reader. We are told about the relationship between a speaking statue and a swallow and the adventures of both as their friendship develops. The way in which the story is told, the *'sujet'*, affords immediately more sophisticated levels of enjoyment. The different elements of narration provide social satire, comedy of manners, moral allegory and a commentary on aestheticism for the cognoscenti.

> High above the city, on a tall column, stood the statue of the Happy Prince. He was gilded all over with thin leaves of fine gold, for eyes he had two bright sapphires, and a large red ruby glowed on his sword-hilt.
>
> He was very much admired indeed. 'He is as beautiful as a weathercock,' remarked one of the Town Councillors who wished to gain a reputation for having artistic tastes; 'only not quite so useful,' he added, fearing lest people should think him unpractical, which he really was not.
>
> (Works, 271)

Reversing the significance of Tennyson's self-obsessed 'Simeon Stylites', Wilde creates a figure removed from the hubbub of every-day life, forced by his passivity to contemplate his past life and surveying the social injustices which his luxurious royal status had helped to maintain. The detail of gilt, sapphire and ruby, as yet ornamental and so pointing towards an aesthete's love of opulent decoration, will become structural elements of the story. Each precious thing is given by the statue to a poor, needy character, in order to salve his stricken conscience and to alleviate the suffering of the poor. The swallow is the statue's reluctant agent, swooping in to hovels and garrets dispensing gifts, and finally giving his own life to the good causes of the Happy Prince. The cold weather comes and the swallow has tarried with the Prince too long to migrate to the warm south; he drops at the feet of the now 'shabby' statue. A spiritual, internal beauty replaces lavish decoration. This moral beauty is invisible to the gallery of burgess snobs within the tale who see only a disfigured statue and a dead bird to legislate against by the end of the story. The reader, privy to the processes of visible change, sees with the eyes of the Angels, and recognises in the statue's leaden heart and the dead bird those two most precious things in the city for which God sends: 'in my garden of Paradise this little bird shall sing for evermore, and in my city of gold the Happy Prince shall praise me' (Works, 277). Transfigured by art, Yeats' *Byzantium* (1933) is just around the corner.

While there is no sense in which the moral of this tale is tacked on to the end, nevertheless, for the child reader, the story effectively ends when the hard frost comes and the swallow dies. The characters of the bird and the statue are fully drawn, and the narrative focus rests with them. When they become passive through the death of the bird, the story is handed over to the Town Councillors, and the Art Professor. These had been choric figures: sharp satires appealing to the knowing intellect of an adult reader, but of little consequence for the child. This results in a double conclusion: one for children, one for adults. The ultimate happy ending in heaven brought about by the *deus ex machina* offers no consolation to the child who has lost the only good characters in the story. A measure of this discrepancy is given by two contrasting responses: the first by Walter Pater in his letter of thanks for the book to Wilde, the second by Michael Mac Liammoir (co-founder of Dublin's Gate Theatre in 1928, and star of a one-man play he wrote about Wilde). Remembering how 'The Happy Prince' affected him as a 12-year-old boy, Mac Liammoir writes:

> I remember wondering as the story drew to its finish why the pages seemed to grow dark, and thinking it was because I was crying. But I had been crying for a long while: ever since the Swallow had plucked out the sapphires that were the eyes of the Prince so that the poor people might have bread. And now, with the swallow's death, I was drowning the stage [sic] with tears.[7]

The child is a victim of the sentimentality of Wilde's plot; the aesthete, by contrast, happily overlooks this dimension of the tale. What

Pater had selected for special praise from this story were what he
called 'your genuine "little poems in prose", those at the top of
pages 10 and 14, for instance, are gems' (Letters, 219). He refers to
two passages of prose which have an ornamental function and little
bearing on the immediate action of the story:

> Soon they will go to sleep in the tomb of the great king. The king
> is there himself in his painted coffin. He is wrapped in yellow
> linen, and embalmed with spices. Round his neck is a chain of
> pale green jade, and his hands are like withered leaves.
>
> All night long he watches the stars, and when the morning star
> shines he utters one cry of joy, and then he is silent. At noon the
> yellow lions come down to the water's edge to drink. They have
> eyes like great beryls, and their roar is louder than the roar of the
> cataract.[8]

Pater seems to be reading a series of prose decorations, discrete
items of lyrical description. He prizes the symbolist technique of the
style: these ornaments are part of a cohesive narrative only in so far
as they evoke an atmosphere of the impossible South to which the
swallow can no longer migrate. But Mac Liammoir, the boy, is
reading a story encumbered with ornament and difficult references.
Within the tales themselves various interpretational practices are
accommodated by describing how characters understand the same
events differently, and follow different lines of 'truth'. The collection
ends with precisely this issue in balance:

> 'Now I am going to explode,' [the Remarkable Rocket] cried. 'I
> shall set the whole world on fire, and make such a noise that
> nobody will talk about anything else for a whole year.' . . .
>
> But nobody heard him, not even the two little boys, for they were
> sound asleep . . .
>
> 'I knew I should create a great sensation,' gasped the Rocket, and
> he went out.
>
> (Works, 301)

The House of Pomegranates

The stories in *The Happy Prince* may be emotionally difficult for young
children, but their ostensive moral credentials, based on exposure of
social inequities, are impeccable. A profoundly ordered world is presented by the collection, through the juxtaposition of dichotomies
such as rich and poor ('The Happy Prince'), love and self-love ('The
Nightingale and The Rose') selfishness and generosity ('The Selfish
Giant'), trust and exploitation ('The Devoted Friend'), arrogance
and humility ('The Remarkable Rocket'). The sentimentality of the

tales manipulates a craving for a moral Utopia, desired in an absence
made painful by the liberal use of dramatic irony. The reader is
teased with omniscience coupled with impotence. This is not the
case with *The House of Pomegranates* (1891), where certainties are overturned and ethical or religious dilemmas of a far more sophisticated
kind are entertained. Witchcraft, lust, sinful pride and cruel punishment are used as narrative components that would stretch a child's
imagination, let alone its patience or vocabulary, beyond the pale.
We can see Wilde losing interest in 'the mind of the child' in the
following account by Montgomery Hyde:

> 'It is the duty of every father,' he said with great gravity, to write
> fairy-tales for his children. But the mind of the child is a great
> mystery ... You humbly spread before it the treasures of your
> imagination, and they are as dross. For example, a day or two
> ago, Cyril yonder came to me with the question, 'Father do you
> ever dream?' 'Why of course, my darling. It is the first duty of a
> gentleman to dream.' 'And what do you dream of?' asked Cyril,
> with a child's disgusting appetite for facts. Then I, believing, of
> course, that something picturesque would be expected of me, spoke
> of magnificent things: 'What do I dream of? Oh, I dream of
> dragons with gold and silver scales, and scarlet things coming out
> of their mouths, of eagles with eyes made of diamonds ...' So I
> laboured on with my fancy, till, observing that Cyril was entirely
> unimpressed, and indeed quite undisguisedly bored, I came to a
> humiliating stop, and turning to my son there, I said: 'But tell me,
> what do you dream of, Cyril?' His answer was like a divine rev-
> elation: 'I dream of *pigs*,' he said.[9]

This zoological catalogue enchants the teller, if not the listening
child. It also exhibits many of the stylistic features typical of *The
House of Pomegranates*. Other indications that this volume addresses
specifically adult tastes are given by its physical appearance, its title
and its dedications. All caught the attention of early reviewers, who
nevertheless dismissed these distinguishing features as purely 'decorative'. Noting that the title of the work bore, apparently, no relation to its contents (although pomegranates recur throughout the
stories like a structuring leitmotif) the reviewer for the *Pall Mall
Gazette* felt mildly cheated. He was unable to recognise the ambiguity of the pomegranate symbol which antiquity saw as the fruit of
Hades and dark captivity, but which Christian iconography revisioned
as the fruit of resurrection and rebirth. Is the reader of *The House of
Pomegranates*, like Persephone, held captive by a Prince of darkness,
entertained by moral uncertainty if not decadence? Or are we presented with another work of the Renaissance, inspired with new life
and vision? And if so, is this modelled on Christian ethics, as *The*

Happy Prince undoubtably was, or conceived according to a more advanced creed of aestheticism? Wilde allows both possibilities to stay constantly in play. The peacock, which figures prominently on the cover design if not in the title itself, enjoys an equally ambivalent symbolic status. In antiquity the birds were kept by Juno: the eyes in their feathers were to be constantly vigilant on her behalf. With Christianity, the symbolism of the peacock changed. Its flesh was reputed never to decay (Wilde makes use of this aspect in one of his 'Poems in Prose'), so it, like the pomegranate, came to symbolise the transfiguring resurrection of the body.

Each of the four stories was dedicated to an aristocratic lady, while the collection as a whole was to 'CONSTANCE MARY WILDE'. Wilde habitually dedicated his works to individual friends, usually men. The most famous example is the gift of *Salome* to Lord Alfred Douglas. In dedicating to a woman a collection of stories that was mistaken as a book for children, it may appear that Wilde was conspiring with the infantilisation of women that had long been the common currency of their cultural construction. But in fact he is celebrating sophisticated taste, creating an aristocracy of intellect among some of his more noble friends and honouring them with print and artifice. And he ensured that the publication of the volume would be more of a social event than was anyway usual for Wilde's work. 'The Young King', which first appeared in the Christmas issue of *The Ladies' Pictorial* in 1888, was for 'Margaret, Lady Brooke': her grander title was the 'Ranee of Sarawak' which she acquired in 1869 when she married Sir Charles Brooke, the Rajah of Sarawak, and lived with him there for a time. She was also a distinguished musician, conducted an amateur orchestra and helped her son to edit his paper *The Planet*. 'The Birthday of the Infanta', first published in French, translated by the symbolist Marcel Schwob, in the *Paris Illustré* on 30 March 1889, was for 'Mrs William H. Grenfell of Taplow Court': of aristocratic descent she was married in 1887 to a notable athlete who became a peer in 1905. Mrs Grenfell became Lady Desborough whose fame, already in 1891, was as a Society hostess. 'The Fisherman and his Soul' was for 'H. S. H. Alice, Princess of Monaco', the boldest statement by Wilde about his social circle. 'Miss Margot Tennant' was the dedicatee of 'The Star-Child'. She did not marry the Rt. Hon. Herbert H. Asquith until 1894 but, both before and after her marriage to the Liberal Chancellor of the Exchequer and later Prime Minister, she enjoyed a high public profile. She was a member of a club of unorthodox women known as the 'Souls' and had a reputation for impulsive behaviour and generosity. Like Wilde, she had reviewed books for the *Pall Mall Gazette* and, also like Wilde, she cultivated a circle of artistic friends.

The dedication of these tales to socially conspicuous women also makes explicit the cultural appeal of aesthetic style for women rather than men and asserts the feminisation of Wilde's tastes. Throughout the 1880s *Punch* had published Du Maurier's satirical cartoons about the creature Mrs Cimabue-Brown and her circle of dandies and aesthetes. She is a Pre-Raphaelite caricature, and she worships at the shrine of The Brotherhood (Rossetti, Burne-Jones, Morris). Du Maurier constructs these men as effete, unmanly specimens, just as an early critic of Wilde's verse had charged him with neglect of proper manly duty in the sphere of action and with having an 'unmanly' poetic voice. As Alan Sinfield has argued, this was not equivalent to the charge of homosexuality, but represented a cultural anxiety about shifting gender roles and behaviour.

Aesthetic criticism

Two kinds of objection stormed from the pens of the reviewers. The first concerned the appearance of the book and the second its supposed readership. Never missing an opportunity to keep hack journalists in their place, Wilde entered into newspaper correspondence. He was particularly provoked when *The Speaker* announced:

> We do not like the outside of the cover of Mr. Oscar Wilde's *House of Pomegranates* ... The Indian club with a housepainter's brush on the top which passes muster for a peacock, and the chimney-pot hat with a sponge in it, which is meant to represent a basket containing a pomegranate, or a fountain, or something of that kind, are grotesque, but not ideally so.
>
> (Letters, 300)

This was not just an insult about the book in hand, but a wholesale attack on the school of aesthetic criticism that Wilde had expounded at length in 'The Critic as Artist'. The reviewer for *The Speaker* had taken it upon himself to share his 'own impression' of the *Pomegranate* design with his readers: a liberty which, as Wilde was quick to point out, exposed the vulgarity of the reviewer's mind rather than the eccentricity of the book's design: 'I do not for a moment dispute that these are real impressions your critic received. It is the spectator, and the mind of the spectator, as I pointed out in the preface to *The Picture of Dorian Gray*, that art really mirrors' (Letters, 301). But clearly, a serious misrepresentation of the aesthetic principles which Wilde practised had been articulated by the *Speaker* reviewer, and Wilde's lengthy reply used a number of strategies to correct it. The arguments are worth considering here because, as Wilde draws round to consider the 'art-criticism' of literature at the end of his reply, they suggest that the stories in *The House of Pomegranates* require response

Cover design by Charles Ricketts for A House of Pomegranates
(London: James R. Osgood, McIlvaine & Co., 1891)
By permission of the British Library (shelfmark: TC4910)

no less aesthetically informed than the exquisite designs and decorations by Ricketts and Shannon.

The first two paragraphs of his letter show Wilde playing the sardonic fool, beginning at an apparent tangent from his real purpose. He advocates the building of newspaper kiosks in London on the model of those in Paris, on the grounds that 'when illuminated at night from within' they look 'as lovely as a fantastic Chinese lantern'

95

(Letters, 300). It is a disarming way of asserting his habitual way of seeing. 'Do not wait for life to be picturesque, but try to see it under picturesque conditions' he had told students at the Royal Academy in 1883.[10] He also anticipates by illustration the main argument of the reply, which is to claim that the cover design of the book is to be viewed primarily in abstract terms as an arrangement of line and colour. In doing this he is following the dogma of aestheticism, taking up, for example, an assertion made by Pater in 1877 at the time of Whistler's libel suit against Ruskin: 'In its primary aspect, a great picture has no more definite message for us than an accidental play of sunlight and shadow for a few moments on the wall or floor.'[11] This was a point of view Whistler developed in his 1885 *Ten O'Clock Lecture*. Furthermore, Wilde anticipates a creed which the designers, Ricketts and Shannon, would themselves articulate in their manifesto for Aestheticism, published in 1892 in the second number of their idiosyncratic journal, *The Dial*. There Ricketts published 'The Unwritten Book', in which he announced:

> These works [paintings, Da Vinci's *Mona Lisa*, Whistler's *White Harmony*] have been chosen for their lack of story, in its common acceptance; and so we come easily to the colour exclamation on some Chinese enamel, dabbed there in vibrant crimson on a liquid purple, where no subject can exist at all.

Wilde's impatient letter to *The Speaker* arrives at the crux of the argument:

> what imitative parallel may be found to them in that chaos that is termed Nature, is a matter of no importance. They may suggest, as they do sometimes to me, peacocks and pomegranates and splashing fountains of gold water, or, as they do to your critic, sponges and Indian clubs and chimney-pot hats. Such suggestions and evocations have nothing whatsoever to do with the aesthetic quality and value of the design. A thing in Nature becomes much lovelier if it reminds us of a thing in Art, but a thing in Art gains no real beauty through reminding us of a thing in Nature.

As if to pre-empt the next round of criticism that would attack the subject matter of the stories, Wilde hammers on, offering the analogy between visual art and literature:

> The primary aesthetic impression of a work of art borrows nothing from recognition or resemblance. These belong to a later and less perfect stage of apprehension. Properly speaking, they are no part of a real aesthetic impression at all, and the constant pre-occupation with subject-matter that characterises nearly all our

English art-criticism, is what makes our art-criticism, especially as regards literature, so sterile, so profitless, so much beside the mark.

(Letters, 301)

Wilde is demanding for his stories an appreciation of literary style, focus not on the tale, but on its telling, on manner not matter. Although both Pater and Wilde assert that attention to style yields the 'primary' aesthetic impression, both as the first thing to notice and as the most important feature to notice, they are cultivating sophisticated tastes. No child will be captivated by style when mermaids are dying and witches are dancing. Just as Cyril was plainly bored by his father's zoological extravaganza, few children will have the patience to unpack the mannered prose of these stories to find what it contains or conceals. As the *Ladies' Pictorial* put it: 'indeed, I do not know to whom I ought to recommend it. It is over the heads of the majority of children, and yet it is not, I imagine, intended for the mature.'[12] The outcome of the second critical debate occasioned by these tales is therefore a forgone conclusion. As Wilde replied to the reviewer for the *Pall Mall Gazette*:

> He starts by asking an extremely silly question, and that is, whether or not I have written this book for the purpose of giving pleasure to the British child. Having expressed grave doubts on this subject, a subject on which I cannot conceive any fairly educated person having any doubts at all, he proceeds, apparently quite seriously, to make the extremely limited vocabulary at the disposal of the British child the standard by which the prose of the artist is to be judged! Now, in building this *House of Pomegranates*, I had about as much intention of pleasing the British child as I had of pleasing the British public.
>
> (Letters, 301–2)

Aesthetic prose: 'The Fisherman and his Soul'

Wilde was writing to please himself. Gone is the popular dimension to his story-telling that had characterised the tales in *The Happy Prince*. The prose style of each tale is an exercise in artificial display. Composition, mood and tone are foregrounded by archaic sentence structure, specialised diction and a deliberate patterning of adventure, forcing storyline and moral into positions of secondary importance. 'The Fisherman and his Soul', the only one to be dedicated to royalty, is the most opulent tale, in which narrative progress is impeded by flights of exotic fancy as the Soul competes with the Mermaid for the Fisherman's heart. These are hung around a version of a traditional tale about love between a mortal and a mermaid, the most familiar of which, then as now, is Hans Christian Andersen's 'The Little Mermaid'. But Wilde's family had extensive knowledge of the folk tradition on which Andersen draws and had already put it into narrative practice. Wilde's brother, Willie, the 'frère sauvage' as he signed himself, had offered one version of it in *Vanity Fair* as far back as 16 December 1879, 'The Story of Mrs Peter Kyne: A Legend of Connemara'. Told in the first person and broad dialect, as an eye-witness account of the sorry fate of the farmer, Peter Kyne, who falls fatally in love with a seal-woman, the narrative voice claims authenticity with one hand and denies it with the other. Dialect places the story in the oral tradition, gossip as much as local legend, but because it is *Irish* brogue, the whiff is of tall tales. Lady Wilde, in her anthology of *Ancient Legends*, returns a number of times to stories about the origins of the Sidhe, or fairy folk, of Ireland, which present them as a host of fallen angels. 'And some fell into the sea . . . the fairies of the earth and sea are mostly gentle and beautiful creatures, who will do no harm if they are let alone . . .'[13] They have no souls and are doomed to annihilation at Judgement Day. But she does recount one tale about a malevolent mermaid, 'The Dead Soldier', in which the appearance of a mermaid on the rocks in the Shannon signals 'ill-luck' or 'crime' near by, and a young fisherman is nearly seduced to his death by her charms in a beautiful underwater country.[14] This story, like the rest of her material, is short and concise, suggesting the polish of many retellings and the storyteller's assurance that brevity will be made up by resonance in the folk imagination.

In form it is therefore quite unlike Wilde's treatment of similar material, which was destined for different ears and eyes. Yet 'The Fisherman and his Soul' also has its roots in oral culture: that generated by Wilde's own fabled skill in talking. Charles Ricketts recollects Wilde's visits to the house he shared with Shannon, 'The Vale' in Chelsea. 'The 'Poems in Prose' were told repeatedly if there were friends present. The several journeys of the spirit in 'The Fisherman and his Soul' would also be described (all have not been printed).[15] Immediately the tale takes on a new aspect: told in the context of private, leisured entertainment, it could be extended or curtailed as the social context required. The published text therefore represents merely one version, expedient or ideal, selected from the alternatives available to the teller. The fact that Ricketts mentions this story in the next breath to the 'Poems in Prose' suggests that the first audience was more like Pater in what it sought to enjoy about narrative than like the youthful Michael Mac Lammoir. The atavistic pleasure in what happens next has been sophisticated into delight in diversion and deferral. Curiosity is replaced by the curious. The more discerning among Wilde's first reviewers were sensitive to this shift in narrative focus and function, if not always approving it:

Among bright colours, sweet sounds, pleasant tastes, Mr.Wilde is like his own Dorian Gray, plunging his hands in gems and letting them run through his fingers. His pages may be cold reading; but their glitter is amazing, and the fineness of the workmanship.

Nor is it merely the sensuous imagery that is decorative. The structure of Mr. Wilde's prose is decorative too . . .

'Her hair was as a wet fleece of gold, and each separate hair as a thread of fine gold in a cup of glass. Her body was as white ivory, and her tail was of silver and pearl. Silver and pearl was her tail, and the green weeds of the sea coiled round it; and like the sea-shells were her ears, and her lips were like sea-coral. The cold waves dashed over her cold breasts, and the salt glistened upon her eyelids.'

Here is a deliberate and successful adaptation of the old Hebrew trick of repeating a phrase to give balance and rhythm to a sentence, or possibly for the mere pleasure of looking a second time on a cluster of beautiful words. Our poets have made splendid use of this device now and again, and perhaps it has been unduly neglected by our prose-writers.[16]

Wary of calling 'The Fisherman and his Soul' a prose poem, the reviewer analyses it in terms that would exactly fit this category of literature. But the commentary does not go far enough. It overlooks the macrocosmic poetry of the narrative structure which, like the sentences, is patterned by repetition and reversal, analogous with that of the oral ballad tradition. The refrain central to the tale is the thrice-repeated dialogue between self and soul,

'Why dost thou call to me?'

And the Soul answered, 'Come nearer, that I may speak with thee, for I have seen marvellous things.'

So he came nearer, and couched in the shallow water, and leaned his head upon his hand and listened.

(Works, 244, 248, 252)

At the Vale this would have drawn Wilde's companions into story, identifying them with the soulless fisherman, and offering the narrator an opportunity for the whole performance to be extended or cut short. Between each of these utterances the Soul woos the Fisherman with tales of elaborate adventure; and on either side of them, at the beginning and the end of the tale, various refrains occur at more frequent intervals and punctuate the narrative to alter its tempo, rhythm or mood. The blocks of narrative or description between refrains can be likened to the masses of colour in a painting where the 'subject is fugitive', or any painting viewed primarily in this

99

abstract way; the refrains themselves can be likened to the arrangement of lines in a design.

One of the most acute reviews of *The House of Pomegranates* was
printed in *The Ladies' Pictorial* (always faithful to Wilde), overlooked
by subsequent critics perhaps because of the modesty of its tone.
Without bafflement or ill-temper, this reviewer observes the dual
focus of the tales:

> The stories are full of fancy and poetic thought, but it is possible
> to read between the lines and to find meanings which, if put into
> the text, would have spoiled the allegories. Mr. Wilde is far too
> wise to allow his morals to be obtrusive.[17]

It is impossible to determine how much weight she wants to give
to the word 'spoiled'. Assuming a radical rather than a conservative
weighting to the term, reading 'between the lines' becomes a dangerous business, and the reviewer's very discretion suggests she recognises that the neatly inferred moral of 'The Fisherman' is not the only
kind of spoiling which such investigation would yield.

Newspaper fiction: Lord Arthur Savile's Crime and Other Stories

Lord Arthur Savile's Crime and Other Stories, clearly destined for adult
readers, was published in 1891. Each tale had been published in
journals during 1887, the title story serialised in the *Court and Society
Review*. The collection addresses the Society of the London Season,
the social group represented by guests at the Wildes' 'At Homes' or
circulating at Private Views in the London Galleries. This was the
most powerful social group in Britain, and also the company which
courted Wilde, inadvertently providing their guest with as much
entertainment as they received. Fads and fashions of the season
are graciously mocked while the narratives also air more serious
aesthetic and political concerns rooted in subjects of immediately
contemporary discussion during the mid-1880s.

The title story belongs to the relatively new genre of crime fiction
which was predominantly popular in appeal when Wilde contributed
his piece. Its literary father was Edgar Allan Poe, and already Wilde
was altering the expectations of what might be expected from crime
writers of the period, such as Wilkie Collins. Instead of focusing on
the solution to the mystery, identifying and punishing the criminal,
Wilde centres his story on how to commit a crime and involves the
reader in the mind of the would-be criminal protagonist. The reader
is made to sympathise with the processes of criminal behaviour from
within, and to urge Lord Arthur forward in his iniquitous pursuits.

The happy ending desired by the protagonist is the same happy end to the tale that the reader is made to desire. The patterning of suspense and relief, the ingenuity of problem-solving, the pacing of discovery rates, mirror those of the more conventional crime story in which the detective hunts the offender – but here they are the function of the criminal in pursuit of his crime. Ultimately we are not even clear that the murder committed by Lord Arthur was a crime, so mischievously is the end made to justify the means of its achievement. But equally questionable, within the frame of the fiction, is whether there is any causal relationship at all between the means and the end: blissful in their urban garden of Eden, it is, as Lady Windermere says, 'nonsense' to suggest that the happiness of the marriage between Lord Arthur and Sybil Merton owes anything to chiromancy. Lady Windermere, after all, has changed her interest like her frock, from the now bankrupt chiromancy to the next voguish scientific spin-off, the new psychology: 'I go in for telepathy now. It is much more amusing' (Works, 182).

Palmistry, like the study of physiognomy, became fashionable and enjoyed brief crazes of plausibility during the Victorian period because it appeared to be based in natural science. The tenets of naturalism held that man was conditioned by genetic heredity and the environment he inhabited; the only unpredictable factor in behaviour was how such a creature would respond to the pressure of the present moment, the third principle of determinism in the governing trinity of naturalist thought. Given that so much of an individual's life appeared to be set down by immovable principles of science, it was not impossible to make a case for a science of augury that could read not just character but also the future from an aspect of physiognomy. Chiromancy was one modish consequence, to which an article by Wilde's friend, Edward Heron-Allen, testified: 'The Chiromancy of Today' appeared in the same issue of *Lippincott's Monthly Magazine* as did the first version of *The Picture of Dorian Gray* (July 1890). A record of Wilde participating in the upper-class entertainment of chiromancy (in a setting that mirrors that of Lady Windermere's party in the story) is given by the Society palmist 'Cheiro' (Count Louis Hamon). He recalls that at a dinner given by Blanche Roosevelt in April 1893 he read Wilde's palms and announced that 'The left hand is the hand of a king, but the right that of a king who will send himself into exile.' The 'king' is said to have left the party immediately (Ellmann, 360).

Although troubled by augury in 1893, with 'Lord Arthur Savile's Crime' six years earlier Wilde was undoubtedly ridiculing enthusiasm for these doctrines. But chiromancy, briefly entertaining as it was, functioned merely as a symptom of a much more sinister movement in social science. This was the developing school of criminal anthropology. Ever since the Italian criminologist, Cesare Lombroso, published *L'Uomo Deliquente* in 1876, the belief that criminal behaviour was genetically determined gained in credibility and influenced wide-ranging debate in Britain as elsewhere about the prevention of crime, appropriate forms of punishment and prison reform. Wilde addressed this debate directly and very seriously during the last five years of his life. Writing to the Home Secretary from prison in July 1896, pleading for early release, he was even willing to consider his own case in the light of principles put forward by the new discipline:

> Such offences are forms of sexual madness and are recognised as
> such not merely by modern pathological science but by much
> modern legislation . . . In the works of eminent men of science
> such as Lombroso and Max Nordau . . . this is specially insisted
> on with reference to the intimate connection between madness
> and the literary and artistic temperament.
>
> (Letters, 401–6)

But in 'Lord Arthur Savile's Crime' Wilde was content to tease a high-society readership with their foibles. The farcical presentation of chiromancy is in keeping with the tenor in which the story represents other serious political movements such as the French Revolution or Russian anarchism. The social context in which the tale is set requires the trivialisation of the serious, since this was the means by which the leisured aristocracy could maintain power in the face of real political threat. Wilde tantalises this class with the possibility of exotic and imaginative misdeeds taking place invisibly at the hub of their own circles. He was gracious in his exposure of the way social territory was policed, and gentle in his ridicule of the notion that character could be read from the shape of an earlobe, or criminal tendencies identified in the structure of the skull. Appearance, as the story repeatedly asserts, is no guide to certainty.

When Wilde changed the subtitle of the story from 'A Study in Chiromancy' to 'A Study in Duty', as he did in preparing the journal publication for its appearance in book form, Wilde was shifting the tonal emphasis of the tale from sensation and mystery to one of more considered irony and moral debate. He was questioning the certainties cherished by participants in the discussion of criminology and the larger metaphysical issues riding on it, such as those expounded by G. H. Lewes (philosopher, physiologist and partner of George Eliot) in an article 'Spiritualism and Materialism' for the *Fortnightly Review* in 1876.

Lewes starts with the observable, with 'what we see', and searches for explanatory causes. Wilde's narrative even follows this method. But as Wilde later suggested in his 'Few Maxims for the Instruction of the Over-Educated', what we see is not just potentially trivial, but unreliable. 'The criminal classes are so close to us that even the policeman can see them. They are so far away from us that only the poet can understand them' (Works, 1243). If chiromancy was to be taken seriously, and for Lord Arthur it was, then it was founded not in the occult but in the disciplines of the natural sciences. And if the path of a man's life was predetermined by observable scientific laws, could the individual ever act as a free agent, responsible for his own actions? Was it even possible to commit a 'crime'? What sense could be made of moral thought or moral action, what meaning could be ascribed to 'duty', in such a scheme? Lord Arthur panics over this dilemma at his first foreboding:

> How mad and monstrous it all seemed! . . . Were we no better than chessmen, moved by an unseen power, vessels the potter fashions at his fancy, for honour or for shame? His reason re-volted against it, and yet he felt that some tragedy was hanging over him, and that he had been suddenly called upon to bear an intolerable burden.
>
> (Works, 165)

Lord Arthur returns to this thought once he knows his fate. Survey-ing the derelicts of London after his dark night of the soul, he muses:

> Were these children of sin and misery predestined to their end, as he to his? Were they, like him, merely the puppets of a monstrous show?
>
> And yet it was not the mystery, but the comedy of suffering that struck him; its absolute uselessness, its grotesque want of meaning. How incoherent everything seemed! How lacking in all harmony!
>
> (Works, 167)

Predestination has no respect for social class; vice or virtue, wealth or poverty, falls to the individual irrespective of breeding. Wilde's satire confronts the growing certainties of criminology with a picture of absurdity which follows logically from its tenets. The hero, on reflection, casts himself in a comedy, rather than the tragedy con-jured forth by his initial instincts. Instead of being expelled from Society by his fate, he will simply be more thoroughly assimilated, his destiny differs from others only by degree and not by kind. The fitting comedic conclusion for such assimilation is marriage, and it is to secure this that the protagonist turns all his efforts. To match the 'comedy' of the plot and its accommodation of Lord Arthur's will to survive, the narrative maintains an ebullient comic tone, ranging through caricature, buffoonery and irony.

Duty, for Lord Arthur, consists no longer in performing good actions rather than bad ones, but in creating order out of the mad and the monstrous. Not his conscience but his aesthetic sensibility has been offended by his insight into human nature and the constraints on human freedom; and so the most that a sense of duty can do for him is to permit him to meet his fate in an orderly, even harmonious, fashion. Rhetoric immediately assists him. On first hearing that he will commit murder he becomes delirious, deranged by profilactic guilt; he 'detects' bloodstains on his hands, he hears the word 'murder' howling on the wind (Works, 167). But after the initial impact of the news, he understands his position differently:

> He wondered how he could have been so foolish as to rant and rave about the inevitable. The only question that seemed to trouble him was, whom to make away with; for he was not blind to the fact that murder, like the religions of the Pagan world, requires a victim as well as a priest.
>
> (Works, 170)

The insouciance of the narrative voice undermines the very concept of crime; the aristocratic hero is not offending against society, he is simply fulfilling his destiny in the most gentlemanly manner possible and becoming the high priest of a new paganism into the bargain. Rhetoric helps him to dress up the grim deed in a noble fashion, to tell himself a new version of his life story and to overcome the 'incoherence' of the human condition as it had been revealed to him. The only freedom that appeared to be available to him was the question of timing: an ultimately aesthetic question about when would be the most opportune moment to commit the crime. To become a murderer after his marriage could have disagreeable consequences that would involve the fate of his wife as well as himself. The most expedient way forward was to find a victim immediately and so preserve the sanctity of his forthcoming marriage and the innocence of his fiancée. The narrative voice informs us that he thereby acquits himself most honourably of the question that is asked 'of us all': whether to live for himself or to live for others. 'He knew that he must not suffer selfishness to triumph over love' (Works, 170).

Throughout 'Lord Arthur Savile's Crime' Wilde delights in exposing the urge to tell explanatory stories about experience as destined to ridiculous failure. When Lord Arthur makes his second attempt at murder he arranges, through a Russian nihilist acquaintance, for an exploding carriage clock to be sent to his uncle, the Dean of Chichester. The bomb is concealed in 'a pretty little French clock, surmounted by an ormolu figure of Liberty trampling on the hydra of Despotism' (Works, 177). Timing is at the heart of Lord Arthur's enterprise. But the device does not work as planned. After waiting for days for news of his uncle's death, he is shown a letter from his cousin Jane about the mysterious gift which arrived for the Dean:

just as the clock struck twelve, we heard a whirring noise, a little puff of smoke came from the pedestal of the figure, and the goddess of Liberty fell off, and broke her nose on the fender! . . . Do you think Arthur would like one for a wedding present? I suppose they are quite fashionable in London. Papa says they should do a great deal of good, as they show that Liberty can't last, but must fall down. Papa says that Liberty was invented at the time of the French Revolution. How awful it seems! . . . I don't think papa likes it so much as he did at first, though he is very flattered at being sent such a pretty and ingenious toy. It shows that people read his sermons and profit by them.

(Works, 179)

Possessed entirely of ignorance about the processes that govern the appearance of the 'toy', hampered by sternly patriarchal and reactionary politics ('Papa says'), the interpretation available to cousin Jane is woefully and comically inadequate when placed against the 'truth' to which the reader is party. What emerges is the egotism that dictates Jane's fabulation, naïve on her part and cunning on the part of 'Papa', coupled with a determination to read appearances allegorically in quest of a moral point. Nothing could be more futile in the context of this story, and that heartening futility illustrates precisely the political, philosophical and aesthetic purposes informing the tale. Wilde's narrative technique makes the reader complicit with the repeated acts of interpreting appearances, piecing together clues, and the construction of fictions masquerading as truth that comprise the tale. He supplies the reader with a kind of literary collage, a sequence of documents: Mr Podgers' Card, the letter from cousin Jane, the newspaper obituary for Mr Podgers – even the silence that follows Mr Podgers' announcement that he is 'quite ready' to read Lord Arthur's palm as Part 1 ends and Part 2 has not begun. All these are inscribed in the text and sit side by side with a disingenuously sage and paternal narrative voice, inviting interpretation from the reader while at the same time defying interpretation as a possibility.

As with so much of Wilde's work, this fiction is Janus-faced and can be viewed from more than one perspective, like Wittgenstein's figure of the duck–rabbit. Depending on the perspective of the reader, the story can be archly conservative, reactionary in politics and form (the *status quo* is restored after difficulty is overcome); or it can be subversively anarchic, a radical attack on a dilettante aristocracy, repressive tendencies in the social sciences and an experiment with frames of fiction and reading practices.

By adopting the perspective of the offender, and by assenting to the rationality of the occult, 'Lord Arthur Savile's Crime' problematises the definition of crime. It can be read as a paradox, a crime story without a crime. The same trick is deployed in 'The Canterville Ghost', which can be understood as a ghost story without a ghost, achieved by the reversal of the expected narrative perspective. Instead of watching a victim of ghoulish apparitions and discovering with the victim some original and secret crime that motivates supernatural disturbance, the reader witnesses the torment of a ghost by the mortal cohabitants of Canterville Chase. 'For some time he was disturbed by wild shrieks of laughter from the twins'; 'His nerves were completely shattered, and he started at the slightest noise' (Works, 191, 193), describe the discomfort of the ghost of Sir Simon de Canterville at his treatment by the American Otis family, republicans and episcopalians, on their arrival in the Old World. Sir Simon died in 1584, having murdered his wife in 1575, and his spirit had been performing 'most conscientious[ly]' ever since (Works, 193). The ghost is fully accommodated within the tolerant parameters of the natural world brought from America; its 'supernatural' status is annihilated by the culture that produces Rising Sun Lubricator (Works, 189). Consequently the pleasing frissons of terror induced by the conventional ghost story are absent from this tale. But some mystery does remain to be solved, and this revolves around the maintenance of power by the English aristocracy. The ghostly quality of the story is simply displaced, represented by an ancient and criminal social class rather than by an individual.

'The Canterville Ghost. A Hylo-Idealistic Romance' was first serialised in the *Court and Society Review* in February and March 1887. It too specifically addresses the readership of that journal, not just with an extravaganza set in the Surrey aristocracy, but also by fortifying the boundaries between the Old World and the New, legitimating the territory of the English upper class against upstart foreigners and the *nouveau riche*. While the catalogue of the ghost's activity shows that it was most concerned to torment members of its own former class – an ostensible target of Wilde's satire – as soon as the ghost itself becomes a victim of American pragmatism, the reader's sympathy is made to close rank with the aristocracy, to despise and resent the newcomers as heartily as does the ghost. But Wilde's first English readers were not the simple beneficiaries of flattery. The whole 'hylo-idealistic' enterprise of the tale satirised another social vogue: not chiromancy, but spiritualism, another sectarian cult riding on the new science.

Spiritualism, itself an import from America, became Society entertainment in London and Paris during the latter half of the nineteenth century. Closest to Wilde's circle of aquaintance was the Society medium, Daniel Home, whose séances inspired Browning's sceptical response with 'Mr Sludge the Medium' (1864). Lady Mount-Temple (then Mrs Cowper) was a devoted participant of Home's séances, and she persuaded Ruskin (ever sceptical) to attend on more than one occasion. Home died in 1886, while Madame Blavatsky settled in London in 1885 to establish there the European Headquarters of the Theosophical Society – so giving the occult a new lease of life. That these circles had their eyes on Wilde is evidenced by the fact that *The Picture of Dorian Gray* was reviewed most earnestly by a spiritualist journal, *Light*. On 12 July 1890 'Nizide' explained what was really happening in that story:

> The only occult explanation of the catastrophe which befalls him [Dorian] is, that he commits astral suicide by the murderous attack he ignorantly makes upon that which is represented to him as his own soul. The blow reverts to his physical body, and he falls dead.

That Wilde in turn had his candid eyes on the spiritualists is inscribed in 'The Canterville Ghost':

> [The Otis family] were clearly people on a low, material plane of existence, and quite incapable of appreciating the symbolic value of sensuous phenomena. The question of phantasmic apparitions, and the development of astral bodies, was of course quite a different matter, and really not under his control.
>
> (Works, 193)

This is what the ghost thinks about the extent of his phantasmic responsibility. He has to keep up appearances, whatever 'Pinkerton's Champion Stain Remover' and 'Paragon Detergent' might be doing to the sixteenth-century bloodstain Sir Simon had been servicing. The ghost is a master of disguise, revelling in the theatricality of his role. ' "Red Ruben, or the Strangled Babe" '; ' "Gaunt Gibeon, the Blood-sucker of Bexley Moor" '; ' "Dumb Daniel, or the Suicide's Skeleton" '; ' "Martin the Maniac, or the Masked Mystery" ' (Works, 188, 191): these are some of the roles of which he feels particularly proud, as he rehearses carefully how to exact revenge on his newly unappreciative audience, incapable of suspending disbelief. Wilde had already signalled his amusement at the sensationalist conventions of melodrama in his sonnet to Ellen Terry, and here amusement is strengthened to good-humoured satire. But in the story it is the very conventionality of the ghost's roles that suggests he is losing his efficacy. A new drama is waiting to be played out. The only member of the Otis family who has not outraged the ghost's sense of self-importance by a failure to be impressed is 'little Virginia', and he reserves judgement about how to deal with her.

The ghost's relationship with Virginia is the only subject of mystery and surprise allowed to flourish in the narrative. She seems at first to be the only one whose imagination is troubled by the ghost. In fact she is the only Otis to have any imagination at all and this is indicated by the fact that she amuses herself by painting. Like the ghost, she engages in some constructive creativity. When the family starts to joke about the 'chameleon-like colour' of the bloodstain, which is removed daily by Paragon Detergent and renewed nightly by phantasmic stealth, 'the only person who did not enter into the joke was little Virginia, who, for some unexplained reason, was always a good deal distressed at the sight of the bloodstain, and very nearly cried the morning it was emerald-green' (Works, 189).

But the reader's relief at greeting a more conventional response to the paranormal is short-lived. For Virginia, it transpires, is not just equipped with imagination, she can also keep a secret. Only she knows that the ghost has been stealing her paints to restore the bloodstain:

> finally I had nothing left but indigo and Chinese white, and could only do moonlight scenes, which are always depressing to look at, and not at all easy to paint. I never told on you, though I was very much annoyed, and it was most ridiculous, the whole thing; for who ever heard of emerald-green blood?

> (Works, 197)

Just as Lord Arthur's insight into an ethical dilemma resolves itself to a point of aesthetics, so too Virginia's moral outrage at the ghost's iniquitous past slides along a spectrum of distaste that ends with an aesthetic complaint. The ghost answers in like fashion, pointing out that Canterville blood is the 'very bluest' in England (Wilde was no doubt joking with his Irish descent, and his homosexuality, when he invented emerald-green blood). And it is precisely because Virginia herself is being courted by blue blood, the 'little Duke of Cheshire' (nevertheless a big cheese, related to the Stiltons (Works, 195)), that she enjoys privilege over the ghost. She is almost his social equal. Her name links the Virgin Queen of Sir Simon's era with the Virgin Mother of spiritual impunity, and the virgin territory of the New World seeking legitimation from the Old. Virginia fulfils the prophecy on the library window: she is the 'golden girl' who can bring peace to Canterville (Works, 198). And doubtless her 'moonlight scenes' have brought her imagination to inhabit similar landscape to the ghost.

Virginia is virtually inconspicuous in the first four sections of the story during which she is mentioned only twice (Works, 185, 189). These two references (to her character, appearance and the proposing Duke; and her response to the restored bloodstain) are crucial clues for the unriddling of the tale. The narrative peripeteia, or reversal of fortunes, takes place during her encounter with the ghost in section five. She then disappears from the narrative again, this time most conspicuously, and what happened to her during this vanishing remains a permanent secret from the reader. But she emerges from her closeting with the ghost carrying a 'little casket' (Works, 200). It contains antique jewels, Canterville heirlooms. Despite her father's attempts to restore them to the Canterville family, she is forced to keep them, so her wealth is transformed from the *nouveau* to the *ancien*. The Venetian ruby necklace is her passport to the upper class, the ultimate theatrical prop deployed by the ghost. The wedded bliss between Virginia Otis and the Duke of Cheshire, on which the tale ends, represents her assimilation by the Old World. It is this foreseen assimilation which conditions her right to lay the ghost, but which is also a condition of her having laid the ghost. The English aristocracy is policed from within. New money cannot buy the status open to the correct temperament, the correct properties, and the correct in-laws. Does the narrative ask its reader to condemn or condone this social law? At the very least, in exposing the machinations of exclusion and entry to Society, its code of conduct becomes questionable. And in giving the role of healer to the 15-year-old girl in her conversation with the 300-year-old Ghost, the fiction does suggest that some habits of class and age require the purge of youth.

'The Canterville Ghost' foreshadows much of the debate between the values of the Old World and the New that Wilde establishes in *A Woman of No Importance*. When Virginia Otis tells the ghost that 'it is very wrong to kill any one' (Works, 196), she betrays 'a sweet Puritan gravity, caught from some old New England ancestor', but in terms that suggest an appealing kind of decadence on her part. She anticipates the fiercer Puritanism of Hester Worsley that is eventually tempered by her marriage into the albeit illegitimate English aristocracy. The banter between the Ghost and Virginia supplies a first run of some of the xenophobic jokes that entertain the Hunstanton guests at Hester's expense.

'I don't think I should like America.'
'I suppose because we have no ruins and no curiosities,' said Virginia satirically.
'No ruins! no curiosities!' answered the Ghost; 'you have your navy and your manners.'

(Works, 197)

Lady Caroline: There are a great many things you haven't got in America, I am told, Miss Worsley. They say you have no ruins, and no curiosities.

Mrs Allonby [*to* Lady Stutfield]: What nonsense! They have their mothers and their manners.
Hester. The English aristocracy supply us with our curiosities, Lady Caroline. They are sent over to us every summer, regularly, in the steamers, and propose to us the day after they land.
(Works, 482–3)

It is no accident that Mrs Allonby, the most amoral among the women, has the version of the Ghost's line; and she is the only major player who remains unchanged by the events of the play. Not all symptoms of decadence are to be purged by a 'golden girl' from across the sea. Wilde's short fiction can be seen as intense commentaries on artistic, social and political topics of the day, rehearsing themes for his plays. Already he subjects the serious to exquisite triviality.

Notes

1   Constance Wilde, *There Was Once! Grandma's Stories* (London: Ernest Nister, 1889) 3.
2   Lady Wilde, *Ancient Legends, Mystic Charms and Superstitions of Ireland* (London, 1887) vii.
3   Ibid., I, 176–7.
4   Mason, *Bibliography*, 334.
5   *Essays and Lectures*, 146–7.
6   Ibid., 170.
7   Michael Mac Liammoir, *An Oscar of No Importance* (London: Heinemann, 1968) 9.
8   *The Happy Prince and Other Tales* (London: David Nutt, 1888) 10, 14.
9   H. Montgomery Hyde, *Oscar Wilde. A Biography* (London: Eyre Methuen, 1976) 107.
10   *Essays and Lectures*, 209.
11   Pater, *The Renaissance*, 104.
12   *Ladies' Pictorial*, 19 December 1891.
13   *Ancient Legends*, I, 169.
14   Ibid., I, 164–5.
15   Charles Ricketts, *Oscar Wilde. Recollections by Jean Paul Raymond and Charles Ricketts* (London: The Nonesuch Press, 1932) 37.
16   *The Speaker*, 2 January 1892.
17   *Ladies' Pictorial*, 19 December 1891.

6   The Picture of Dorian Gray

The story exists in two forms. The first was published in the American journal *Lippincott's Monthly Magazine* in July 1890; the next year an expanded version came out in London as a book, after the publication of maxims as the 'Preface' in the *Fortnightly Review* in March 1891. Wilde called it 'my first long story', formally linking it with the short stories he had written for journals during 1887. It displays both the precision required of the short-story form, and the discursiveness permitted by length. Many of the themes entertained earlier recur: the relationship between the artist and his model ('The Model Millionaire'); the relationship between art and morality, or, put differently, between form and content ('The Sphinx without a Secret'); the question of influence, criminal propensity, and determinism ('Lord Arthur Savile's Crime'); the relationship between empiricism and the occult ('The Canterville Ghost'). Characteristic of the perspectival reversals which Wilde deployed in the tales of *Lord Arthur Savile's Crime and Other Stories*, he presents in *The Picture of Dorian Gray* a story which begins to be about the relationship between an artist and his model, and turns into a story about the relationship between art and its model.

Wilde chose to cast his ideas into the form of a 'magic picture' story. 'This portrait would be to him the most magical of mirrors. As it had revealed to him his own body, so it would reveal to him his own soul' (Works, 84). Dorian is the ultimate 'poser', as Wilde described a species of artist's model in 'London Models' (1889): 'professional posers of the studio' and 'posers of the Row, the posers at afternoon teas' (Works, 978), since he presents not just in the studio, but also in life itself, a false self-image, turning the world at large into an artist's studio fit for experiment and larger vision. The 'magic picture' genre enjoyed a vogue of popular circulation during the 1880s: Kerry Powell points to four examples from this decade: *The Picture's Secret, The Portrait and the Ghost, The Veiled Picture* and *His Other Self*.[1] As Walter Pater stated in his review of *The Picture of Dorian Gray*, the 'interest turns on that very old theme, old because based on some inherent experience or fancy of the human brain, of a double life: of Doppelgänger' (Critical Heritage, 85). One reason for the closer and more fantastic scrutiny to which the 'human brain' was subjected in literature at this time was the contemporary development of the discipline of psychology. It was not just articles like 'The "New" Psychology and Automatism' in the *Contemporary Review* in April 1893, but also Stevenson's *Dr Jekyll and Mr Hyde* (1884),

Wilde's *Portrait of Dorian Gray* and Bram Stoker's *Dracula* (1897) that signposted the way to Freud's publication of *The Interpretation of Dreams* in 1900. The psyche was fragmenting, and art – intoxicated by the Gothic possibilities of rupture – still offered a way to reassemble it.

This was not the way in which Wilde's story was greeted. It met with a storm of revolted abuse: 'not being curious in ordure, and not wishing to offend the nostrils of decent persons, we do not propose to analyse *The Picture of Dorian Gray*'; 'it is a tale spawned from the leprous literature of the French Decadents'; 'why go grubbing in muck-heaps?'; 'a truer art would have avoided both the glittering conceits, which bedeck the body of the story, and the unsavoury suggestiveness which lurks in its spirit'.[2] Wilde fired off a sequence of incandescent letters to the press and later put his rage into the gnomic 'Preface', published in advance of the appearance of the book in Britain ('My preface should teach them to mend their wicked ways' (Letters, 290)). The epigrammatic form of the Preface defies simplistic interpretation, and places the work firmly in the French 'art for art's sake' tradition. The concluding *homage* is to Gautier's Preface to *Mademoiselle de Maupin*, in which the French poet had defended his own aestheticism to a utilitarian age: 'all art is quite useless'. The baying public Wilde characterises as 'Caliban', enraged equally by its own reflection as by its lack. He draws particular attention to the vexing relationship between art and morality, the issue which had so supremely lathered his detractors. 'Vice and virtue are to the artist materials for an art' (Works, 17) points the reader back to the kind of naturalist doctrine explicated by Taine, practised by Zola and defended in his preface to *Thérèse Raquin* (1867), a novel which figures as a significant precursor to *Dorian Gray*.

The assertions 'There is no such thing as a moral or an immoral book. Books are well written or badly written. That is all' call attention to style at the expense of content in a provocative gesture of amorality. Wilde had already used it once in self-defence, when asked by an interviewer during his American lecture tour to respond to the charge that his poetry was 'immoral'. He replied: 'A poem is well written or badly written. In art there should be no reference to a standard of good or evil'.[3] Nevertheless this was the aphorism which Wilde claimed during his trial, when asked whether the novel was 'proper' or 'improper', to have added at the advice of Walter Pater. His Oxford mentor had pointed out to him that certain features of the story were open to misconstruction of precisely the kind for which Wilde later stood in the dock. Within *Dorian Gray* itself the mephistophelean voice of Lord Henry explains the prefatory maxim further: 'Art has no influence upon action. It annihilates the desire to act. It is superbly sterile. The books that the world calls immoral are books that show the world its own shame' (Works, 156). The appeal of art, Wotton implies, is to a Kantian mental state of disinterested contemplation. Gilbert, in 'The Critic as Artist', also engages with this point, declaring that 'Art does not hurt us. The tears that we shed at a play are a type of the exquisite sterile emotions that it is the function of Art to awaken'; Gilbert uses this to lead up to his statement that 'All art is immoral' (Works, 1135, 1136), seeming to contradict the terms of the 'Preface to Dorian Gray'. But both pieces mean the same: responsibility for interpretation and any consequent action must lie with the individual who has misconstrued the ideal terms in which art operates. Within the novel, Wotton's utterance is untrustworthy. Delivered by one who has 'poisoned' Dorian with a book, to the now middle-aged protagonist who has spent 18 years experimenting with the face of his portrait, the dictum is both chastening and ironical. Outside the novel Wilde stood firm, writing to the press: 'Each man sees his own sin in Dorian Gray. What Dorian Gray's sins are no one knows. He who finds them has bought them' (Letters, 266).

Wilde's perplexity at the reception of the book was justified and real. To Arthur Conan Doyle he wrote: 'I cannot understand how they can treat *Dorian Gray* as immoral. My difficulty was to keep the inherent moral subordinate to the artistic and dramatic effect, and it still seems to me that the moral is too obvious' (Letters, 292). On 26 June 1890 he had even spelled it out to the readers of the *St James's Gazette*:

> the moral is this: All excess, as well as all renunciation, brings its own punishment. The painter, Basil Hallward, worshipping physical beauty far too much, as most painters do, dies by the hand of one in whose soul he has created a monstrous and absurd vanity. Dorian Gray, having led a life of mere sensation and pleasure, tries to kill conscience, and at that moment kills himself. Lord Henry Wotton seeks to be merely the spectator of life. He finds that those who reject the battle are more deeply wounded than those who take part in it.
>
> (Letters, 259)

The stakes were high because the issues were so confused by the hypocritical mores and punitive legislation of the period. Nobody could bring themselves to say that *Dorian Gray* was a passionate homosexual love story. It did for homosexuality what *Thérèse Raquin* had done for heterosexuality. And while the same-sex passion that drives the plot of the novel results in two terrible *crimes passionelles*, the murder of Basil Hallward, comparable to the murder of Camille in *Thérèse Raquin*, and the suicide of Dorian, comparable to the deaths of the lovers at the end of Zola's novel, homosexuality is also represented as a force of possible redemption, with a noble pedigree:

He shuddered, and for a moment he regretted that he had not told Basil the true reason why he had wished to hide the picture away. Basil would have helped him to resist Lord Henry's influence, and the still more poisonous influences that came from his own temperament. The love that he bore him – for it was really love – had nothing in it that was not noble and intellectual. It was not the mere physical admiration of beauty that is born of the senses, and that dies when the senses tire. It was such love as Michael Angelo had known, and Montaigne, and Winckelmann, and Shakespeare himself. Yes, Basil could have saved him.

(Works, 92)

The mythic analogies for Dorian are predominantly female: Eve, Pygmalion's sculpture, Salome, or, like Narcissus, given to feminised interpretation. Wilde can be seen to structure an epic for the homosexual Fall, to parallel that of the heterosexual expulsion from Eden and the subsequent idolatry on the way to redemption. The real pathology which Wilde scrutinises in the story lies not in the delineation of same-sex passion, but in the way Dorian's character is structured by vanity, so extreme that it heralds a Freudian analysis of narcissism. Further critical confusion arises from the way in which the love story is knitted together with aesthetic doctrine so that the two appear to become inseparable. The failure of the early critics to distinguish between the 'moral' of the story and the ethical foundation on which the fiction is built contributes to further obfuscation.

The distinction between superficial 'moral' and profound ethical vision starts to enter the public debate more clearly with responses to the book in 1891. Some, like the *Athenaeum*, continued with the line that it was 'unmanly, sickening, vicious . . . and tedious' (27 June 1891). But it was Pater who, unsurprisingly, soared above the shrill hysteria and gave the novel balanced attention. Noting the effect which Dorian produces in Hallward at the start of the novel, Pater states,

How true, what a light on the artistic nature, is the following on actual personalities and their revealing influence in art. We quote it as an example of Mr. Wilde's more serious style.

I sometimes think that there are only two eras of any importance in the world's history. The first is the appearance of a new medium for art, and the second is the appearance of new personality for art also. What the invention of oil-painting was to the Venetians, the face of Antinous was to late Greek sculpture, and the face of Dorian Gray will some day be to me . . . in some curious way his personality has suggested to me an entirely new manner in art, an entirely new mode of style. I see things differently. I think of them differently. I can now recreate life in a way that was hidden from me before.

(Critical Heritage, 85)

The final version of the novel is an extraordinary anthology of styles, dovetailed to express the central ethical idea that art, serving as a repository for the conscience of a culture, extends or constrains the perceptual range of humanity. Cumulatively, the 'more serious style' and the more flippant or experimental styles of narrative voice make manifest Dorian's statement that 'if one doesn't talk about a thing, it has never happened. It is simply expression . . . that gives reality to things' (Works, 85). This is a belief which promotes artistic expression to a functional necessity in order for any culture to see itself, to be self aware. It was a creed to which Wilde held, writing in 'The Decay of Lying', '[t]hings are because we see them, and what we see, and how we see it, depends on the Arts that have influenced us' (Works, 1086), and amplifying this in 'The Critic as Artist' with 'language . . . is the parent, and not the child, of thought' (Works, 1121). The expressive range of an individual, as of a culture, defines the boundaries of possible experience. This is the Faustian pact which the novel makes with its reader, taking us through a universe of experience, occult, mundane, melodramatic, sophisticated, but always emphasising the stylistic lens through which apprehension is made possible. The Faustus legend which informs both the plot and the fabric of the novel comes from the Renaissance, not from the Romantics; it is Marlowe's damned Faustus, hungered by curiosity for forbidden knowledge, not Goethe's Faust ultimately redeemed, which governs the pessimistic aesthetic–ethical horizons of the tale. There is no transcendent vision other than what man can make or muster for himself. ' "Each of us has Heaven and Hell in him, Basil," cried Dorian, with a wild gesture of despair' (Works, 116).

One of the clearest examples of the way art fashions the self-knowledge of the individual is given by the account of Sybil Vane and her family in Chapter 5, an addition for the expanded English version. The whole episode is written in a style that parodies the conventional melodrama of the period, and the kind of theatre that had nurtured Sybil's mother in her acting days. The mother is portrayed as a victim of this style, unwilling and unable to experience anything that does not fit the mould:

'Ah! Mother, mother, let me be happy!'
Mrs Vane glanced at her, and with one of those false theatrical gestures that so often become a mode of second nature to a stage-player, clasped her in her arms. At this moment the door opened, and a young lad with rough brown hair came into the room . . . Mrs Vane fixed her eyes on him, and intensified the smile. She

115

mentally elevated her son to the dignity of an audience. She felt
sure that the *tableau* was interesting.

(Works, 56)

It is not simply the case that Mrs Vane is morally culpable in failing
to distinguish between art and life; she has no other medium of
expression with which to represent life to herself. The consequences
are disastrous, as she encourages her daughter towards an affair
with an unknown but wealthy 'Prince Charming'. The outcome,
dictated by melodrama, is as predictable as James Vane dreads it to
be. Similarly, Sybil, an empty vessel to be filled with the Shakespear-
ean repertoire, can impersonate every romantic heroine from Juliet
to Imogen. But once she feels an emotion that seems to be 'real', she
has no medium in which to express it. 'I might mimic a passion that
I do not feel, but I cannot mimic one that burns me like fire' (Works,
72). She loses her audience, and she loses Dorian:

> You simply produce no effect. I loved you because you were
> marvellous, because you had genius and intellect, because you
> realised the dreams of great poets and gave shape and substance
> to the shadows of art. You have thrown it all away. You are
> shallow and stupid . . . Without your art you are nothing.
>
> (Works, 72)

Sybil cannot understand him: 'You are acting,' she says, as her own
performance of the process of desertion approaches melodramatic
climax. 'In a few moments he was out of the theatre' (Works, 72,
73); Dorian leaves the house of illusion, and will go to other forms
of expression to satisfy his hunger for a life of sensation.

Other modes of expression represented in the novel permit their
users more sophisticated freedom, but contain ultimately no better
earthly redemption. Hallward, as we have noted, 'sees things differently' as a consequence of meeting Dorian, and creates his master-
piece, the fateful portrait. The 'new medium for art' which he
discovers at the unwitting inspiration of Dorian supplies the central
conceit of the novel. It is painting which spectacularly defies the
laws that hitherto governed the creation of the visual arts. Instead of
preserving on canvas a glorious, timeless moment, 'a single exquisite
instant, eternal indeed in its beauty, but limited to one note of passion or one mood of calm' (Works, 1123), Hallward's portrait also
acquires the temporal powers of narrativity. 'Movement, that problem of the visible arts, can be truly realized by Literature alone.
It is Literature that shows us the body in its swiftness and the soul
in its unrest' (Works, 1124). Not so, if the subject is Dorian and the
painter his idolatrous lover, Hallward. The novel explores a painterly
fantasy of exercising an art that overcomes this 'problem of the

visible arts' identified by Wilde in 'The Critic as Artist'. It toys with the notion of *Anders-streben* [striving to be different, striving towards the other] within the arts.

This was an impulse which Pater and the aesthetic philosopher before him, Hegel, no less than the practitioners Wagner and Baudelaire, had identified as a force by which the arts could lend each other expressive powers properly specific to distinct media. The only medium, Pater argued, which could liberate itself from the constraints by which a specific art form is limited to a specific kind of content, was music. In music alone the dichotomy between form and content collapses. Hence Pater's maxim 'all art constantly aspires towards the condition of music'. Wilde's 'magic picture' conceit in the novel fantasises over how this aspiration may really affect the visual arts. The consequences of over-reaching are not less terrible for Hallward than they are for Marlowe's Faustus. The portrait, revelatory in its pristine form, is horribly disfigured by its acquisition of the expressive powers that belong properly to literature. When Dorian first sees the portrait, 'a look of joy came into his eyes, as if he had recognised himself for the first time' (Works, 33). When Hallward sees it next,18 years later '[a]n exclamation of horror broke from the painter's lips as he saw in the dim light the hideous face on the canvas grinning at him' (Works, 115). His work is identifiable only by the 'brushwork', the frame and the signature. Over-reaching its medium, the portrait is destroyed, the artistry and vision which went into it are travestied. But just as Marlowe, in *Faustus*, is unable to reveal to the audience a serious dimension to the forbidden knowledge Faustus acquires by his pact, and shows instead the effects of the 'fall' on the protagonist, consequences which drama is fully able to show, so Wilde can only reveal the portrait through literature. In showing the defiance of one art form within the fabric of another, Wilde eschews the difficulty of displaying the impossible while he also endorses the legitimacy of proper aesthetic constraint. *The Picture of Dorian Gray* contains a 'moral' about aesthetic over-reaching just as much as it contains a rather more trite 'moral' about how to live.

The most entertaining style contained by the narrative voice is the epigrammatic wit of Lord Henry Wotton. His voice is so important as a catalyst for events within the novel, yet his form of wit is also the most detachable from the plot, as he himself practises social detachment as an art. Much of his dialogue was used again by Wilde three years later to create Lord Illingworth in *A Woman of No Importance* (and some of it had appeared already, in *Vera*, and elsewhere). Wotton is a Mephisto, a cynic, a dandy who treats life as a spectator sport and exercises malign influence on Dorian in the interests of vivisection. The function of his style is recognised by Dorian, who accuses 'You cut life to pieces with your epigrams' (Works, 78). The dangerous temptation of the style is confessed by Wilde: 'the chance of an epigram makes me desert truth' he wrote to Conan Doyle (Letters, 291–2). Lord Henry Wotton's use of epigram would be less disturbing for the reader if it were a style that Wilde had used solely to delineate an obviously corrupt character within the novel. But epigram and paradox were the hallmarks of Wilde's own style in his non-fiction as well as his fiction, and much of Wotton's philosophy is repeated in the critical discourses which Wilde was composing at the same time as the two versions of *Dorian Gray*. For example, 'The Soul of Man Under Socialism' begins with an attack on charity, and returns repeatedly to the morally corrupting tendency to have sympathy with other people's suffering:

> Up to the present man has hardly cultivated sympathy at all. He has merely sympathy with pain, and sympathy with pain is not the highest form of sympathy . . . One should sympathize with the entirety of life, not with life's sores and maladies merely, but with life's joy and beauty and energy and health and freedom.
>
> (Works, 1195).

At Lord Henry's second meeting with Dorian he sets out to divert Dorian from the social activity in which he is engaged: that of being charitable to the poor in the East End. Lady Agatha laments,

> 'Harry, I am quite vexed with you. Why do you try to persuade our nice Mr. Dorian Gray to give up the East End?'
>
> 'I can sympathize with everything, except suffering,' said Lord Henry . . . 'I cannot sympathize with that. It is too ugly, too horrible, too distressing. There is something terribly morbid in the modern sympathy with pain. One should sympathize with the colour, the beauty, the joy of life. The less said about life's sores the better.'
>
> (Works, 42)

The distinction is blurred between what Wilde professes as a radical, wholesome, philosophy of life outside the novel, and what an iniquitous character holds within the fiction. This subverts the framing device of the fiction which places, contains and evaluates Wotton's views unambiguously.

Epigram is not exclusively the symptom of Wotton's moral vision, but also of the corrupt aristocratic society in which he stars, portrayed, Pater says, so 'mercilessly' by the novel. In Chapter 17, which describes the party at Dorian's country estate, Selby Royal, clever quips take over the narrative completely. Who says what is less important than the sheer sequence of utterance. The languid conversational pattern controlled by Wotton (here a self-professed Minotaur in a cravat) is all important:

'Decay fascinates me more.'
'What of Art?' she asked.
'It is a malady.'
'Love?'
'An illusion.'
'Religion?'
'The fashionable substitute for Belief.'
'You are a sceptic.'
'Never! Scepticism is the beginning of Faith.'
'What are you?'
'To define is to limit.'
'Give me a clue.'
'Threads snap. You would lose your way in the labyrinth.'

(Works, 141)

This open technique of inscribing free direct speech creates a public atmosphere of the idle debonair. This style, by which the narrative voice appears to retreat into the mere notation of inverted commas, contrasts starkly with the elaborate descriptions of Chapter 11. Here the narrative voice is foregrounded to mediate Dorian's private sensory escapades and creation of occult 'worlds':

He would often spend a whole day settling and resettling in their cases the various stones that he had collected, such as the olive-green chrysoberyl that turns red by lamplight, the cymophane with its wire-like line of silver, the pistachio-coloured peridot, rose-pink and wine-yellow topazes, carbuncles of fiery scarlet with tremulous four-rayed stars, flame-red cinnamon stones, orange and violet spinels, and amethysts with their alternate layers of ruby and sapphire.

(Works, 102)

In fact, the narrative voice has retreated even more radically from this section of the novel than from that of the reported society conversation. That this description is based on a South Kensington Museum Art Handbook, *Precious Stones* (1882), or that as Isobel Murray has indicated, Wilde plagiarised word for word the 'stories' which bring these gems to life in the subsequent three paragraphs of the chapter from William Jones' *History and Mystery of Precious Stones* (1880),[4] and did the same for every other branch of sensory knowledge Dorian pursues, reveals an audacity of composition. But it compounds, almost comically, the governing idea that the experiential range of mankind is constrained by expression, in this case not by what art might express but by what science has already expressed. Dorian, and the reader, are cheated together in the Faust pact of the novel.

The stolen ventriloquism of this section of the novel also illustrates, as a narrative device, the principles of naturalist doctrine which govern the ethical pessimism of the novel. The fabric of the novel itself, no less than the flesh of its protagonist, is the product of precedence:

> Man is the most complex of the products of nature. Character merges into temperament; the nervous system refines itself into intellect. Man's physical organism is played upon not only by the physical conditions about it, but by remote laws of inheritance, the vibration of long-past acts reaching him in the midst of the new order of things in which he lives. When we have estimated these conditions he is still not simple and isolated; for the mind of the race, the character of the age, sway him this way or that through the medium of language and current ideas. It seems as if the most opposite statements about him were alike true: he is so receptive, all the influences of nature and of society ceaselessly playing upon him, so that every hour is unique, changed altogether by a stray word, or glance, or touch.[5]

Pater uses this summary of the tenets of naturalism to justify his belief that under such circumstances as have been revealed by empirical science, the 'speculative instinct in our modern minds' can only be exercised to the full by attention to 'subtleties of effect' or 'individual knowledge' in 'the world of form, colour, and passion'.[6] This is how Wilde effects the provocative blend of naturalism and aestheticism, summarised in Wotton's dictum that 'nothing can cure the soul but the senses, just as nothing can cure the senses but the soul' (Works, 30). The saying takes root in Dorian who uses the determinist doctrines of naturalism to justify devotion to sensory experience and indulgence in passions known only by scandalous rumour. But as Dorian's sensibility, like that of the reader, is circumscribed by the limits of aesthetic expression, so Dorian himself is the product of a complicated and doom-laden past.

Henry Wotton, the scientific investigator of the piece – the vivisector – takes the trouble to find out about Dorian's heredity. It emerges (in Chapter 3) that he is an orphan, born out of an ill-starred romance, and Dorian himself takes pleasure in strolling through the 'gaunt cold picture-gallery of his country house', looking at the 'various portraits of those whose blood flowed in his veins'. This is a more oblique exercise of his narcissistic passion, and it arises from his Paterian insight that 'to him, man was a being with myriad lives and myriad sensations, a complex multiform creature that bore within itself strange legacies of thought and passion, and whose very flesh was tainted with the monstrous maladies of the dead' (Works, 107). The reader becomes privy to more information about his immediate past, which also exercises a malign influence over the present. The secrets of his childhood are contained in the attic nursery where he chooses to conceal the portrait:

> He had not entered the place for more than four years – not, indeed, since he had used it first as a play-room when he was a child, and then as a study when he grew somewhat older. It was a large, well-proportioned room, which had been specially built by the last Lord Kelso for the use of the little grandson whom, for his strange likeness to his mother, and also for other reasons, he had always hated and desired to keep at a distance. It appeared to Dorian to have but little changed . . . How well he remembered it all! Every moment of his lonely childhood came back to him as he looked round. He recalled the stainless purity of his boyish life, and it seemed horrible to him that it was here the fatal portrait was to be hidden away.
>
> (Works, 94)

Having no one to love him as a child, Dorian devotes himself to self-love as an adult.

The absent relationship of mother–father–child is recreated in grotesque parody through portrait–mirror–subject: 'he . . . would stand, with a mirror, in front of the portrait that Basil Hallward had painted of him, looking now at the evil and ageing face on the canvas, and now at the fair young face that laughed back at him from the polished glass' (Works, 98). His favourite mirror, 'an oval glass framed in ivory Cupids', was a gift from Lord Henry (Works, 74), making the perverse family comprise of Dorian, Basil and Wotton. Both nursery and portrait function as a repository for Dorian's 'soul'. The contrast between the unchanged playroom and the foul toy it now contains becomes a source of pleasure to Dorian as he slides further and further into sterile dereliction and vapid diversion. The repeated references throughout the novel to one of Wilde's favourite myths – that of Narcissus – and the analogy we can draw between the locked attic and what Freud would soon term the subconscious (both must be entered from above; the servants get in from the roof, for all the bars with which Dorian bolted the door), invite a psychoanalytic interpretation of the novel in terms of Freud's deployment of the figure of Narcissus.

Such a reading may clarify the latent psychological content of the story, but it overlooks the critique of Platonism which Wilde also engaged with in the process of writing the novel. This deals not with the literal, immediate past of the protagonist, but with the strand of archetypal, Hellenic, past contained in the iconography of the character Dorian Gray. The importance of childhood influences in the formation of character was viewed by Wilde (at least in part) in the terms Plato set out for the education of the young in his Utopian vision, *The Republic*, which informed his experiment in the composition of fairy tales for children in *The Happy Prince*. But for Wilde the simple equation between sensitivity to beauty and the propensity to good action is thoroughly overturned by 1890. *The Portrait of Dorian Gray*, like its companion story 'The Star-Child' (*The House of Pomegranates*), depicts a protagonist whose source of the perception of beauty comes from his own image – and it exercises an exaggeratedly malign influence. Dorian, unlike the Star-Child, takes no opportunity for redemption by the discovery of love for others.

The name of the protagonist, Dorian Gray, alerts the reader to a certain revision of ancient Greek culture. 'Dorian' can mean simply 'gilded' or 'golden', itself a paradox in its coupling with the colour 'gray' which points to the split personality of the hero. The divided name shows off the gilded beauty more vividly, and makes the crimes more gross by contrast. The name of Wilde's protagonist also refers to the ancient Dorian culture: an early civilisation that centred on the city of Sparta from which Plato drew many features that govern his conception of the ideal state described in *The Republic*. In a scholarly work of 1824, *The Dorians*, K. O. Müller states that 'the whole life of the Lacedaemonian [Spartan] community had a secluded, impenetrable, and secret character'.[7] As Pater comments, 'You couldn't really know it unless you were of it.'[8] The secrets of Dorian Gray remain his even at the end of the novel. The ancient Dorian culture prized the physical fitness and beauty of its male youth; it trained a vigorous warrior race. It 'found proportion, Pythagorean symmetry or music, and . . . forbade all that was likely to disfigure the body'.[9] This is how Wilde's protagonist begins his story, and would even 'give [his] soul' (Works, 33) to preserve his own physical beauty.

As a people the Dorians found themselves 'very susceptible to the influences of form and colour and sound, to external aesthetic influence'[10] and disciplined their susceptibility by 'self-denial' in the nurture of a martial creed. Dorian Gray is equally susceptible, but he lacks the discipline of the cultural purposiveness which governed the ancient Dorians. Its absence permits the excessive vagaries of his self-directed experiments. He is an orphan both in terms of family and culture. The ancient Dorians, basing their religion in Pythagoreanism, held to the belief in metempsychosis, or the transmigration of souls. What to the ancients was a matter of mysticism became to the nineteenth century a question of heredity. The blood that flows through the veins of Dorian Gray was mingled with that of his ancestors visible in his portrait gallery: he embodies the last flowering of his family's transmigrating soul. Throughout the novel vice and virtue are described by the rhetoric of aesthetics. 'I want to be good. I can't bear the idea of my soul being hideous,' Dorian protests to Wotton (Works, 78). Basil, pleading with Dorian to lead a virtuous life, informs him about 'all these hideous things that people are whispering about you' (Works, 112) and is at a loss to put the rumours together with Dorian's physical beauty. The inference that appearance creates reality is grotesquely naïve in the context. With it, Plato's belief that 'all . . . visible things . . . exercise an aesthetic influence on character',[11] culled from Dorian lore, is modified. Aesthetic influence remains, but beauty no longer equates unambiguously with goodness.

The fabric of the novel negotiates a highly complex set of inter-textual relationships with other works. Sometimes these are considered as 'influences' on the novel, or 'sources' for the novel, or sometimes they are viewed as texts on which Wilde chose to comment in the potentially parodic form of selective quotation and misquotation in the service of a bizarre plot. Critical opinion must choose a judicious emphasis among the range of possibilities. There is the 'magic picture' topos, with its garnish of Gothic effects that Wilde could produce with such facility. There are the apparently conflicting ideologies of naturalism in *Thérèse Raquin* and aestheticism in *Mademoiselle de Maupin* brought together in such a fertile mix by the plot:

> he found himself at first gazing at the portrait with a feeling of almost scientific interest. That such a change should have taken place was incredible to him. And yet it was a fact. Was there some subtle affinity between the chemical atoms that shaped themselves into form and colour on the canvas, and the soul within him? Could it be that what that soul thought, they realized? – that what it dreamed they made true? Or was there some other, more terrible reason?'
>
> (Works, 77)

Two of the most important works which structure an ideology within the novel are Pater's *Studies in the History of the Renaissance* (1873) and Huysmans' *A Rebours* (1884). Both are represented in the gospel of 'new hedonism' preached by Wotton and practised by Dorian under his influence. The seduction which Wotton practises on Dorian begins with a panegyric on youth uttered in the June garden at the studio of Basil Hallward. Wotton is the serpent in the garden of Eden, beguiling his youthful victim Dorian; although Wotton himself is described as 'the tall, graceful young man' (Works, 30), the experienced cynicism of his voice always makes him seem significantly older than Dorian. The effect of this is to make real for the reader the sense of terrible brevity about the poise of youth about to embark on manhood as

Wotton portrays it. Dorian begins the novel at that moment of poise and, under the joint influence of Wotton and Hallward, his physical form is arrested there. Two of the essays in Pater's collection speak with the same plangent tone of the romance of youth, 'Winckelmann' and the 'Conclusion':

> realize your youth while you have it . . . Live! Live the wonderful life that is in you! Let nothing be lost upon you. Be always search- ing for new sensations. Be afraid of nothing . . . A new Hedonism – that is what our century wants . . . Youth! Youth! There is absolutely nothing in the world but youth!
>
> (Works, 31)

These are the words with which Wotton prepares Dorian to meet his own image for the first time. The sentiments echo Pater's infamous dictum 'to burn always with this hard, gem-like flame, to maintain this ecstasy, is success in life . . . Not to discriminate every moment some passionate attitude . . . is, on this short day of frost and sun, to sleep before evening.'[12] Time, life itself, is a destroyer, and the only existential answer is to steal eternity away from time, 'to dis- criminate every moment'.

The adoration of youth pervades Pater's essay about the eighteenth- century German archaeologist, Winckelmann. His discovery of ancient Greek art becomes an iconic image for the cultural signific- ance of the delayed Renaissance that Pater posits, and Winckelmann's homosexuality (his 'fervent friendships with young men')[13] becomes an instrument of divination which permits him, by a special personal affinity with ancient culture, to discover laws governing the aesthetics of antiquity. Pater argues that Winckelmann discovered the youth of Western culture; he became acquainted with an age when 'the youth tried to rival his gods; and his increased beauty passed back into them'. It was:

> a perfect world, if the gods could have seemed for ever only fleet and fair, white and red! Let us not regret that this unperplexed youth of humanity, satisfied with this vision of itself, passed, at the due moment, into a mournful maturity; for already the deep joy was in store for the spirit, of finding the ideal of that youth still red with life in the grave.[14]

Pater argues that 'Greek sculpture deals almost exclusively with youth, where the moulding of the bodily organs is still as if suspended between growth and completion.' He singles out an example,

> the *adorante* of the museum of Berlin, a youth who has gained the wrestler's prize, with hands lifted and open, in praise for the

victory, Fresh, unperplexed, it is the image of man as he springs first from the sleep of nature.[15]

The living Dorian is hailed by Wotton as having '[a]ll the candour of youth . . . as well as all youth's passionate purity. One felt that he had kept himself unspotted from the world' (Works, 27). After years of crude experiment with his 'soul' Dorian's look is still the same and has the same social effect:

> He had always the look of one who had kept himself unspotted from the world. Men who talked grossly became silent when Dorian Gray entered the room. There was something in the purity of his face that rebuked them. His mere presence seemed to recall to them the memory of the innocence that they had tarnished.
>
> (Works, 97–8)

The figure of Dorian Gray becomes a living sculpture, a token of the magnificent vision of the fifth-century BC Greek artists and the cultural significance of its rebirth, 'renaissance', or rediscovery in the late nineteenth century by Pater in his celebration of Winckelmann. Dorian's appearance symbolises not just the lost personal innocence of the individual, but a primal innocence of mankind. It effects a poignant recollection of the myth of arcadian purity and its loss in the context of his '*fin de siècle, fin du globe*'. Dorian's self-destructive urge ('I wish it were *fin du globe*,' said Dorian, with a sigh. 'Life is a great disappointment' (Works, 130)), stands for the death wish of his culture. Like Dorian it has a double life: it can see beauty and innocence, but it knows them as irrecoverably lost. Mankind is out of Eden, but it can see no Second Coming, no source of redemption. Wotton prophesies that Dorian might be the 'visible symbol' of the 'new Hedonism' for which the era seeks (Works, 31). And at the end of the novel he summarises: 'You are the type of what the age is searching for, and what it is afraid it has found' (Works, 155).

The relationship Wilde constructs with Huysmans' novel *A Rebours* in *The Picture of Dorian Gray* has two facets. On the one hand there is the content of *A Rebours*. It is a story about the perversely reclusive dandy and decadent, Des Esseintes, the adventures of whose soul become so inspirational to Dorian's vice when he reads the 'strangest book' (Works, 96) that Wotton leaves as a gift to spur on his seduction after Dorian abandons his infatuation with Sybil Vane. The poisonous book is never named in the novel, although the typescript of the story Wilde submitted to *Lippincott's Monthly Magazine* did name an invented novel, 'Le Secret de Raoul, par Catulle Sarrazin', deleted from both published versions. *A Rebours* was identified by Wilde at his trial as the work he had in mind for the novel

Wotton gives Dorian. The description within *Dorian Gray* of the mysteriously infectious novel certainly matches with Huysmans' text. The hero, Des Esseintes, withdraws from conventional social intercourse to his *château* in order to pursue a life of exquisite or perverse sensation, exhausting passions for a catalogue of sensory disciplines from interior design to exotic cuisine.

Dorian's private sensory adventures, based quite literally on catalogues or their literary and scientific equivalents, are modelled on these, as are small details of his behaviour like his choice of Parma violets for a buttonhole: one of Des Esseintes's favourites. The Parisian's motive philosophy for his curious behaviour is based on a famous dictum by Villiers de l'Isle-Adam, 'As for living, our servants do that for us.' The life of action, subordinate to the life of contemplation, was abandoned. In its place the individual discovered a full intellectual and soulful life through disciplined but uninhibited sensory experience and experiment. This choice of life anticipated in perverse and parodic form the philosophy of the Flemish symbolist dramatist, Maeterlinck, whose work supplied Wilde with wide-ranging inspiration (clearest in *Salome* and *A Woman of No Importance*). In 1896 Maeterlinck published an essay, contained in *The Treasure of the Humble*, in which he stated his belief in the superiority of the contemplative life:

> I have grown to believe that an old man, seated in his armchair, waiting patiently, with his lamp beside him; giving unconscious ear to all the eternal laws that reign about his house . . . I have grown to believe that he, motionless as he is, does yet live in reality a deeper, more human and more universal life than the lover who strangles his mistress, and captain who conquers in battle, or 'the husband who avenges his honour'.[16]

That such vision is not far from Huysmans' decadent experiment with *A Rebours* is clear from the fact that this novel is the first of a trilogy – and in the last, Des Esseintes completes his quest for spiritual fulfilment by taking holy orders. However, this is a far cry from the manifestation of *A Rebours* in *Dorian Gray*: the closest Dorian gets to finding solace in conventional religion is his profane collection of 'ecclesiastical vestments' (Works, 105).

The second aspect of the relationship between *A Rebours* and *Dorian Gray* concerns not the content of either novel, nor the supply of an iniquitous philosophy to Dorian through Wotton, but the form of both novels. Dorian is captivated by 'a novel without a plot, and with only one character' (Works, 96). While it would be nonsense to suggest that *Dorian Gray* is similarly 'a novel without a plot', Wilde's handling of action and plot is unusually perfunctory. Crowded with melodramatic incident, five deaths (three of them suicides: Sybil Vane, Alan Campbell, Dorian Gray; one murder, Basil Hallward; one accident, James Vane), two dreadful oaths which find fulfilment in action (that of Dorian to give his soul to keep the beauty of his image intact, and that of James Vane to kill the callous seducer of his sister), yet Wilde could describe it as 'rather like my own life – all conversation and no action. I can't describe action: my people sit in chairs and chatter' (Letters, 255). (Admittedly Wilde was here describing the first version, which contained only three deaths.) He judges the focus of the novel accurately. It is not action, nor plot, which dominate the experience of reading the novel, but attention to conversation, to psychological interaction, to the mental effects of action, to impressions in an interior mental landscape. 'Action! What is action? It dies at the moment of its energy. It is a base concession to fact. The world is made by the singer for the dreamer', he said in 'The Critic as Artist' (Works, 1123).

This is an important and striking feature of technique which the novel shares with *A Rebours* and in which it finds affinity with the impressionistic prose becoming fashionable at the *fin de siècle*. This in turn pointed forward to some major achievements of modernism in the work of Woolf, Joyce and Beckett. It is as though Wilde regarded plot as a necessary evil for fiction, and he said as much when the plot of *A Woman of No Importance* was admired by Beerbohm Tree: 'Plots are tedious. Anyone can invent them. Life is full of them. Indeed one has to elbow one's way through them as they crowd across one's path.' He went on to say, 'I took the plot of this play from the *Family Herald*, which took it – wisely, I feel – from my novel *The Picture of Dorian Gray*' (Ellmann, 359).

The result of Wilde's impatience with action and plot, on a par with his disgust of 'facts', is a fiction woven out of curious lacunae or gaps, unconventional moments of emphasis and anti-climaxes. The account of the relationship between Dorian and Sybil is deflected by Dorian's reports on her abilities as an actress to Wotton, and by the description of her family environment. Similarly, the revenge assault which James Vane attempts to make on 'Prince Charming' towards the end of the novel is deflected by conversation between the would-be murderer and his victim, as Dorian talks his way under a street lamp to show off his youthful face. Of the five deaths that occur, we see only one: that of Basil Hallward at the hand of Dorian. But this one is certainly spectacular, driving home the full inhumanity of the protagonist and his skill at disassociating himself from the actions he performs. Even as he stabs his friend, Basil is not seen as one known but becomes anonymous, 'the man'. And Dorian's reaction is one of suppression: 'he felt that the secret of the whole thing was not

to realise the situation' (Works, 117–18). Wilde and Dorian share
the problem of how to dispose of the body. Dorian calls in the assistance of a former lover, Alan Campbell. The interview between the
two estranged men is charged with various tensions. The reader is
made hungry for information never supplied. What happened in
their relationship? What exactly are the experiments that Campbell
engages in?

Most tantalising of all is the brutally effective information that
Dorian possesses with which he blackmails Campbell into helping
him: 'he stretched out his hand, took a piece of paper, and wrote
something on it. He read it over twice, folded it carefully, and pushed
it across the table' (Works, 125). We never discover that 'something':
it remains one of Dorian's many secrets. Wilde is exclusively concerned with the effects of action, rather than action or fact themselves. The consequence of this allusively described action of blackmail
is that by the end of the chapter, 'the thing that had been sitting at
the table was gone' (Works, 127). How it went is again left to the
reader's imagination. This too is the fate of Dorian's rumoured sins,
which are more interesting in their effects (on the portrait, on the
way society within the novel responds, and on the reader) than in
their performance. And it is the fate of Dorian's ultimate demise.
Dorian picks up the knife that killed Basil, and stabs the picture.
Immediately Wilde changes location. The reader is taken into the
servants' quarters, where 'there was a cry heard, and a crash'. The
next and last we see of Dorian is:

> Lying on the floor was a dead man, in evening dress, with a knife
> in his heart. He was withered, wrinkled, and loathsome of visage.
> It was not till they had examined the rings that they recognized
> who it was.
>
> (Works, 159)

The murder that Dorian predicted in Hallward's studio when the
artist takes a knife to the portrait is consummated. The subject
acquires unity and stability only through death.

> Tired of being on the heights I deliberately went to the depths
> in the search for new sensations. What paradox was to me in the
> sphere of thought, perversity became to me in the sphere of pas-
> sion . . . I forgot that every little action of the common day makes
> or unmakes character and therefore what one has done in the
> secret chamber one has some day to cry aloud on the housetops.
>
> ('De Profundis', Letters, 466)

So Wilde confessed to his lover from prison. Although within the
novel itself, Wilde's artist, Hallward, announces with contempt that

'we live in an age when men treat art as if it were meant to be a form of autobiography' (Works, 24) yet *Dorian Gray* contains an uncanny sort of prophecy of the pattern that Wilde's life would take. The personal quality of the novel is compounded by the instability of the narrative voice which once even addresses the reader in the first person. 'Is insincerity such a terrible thing? I think not. It is merely a method by which we can multiply our personalities' (Works, 107). A more cautiously conventional voice immediately breaks in: 'Such, at any rate, was Dorian Gray's opinion.' The care Wilde takes to frame and distance the poisonous doctrines of aestheticism within the novel is disrupted by this gesture of authorial approval. Who is 'I' supposed to be if not Wilde himself? The transgression is compounded by the fact that Gilbert, in 'The Critic as Artist', also announces 'What people call insincerity is simply a method by which we can multiply our personalities' (Works, 1145). This illustrates the disruption of the fictional frame brought about by the acts of self-plagiary in which Wilde engaged, lifting and polishing epigrams used before in a wide variety of work from drama to journalism, only to recycle them again in later work. Consistency of voice over time and across works goes beyond the mere economy of not wishing to waste a good joke or saying. It lends Wilde's authority to the utterances and turns them into life-informing maxims. He was frank about this dimension of the novel in a letter to a friend: 'Basil Hallward is what I think I am: Lord Henry what the world thinks me: Dorian what I would like to be – in other ages, perhaps' (Letters, 352).

Notes

1 Kerry Powell, 'Tom, Dick and Dorian Gray: Magic Picture Mania in Late Victorian Fiction', *Philological Quarterly* 62 (1983) 147–70.

2 Respectively: *St James's Gazette*, 24 June 1890; *Daily Chronicle*, 30 June 1890; *Scots Observer*, 5 July 1890; *Punch*, 19 July 1890.

3 *The Daily Examiner*, San Francisco, 27 March 1882.

4 *Oscar Wilde*, ed. Isobel Murray (Oxford: Oxford University Press, 1989) 583.

5 Pater, 'Coleridge', *Appreciations*, 67.

6 Ibid., 68.

7 K. O. Müller, *The History and Antiquities of the Doric Race*, translated [from *Die Dorier*, 1824] by H. Tufnell and G. C. Lewis (Oxford, 1830). Cited by Pater in *Plato and Platonism*, 199.

8 *Plato and Platonism*, 215.

9 Ibid., 219.

10 Ibid., 211.

11 Ibid., 209.

Critical survey

12 Pater, *The Renaissance*, 189.
13 Ibid., 152.
14 Ibid., 166–7.
15 Ibid., 174–5.
16 Cited in Katherine Worth, *The Irish Drama of Europe from Yeats to Beckett* (London: Athlone Press, 1978) 78.

7 *Salome,* Salome, *and symbolist theatre*

Salome can seem strange in Wilde's corpus. The play appears to be an uneasy bedfellow with the society comedies which dominate our received picture of his dramatic work, compounded by the fact that *Salome* has been so rarely performed since its publication in French in 1893. The features which set *Salome* apart are obvious. It was written in French; its subject matter is mythological, spiritual, symbolist; its dialogue is oddly inflected and reminiscent of 'The Song of Songs'; it is a tragedy; it was never performed in Britain during Wilde's lifetime yet it managed on two occasions to create a sensation in the press.

The first storm that erupted around *Salome* occurred in June 1892. Wilde, Sarah Bernhardt who was playing Salome, Charles Ricketts who designed a set and Graham Robertson who designed Salome's costume, were two weeks into rehearsal for a production in French at the theatre Bernhardt had hired for her London season, the Royal English Opera House (shortly to be renamed the Palace Theatre) when the Lord Chamberlain, one Edward Pigott, refused to license the play for performance. Its censorship continued until 1931. The second debate that centred on the play concerned its 1894 reception in Britain as a text published in English, effectively as a dramatic poem, with illustrations by Aubrey Beardsley substituting for full-scale dramatic production. Three of Beardsley's illustrations, including the frontispiece, were themselves censored and had to be removed or replaced, while Wilde and Lord Alfred Douglas fought over the translation of the play. Douglas was to have written the English text but Wilde, dismayed by his lover's command of French, intervened. Even so, we cannot be sure how much of the English is by Wilde, and how much survives by Douglas. All these seem alien features in the work of a dramatist remembered for English comedy of manners, fast dialogue, political and contemporary subject matter, and huge commercial success in production.

Yet the play, even superficially, is not so foreign to Wilde's corpus as a whole. Situated, as it is, between *The House of Pomegranates* (1891) and the 'Poems in Prose' (1894), themselves followed by the dramatic fragments composed in 1894, 'The Florentine Tragedy' and 'La Sainte Courtisane', we can find in these works a kinship of style, diction and subject matter all pointing to Wilde's emulative interest in French aestheticism, coupled with his concern for adventures of the spiritual imagination. Only the tragic form remains unique.

Nevertheless, one temptation in criticism is to emphasise the resemblances of *Salome* to the social comedies, to make the play seem less strange.

Approaching the play from work Wilde had completed in similar vein, it is apparent that in 'The Fisherman and his Soul', Wilde had already tempted his readers with images of exotic and corrupt Byzantine worlds holding all the riches a Soul, though not a Heart, could desire. The Soul entices the fisherman with marvels that resemble those which Herod, in *Salome*, offers to the young Princess in place of the Baptist's head. The encounter between the Soul and the Emperor in the city of Ashter in the land of the Bedouins directly anticipates the contest between Herod and Salome for possession of the Baptist (the Soul functions as a composite of Jokanaan and Salome, before turning into Herod to tempt back his Heart from the fisherman). The Emperor says to the Soul:

> 'Art thou a prophet, that I may not harm thee, or the son of a prophet, that I can do thee no hurt . . .? I pray thee leave my city to-night, for while thou art in it I am no longer its lord.'
> And I answered him, 'I will go for half of thy treasure. Give me half of thy treasure, and I will go away.'
> He took me by the hand . . .
> Thou couldst not believe how marvellous a place it was. There were huge tortoise-shells full of pearls, and hollowed moonstones of great size piled up with red rubies. The gold was stored in coffers . . . There were opals and sapphires . . . And yet have I told thee but a tithe of what was there.
>
> (Works, 251)

But the fisherman, like Salome, is unimpressed. Like the Princess, he wants what he loves. What finally tempts him back to the land is the promise of a dancing girl which his Soul has seen:

> And when he had laid out the carpet on the floor, he struck with a quill on the wire strings of his lute, and a girl whose face was veiled ran in and began to dance before us. Her face was veiled with a veil of gauze, but her feet were naked. Naked were her feet, and they moved over the carpet like white pigeons . . .

> Now when the young Fisherman heard the words of his Soul, he remembered that the little Mermaid had no feet and could not dance. And a great desire came over him.
>
> (Works, 252)

The fisherman leaves the mermaid and journeys with his Soul towards an image of the dancing girl which, like a chimera, always eludes him. The Soul continues to woo him with stories:

And she who feeds [the peacocks] dances for pleasure, and sometimes she dances on her hands and at other times she dances with
her feet. Her eyes are coloured with stibium, and her nostrils are
shaped like the wings of a swallow . . . She laughs while she dances,
and the silver rings that are about her ankles tinkle like bells of
silver. And so trouble not thyself any more, but come with me to
this city.

(Works, 255)

Wilde models this entrancing dancer on the legend of Salome. She
performs a discreet version of the dance of the seven veils, and she
also dances on her hands, just as the earliest representations of Salome
in the visual arts of the medieval period pictured her, and as Flaubert
presented her in *Herodias* (1877). She shows a world turned on its
head, yet with perfect equilibrium. While the first girl seen by the
Soul dances at the bidding of another, the second, observed it seems
voyeuristically, dances for her own pleasure and laughs. Wilde is
already enlarging the Salome legend: a new self-will and self-delight,
such crucial factors in his play, are coupled with an unpossessibility.
The fisherman never sees her, except in his mind's eye, and Herod,
in the play, never possesses her, except through death. The scenario
which we read in 'The Fisherman and his Soul' heralds the vision
of the Young Syrian at the start of *Salome* who says of the moon:

She has a strange look. She is like a little princess who wears a
yellow veil, and whose feet are of silver. She is like a princess who
has little white doves for feet. You would fancy she was dancing.

(Works, 583)

Like the fisherman, he dies for what he sees and without consummat-
ing the desire. While this story anticipates something of the dynamics
of the play to come, the jewelled style of diction (like that of the
other tales in the collection), with pseudo-archaic grammar, emphatic
inversions of conventional word order and rhythmic repetitions, also
looks forward to the mannered language of *Salome* which creates a
sort of dance in the language itself. An important stylistic distinction
is to be made, however, in the effect achieved by shifting the descript-
ive powers of the narrative voice (the voice of the Soul) into dialogue
which is actually spoken by characters of the play.

While it is possible to look back at the kind of prose Wilde was
writing immediately before embarking on *Salome,* and remembering
too that 'The Fisherman and his Soul' appeared in French (translated
by Marcel Schwob) simultaneously with the English version, it is also
possible to look forward to the 'Poems in Prose' published two years
later, to see the direction which this kind of prose would take. Narrative complexity is cast aside. These short pieces are suggestively spare,

resembling the narrative style of the Gospels. An abstract vision which gives the reader only what is necessary and works by the trope of metonymy, foregrounds the symbolic value of what is described, and sharpens the symbolist's sense of the unseeable but apprehendable forces governing human life. Bold sweeps of colour used in *Salome* (both in the language, and as the set was first conceived) recur. These paradoxical meditations about the parameters of spiritual and carnal desire come to the same kind of abrupt and shocking conclusions that mark the closing lines of the play. The 'Poems in Prose' are self-standing parables, resonant precisely because they work with abstracts. They proffer universal truths, yet Wilde, working consciously with revision of the Biblical exercises, acknowledges implicitly the provisional and temporary nature of their poised universality.

Among the figures that occur, some of the spiritual territory suggested by *Salome* can be traced further, leading into the larger spheres adumbrated by the play. 'The Artist', whose medium is bronze, as Salome's is dance, melts down his image of *The Sorrow that Endureth for Ever* in order to make another one of *The Pleasure that Abideth for a Moment*. Impossible to picture this 'image', just as Salome's dance is impossible to see outside the production of the play, this poem in prose asks where the proper emphasis of experience lies: in momentary rapture for possession, or eternal mourning for loss? In a kiss or in a severed head? 'The Doer of Good' presents a female figure who resembles Salome in her combination of the whorish and the naïve, and mocks her saviour; 'The Disciple' muses on the complex and entrancing relationship between a man and his mirror, providing potential commentary on the relationship of the moon to all characters, or between Salome and the Prophet, Salome and herself, or Herod and his court; 'The Master' offers a picture of a Baptist figure who longs for martyrdom, as the Prophet might be seen to invite his own fate in the play. 'The House of Judgement' provides a most significant gloss on *Salome*, for in it Wilde considers that man's spiritual journey will take him no further than the limits of his own imagination, and God is silenced:

> And after a space God spake, and said to the Man, 'Seeing that I may not send thee into Hell, surely I will send thee unto Heaven. Even unto Heaven will I send thee.'
>
> And the Man cried out, 'Thou canst not.'
>
> And God said to the Man, 'Wherefore can I not send thee unto Heaven, and for what reason?'
>
> 'Because never, and in no place, have I been able to imagine it,' answered the Man.
>
> And there was silence in the House of Judgement.
>
> (Works, 903)

'The Teacher of Wisdom' concerns the education of a holy man changed from charismatic figure to hermit before, in mortal combat to save a Robber's soul, he learns that knowledge of God is nothing without the transfiguring love of God. In his selfish rejection of the world and his transfiguration through death, we can see something of the ambiguity of Wilde's Baptist.

The figure of John the Baptist also occurs in the dramatic fragment 'La Sainte Courtisane or The Woman Covered with Jewels', in which Wilde embarks on one of the many Salome stories for which he was conversationally famous (Ellmann, 325). In this fragment the prophet is called Honorius, 'the beautiful young hermit' who 'will not look on the face of woman' (Works, 734). Myrrhina is the name of La Sainte Courtisane, the Salome figure, which the hermit particularly refuses to behold. The dialogue of the play begins:

> *First man*: Who is she? She makes me afraid. She has a purple cloak and her hair is like threads of gold. I think she must be the daughter of the Emperor. . . .
>
> *Second man*: She has birds' wings upon her sandals, and her tunic is the colour of green corn. It is like corn in spring when she stands still. It is like young corn troubled by the shadows of hawks when she moves. The pearls on her tunic are like many moons.
>
> (Works, 734)

The winged sandals, the youth, and especially the colours of the 'Emperor's daughter' are reminiscent of *Salome*. When the French text of *Salome* was published in February 1893 Wilde had the volume bound in 'Tyrian purple' as he pointed out in letters to friends who were to receive copies (Letters, 332): To Campbell Dodgson he joked, 'Bosie is very gilt-haired and I have bound *Salome* in purple to suit him' (Letters, 333). The green tunic of Myrrhina is recalled by Charles Ricketts' account of design discussions held with Wilde. 'Over Salomé the discussions were endless; Should she be clothed in black – like the night, in silver like the moon or – the suggestion was Wilde's – green, like a curious poisonous lizard?'[1]

When Myrrhina asks why the hermit, and the two men, will not look at her, the reply is: 'You are too bright to look at. It is not wise to look at things that are very bright. Many of the priests in the temples are blind, and have slaves to lead them' (Works, 734). Eventually Myrrhina and Honorius do look at each other. The result is that they wish to exchange roles, the courtisane wishes to become a hermit saint, and Honorius declares: 'Myrrhina, the scales have fallen from my eyes and I see now clearly what I did not see before. Take me to Alexandria and let me taste of the seven sins' (Works, 738). Here Wilde exposes one of the reasons for the compulsive attention to the Salome legend for his *fin de siècle* era. The urge for self-destruction, transfiguring, but simultaneously purging and annihilative, motivated by the experience of ravishing beauty, overwhelms the players. A death wish of the period is encapsulated in the legend, and had already been articulated by Wilde in the long poem 'Charmides':

> The joy of passion, that dread mystery
> Which not to know, is not to live at all,
> And yet to know is to be held in death's most deadly thrall.
>
> (Works, 810)

Salome, William Archer said, was an 'oriental Hedda Gabler' (Critical Heritage, 142).

The play *Salome* in Wilde's corpus is not, therefore, so anomalous as it might at first seem. This is not to belittle the exceptional achievement of the drama, but simply to indicate that it does not occupy unusual terrain. It arises from work he had done and it leads to further endeavour.

Equally characteristic of Wilde's method of composition was the fact that in offering his treatment of the Salome legend he was contributing to one of the most conventional topoi of his era's artistic *avant garde*. Just as he plundered the boulevard successes of the well-made play for his social comedies, so he allowed others to organise the material from which he would negotiate a new relationship with the most notorious *femme fatale* of the *fin de siècle*.

There are many cultural reasons for the cult of Salome at this period. The decadent urge for collective self-destruction has already been mentioned. Alternatively, patriarchal anxiety about the emergence of women as a political force during the nineteenth century also crystallised around the image of Salome, and this is part of its appeal. Young, innocent, of astonishing beauty, eliciting voyeuristic sexual response from a male court, Salome could sum up all the decorative and diverting qualities requisite of woman. But she was equally fury, harridan and whore, a dangerous, capricious murderer, to be castigated for revelling in her own monstrous desires. Concomitant with this was the way in which the figure of Salome could simultaneously represent two divergent but equally strong drives in nineteenth-century culture: the fascination with the mystical and the obsession with the physical. Lemaitre characterised 'the fantastic queens of Gustave Moreau' as 'those dream figures, in turn hieratical and serpentine, possessing a mystical and sensuous attraction'.[2] Setting a certain cultural misogyny aside, the larger Biblical context in which Salome plays her part offered a mirror for Europe on the brink of a new century.

Salome's dance is a watershed between the Old and the New Testaments, between the reign of Judaism and the coming Christianity. Dancing on her hands is a visually succinct way of representing the overturning of the old. In the Gospels, her story is told by Herod – recalling the events that led to the Baptist's execution – in a kind of flashback when he hears of miracles performed by the new prophet, Christ. The Tetrarch fears that John, whom we recognise as the last prophet of the Old Testament directly heralding the Messiah, has come back to life. Wilde's *fin de siècle* was an age when, as Pater's *Renaissance* and Ibsen's *Ghosts* proclaimed in their different ways, the dead would not stay dead. The *avant-garde* projected an age of artistic rebirth and rejuvenation, when everything from woman to journalism was 'new', yet it was painfully aware of an inherited burden from the momentous century it concluded. The material of the Salome legend therefore focuses on the moment of poise before the old sectarian confusions could be swept aside and the new century ushered in. Wilde's selection of the 47-year-old actress Sarah Bernhardt (who had been 'immortal' since the age of 24) to play the part of the child Salome illustrates precisely this mutual embarrassment of the old and the new. Two months before his death, Wilde returned impatiently to the subject: 'What has age to do with acting? The only person in the world who could act Salome is Sarah Bernhardt, that "serpent of old Nile", older than the Pyramids.'[3] Like Pater's Mona Lisa, as 'symbol of the modern idea', Wilde's Salome was 'older than the rocks among which she sits'.[4] Age was an advantage for what he wished the actress to express through Salome.

'In art as in life the law of heredity holds good. *On est toujours fils de quelqu'un,*' Wilde had written in a review in 1886;[5] but he also declared that '*Dans la littérature il faut toujours tuer son père*' in conversation with Will Rothenstein who noticed the likeness between Flaubert's *Herodias* and *Salome.*[6] If Pater could elicit the 'symbol of the modern idea' from the *Mona Lisa,* then Wilde could conjure its more culturally resonant partner from Salome. Few among Wilde's early critics were alert to his radical interpretation of the legend. Missing the point entirely while oddly stating it, the *Pall Mall Gazette* reviewer announced that 'She is the daughter of too many fathers. She is a victim of heredity. Her bones want strength, her flesh wants vitality, her blood is polluted. There is no pulse of passion in her.' Wilde had just listed Gautier, Maeterlinck, Anatole France, Marcel Schwob and Flaubert as the real authors of this 'mosaic' piece (Critical Heritage, 136). Subsequent critics have added to the list of literary contexts Heine, Mallarmé, Laforgue and, most significantly, Huysmans' descriptions of Gustave Moreau's two paintings of Salome in *A Rebours.* For Wilde, it was not a question of influence, but of joining in.

Overlooked in this glittering constellation is the hardly famous but certainly significant sonnet by Willie Wilde, 'Salome (For a Picture),' published in *Kottabos* in 1878. This is not to make the laughable suggestion that Wilde borrowed from his brother, but to indicate a long-standing interest in the legend close to home:

> The sight of me was as devouring flame
> Burning their hearts with fire, so wantonly
> That night I danced for all his men to see!
> Fearless and reckless; for all maiden shame
> Strange passion-poisons throbbing overcame
> As every eye was riveted on me,
> And every soul was mine, mine utterly, –
> And thrice each throat cried out aloud my name!
> 'Ask what thou wilt,' black-bearded Herod said.
> God wot a weird thing do I crave for prize:
> 'Give me, I pray thee, presently the head
> Of John the Baptist.' 'Twixt my hands it lies.
> 'Ah, mother! see! the lips, the half-closed eyes –
> 'Dost think he hates us still now he is dead?'

'W.C.K.W.' achieves a significant adjustment of the legendary material which his brother would take further with incomparable panache.

Alone among the description of events from Salome's perspective, allowing the dancer to be the centre of her own performance is a fresh approach. And while she does dance for the male gaze ('for all his men to see'), she is enthralled by the sheer intoxication of her own self-directed power. Instead of the traditional surrender of the dancer to her audience, she finds that 'every soul was mine'. With the discovery of a captivating and commanding self through the process of dance, Salome does not first ask her mother what to request (as she does in the Bible, and in Flaubert's *Herodias*), but makes her own demand. She is neither Herod's plaything, nor the instrument of Herodias' revenge in claiming the Baptist. Only in the final question does Salome draw her mother into the scene, aligning the two women as like objects of the prophet's hatred, while also anatomising his parts to brand him with the same kind of allure with which he charged the whorish pair. The shift of the balance of emotional power away from Herod and his Queen towards the Princess is the same shift that Wilde would deploy: and a departure that the brothers share in their handling of conventional material. Only Heine, among the significant forbears, had allowed this slant into the legend, asking with skilful satire, 'What woman would demand the head of a man she did not love?'

Another feature of Willie Wilde's innovation is the use of dialogue to structure the tale. The Bible itself uses little dialogue in the telling, and it is recounted in the third person. 'And she, being before instructed of her mother, said, Give me here John Baptist's head in a charger' (Matthew 14.8). Flaubert and Huysmans also describe Salome's dance from the outside, without the dynamic unfolding of events through first-person speech. This points the way to Wilde's most provocative innovation which was to choose the medium of drama for his version of the legend. Only Maeterlinck, among his obvious models, had used drama – and he had not written a Salome play.

The reference to Maeterlinck is apposite for an understanding of the artistic project to which Wilde committed himself with *Salome.* The Flemish playwright was the only thoroughgoing practitioner of symbolist theatre among Wilde's 'influences' listed by the *Pall Mall Gazette,* and in 1892 he was just becoming known in London. In December 1891, Herbert Beerbohm Tree, later an apologist for Maeterlinck, ridiculed his first play *La Princess Maleine* (1889) for its preposterous plot and inarticulate language. At that stage Tree was unable to see that Maeterlinck's drama was shaped by the same priestly ambition as that which he assumes for himself at the end of his lecture:

> In an age when faith is tinged with philosophic doubt, when love is regarded as but a spasm of the nervous system, and life itself but as the refrain of a music-hall song, I believe that it is still the function of art to give us light rather than darkness.[7]

Maeterlinck shared the honour of being parodied along with Wilde in the burlesque *The Poet and the Puppets* which was running, despite Wilde's request to the Lord Chamberlain to ban it, as a box-office hit at the time when the same Pigott refused to license *Salome.*

The authors Charles Brookfield and J. M. Glover could not have known how prophetic their travesty would be. When the Fairy offers to help the Poet (Wilde) with his next play she conjures 'expert advice': the Flemish playwright is not among the advisors, but the Poet says in an aside: 'The man I thought would come was Maeterlink' (*sic*).[8] Scene two of the burlesque opens on 'Lord Winterstock's Ball Room. Six ladies lying in a heap like marionettes. Enter POET L., shown on by PARKER.'

> *Poet:* . . . how can I rouse these charming ladies to life? Music might do it . . . It must be some delightful Orphean music coaxed from tambour and panpipes . . .

Song

> Little tiny puppets here to dance and sing,
> We will do our best if you will pull the string.[9]

Although Brookfield thought he was parodying Wilde's statement, made in the *Daily Telegraph*, that 'The stage is only a frame furnished with a set of puppets' (Ellmann, 349) the joke is unwittingly and prophetically more complex – and potentially also at Maeterlinck's expense. Three of his experiments with dramatic symbolism, published in 1894, *Alladine et Palomides*, *Intérieur* (Interior) and *La Mort de Tintagiles* (The Death of Tintagiles), took the shape of 'plays for puppets'. By this he meant quite literally that marionettes were to be used in performance, but also that human beings were manipulated by invisible forces that could only be apprehended by their fateful effects. The use of puppets became a favourite device of French *avant-garde* theatre during the 1890s; the inanimate dolls could impersonate both the supra-human and the sub-human without straining credibility, thereby extending the perceptual range of an audience.

Looking back in 1902 Maeterlinck wrote:

> The keynote of these little plays is dread of the unknown that surrounds us. I . . . seemed to believe in a monstrous, invisible, fatal power . . . Its intentions could not be divined but the spirit of the drama assumed them to be malevolent always . . . The problem of existence was answered only by the enigma of annihilation.[10]

Not all Symbolists shared this sense of humanity as victim, but they did espouse the creed, inherited from Baudelaire, whose poem 'Correspondances' is a crucial symbolist document, and practised most famously by Mallarmé, that spiritual forces governed human life and penetrated the whole of the natural cosmos. A higher plane of spiritual awareness could be suggested by the arts; the artist was envisioned as priest with a duty to adumbrate the secret forces at work. 'What is Symbolism if not an establishing of the links which hold the world together, the affirmation of an eternal, minute, intricate, almost invisible life, which runs through the whole universe?' asked Arthur Symons.[11]

Maeterlinck developed particular strategies for communicating the agency of 'the invisible life' in the theatre, which he justifies in *The Treasure of the Humble* (1896). He practised a drama of stasis, a theatre of inaction, to induce a meditative effect and to convey a sense of the futility of human volition in the sphere of action. He wrote what he called 'second degree dialogue' in which characters use language not to refer to events, or to propel events around them, but with which they themselves muse on the cosmic forces operating on them. Long silence and portentous pauses punctuate the words spoken so that the dialogue itself seems insignificant in comparison to what cannot be uttered, and cultivates a profound interiority of vision. Within this dialogue Maeterlinck deployed a limited range of diction, preferring the rhythmic repetition of key words, tossed from one character to another. This again had a mesmerising effect on character and audience alike, creating a false calm in the face of impending doom, while also suggesting that an articulate command was no answer to the mysterious and ineluctable. All these are techniques which Wilde used in *Salome,* but they are not, significantly, the only techniques at his disposal.

One aspect of Maeterlinck's work which Wilde adapted with extraordinary sophistication was the Fleming's use of dramatic irony. Maeterlinck was often careful to frame his dramas in such a way that the audience was always in possession of more information than the characters themselves. By analogy with their own larger understanding, the audience could assume that an intelligence higher even than their own looked at the affairs of humanity with a dispassionate eye. While in *Salome* the audience never knows more than the characters (apart, that is, in the epic sense of knowing the legend before its enactment begins), yet each character sees something unique to their own imaginative horizons. It is a manipulation of Maeterlinck's ironic technique, making knowledge a matter of perspective so that each character is both the agent and the victim of dramatic irony, and the audience is the recipient of collective knowing and unknowing. The blend of registers, literary and dramatic, which Wilde actually deploys makes Graham Robertson forgivable for his assumption on hearing Wilde read the play that it, no less than the *Poet and the Puppets,* was 'a burlesque of Maeterlinck, very clever, very delicate, but nevertheless a burlesque'.[12] But that Wilde took the symbolist dimension of the play very seriously is clear from his hurt response to this suggestion.

It was fitting that the only production of *Salome* to take place during Wilde's life occurred in 1896 at Lugné-Poë's Théâtre de l'Œuvre in Paris. This was the home of symbolist theatre, successor of Paul Fort's Théâtre d'Art (founded in 1890) which had staged Maeterlinck's *L'Intruse* (The Intruder) on a benefit night for Verlaine and Gauguin in May 1891, and *Les Aveugles* (The Blind) in December the same year. Lugne-Poe performed in both pieces. Also on the programme for December 1891 was the extravagant experiment by Paul-Napoléon Roinard whose stage adaptation of the *Song of Songs* pushed the expressive range of symbolist theatre beyond anything hitherto seen. The performance of the Biblical text was accompanied by an 'orchestration' of music, colour and perfume. The stage directions specified that the performance of each section of the play ('*huit devises mystiques et trois paraphrases*') should be structured by a dominant verbal sound, a colour, a musical note and a perfume sprayed over the audience.[13] The inspiration was Wagnerian, taking forward Wagner's key notion of opera as *Gesamtkunstwerk* or 'total theatre', engaging all the senses simultaneously; it also drew on Baudelaire's theory of correspondences, seeking sensory equivalents across media. The evening at the Théâtre d'Art collapsed in uproar among performers and their olfactorily fatigued audience. But this is the context in and for which Wilde wrote *Salome*. During 1891 his visits to Paris cemented friendships with many symbolists; he attended Mallarmé's *mardi* salons in February and November, and therefore circulated among those who participated in the ventures at the Théâtre d'Art. French, in the cultural context of symbolism, is the only language in which the play could have been written. Wilde justified it, claiming: 'I wanted to touch this new instrument to see whether I could make a beautiful thing out of it'.[14] *Salome* was largely completed during his stay in Paris in the winter of 1891. During the London rehearsals in 1892 his excitement at the possibility of burning braziers of incense during performance, 'a new perfume for each emotion', was in harmony with the enterprise of his French colleagues, if not with his English ones. Graham Robertson feared prosaically that the auditorium could not be aired between emotions (Ellmann, 351).

Two sketches for the set design of the aborted 1892 production of *Salome* have survived. One is by Wilde himself: a ground plan in pencil, attached to a manuscript of the play. It shows, as Richard Allen Cave suggests, the playwright apparently 'deciding what would be the ideal disposition of cistern and staircase within the stage space'.[15] The other is by Charles Ricketts, made during later discussion with Wilde, in preparation for the production, and it matches his later description of the set. The cistern is foregrounded off-centre to the left, the stairs curving up to the back right, with the moon, off-centre to the right and half eclipsed by what were to be 'gilded strips of Japanese matting', looming high above the foot of the stairs. The sky was to be a 'rich turquoise green' and the floor black 'upon which Salome's feet could move like white doves'.[16] The centre of the set is empty, attention focused there by the essential elements – cistern, moon and stairs – which embrace the area. The structure of this design is symbolist in function and effect. The audience (ideal in this case), presented with nothing inessential, contemplates a suggestive rather than a mimetic picture. An invitation is given to focus on the thereby uninhibited language and spectacle that may lift the audience to a similarly abstract level of understanding.

Ricketts goes on to mention the other colour notes that would be introduced to the black, gold and turquoise set as the action evolved: 'Did Wilde suggest the division of the actors into separate masses of colour? To-day I cannot decide. The Jews were to be in yellow,

John in white, and Herod and Herodias in blood-red.'[17] The discussion over Salome's colour was, as we have seen, inconclusive. But we also know that Graham Robertson designed for her a 'golden robe with long fringes of gold, sustained on the shoulders by bands of gilt and painted leather' (Ellmann, 351), so that none of the colours entertained by Ricketts and Wilde – black, silver or green – would have succeeded. For *Salome*, this use of colour was more than picturesque, symbolic or symbolist. It would also help the audience to identify the different factions within the play and to link them to the successive colour changes of the moon. The young Syrian sees a yellow moon, Salome a silver moon, Herod the blood-red moon which Jokanaan foretells. Finally, the audience sees a black moon with a single beam to illuminate the death of Salome.

To see Wilde so engaged with the practical and collaborative enterprise of production is to discover why his stage direction governing the central spectacle of the play, Salome's dance, is so matter of fact. Critics have been puzzled by the laconic, off-hand, tone of the direction '(SALOME *dances the dance of the seven veils*)' (Works, 600). Even Ibsen, in his version of Salome's dance in *The Doll's House* (1879), had prescribed something of the style in which Nora should dance the tarantella. But if Wilde's direction seems curt it is because dance is the business of performance. Wilde controls the metaphorical dance within the dialogue of the play, the linguistic concealments and revelations, and he controls the position of the dance in the drama. But he delivers the visual analogue of the linguistic dance into the hands – and feet – of the performer.

Wilde was only half joking when he announced that the most important character in the play was the moon. If the symbolist enterprise was to animate the apparently inanimate, to dwarf human endeavour and perspective in the face of larger cosmic forces, then this is achieved by Wilde's moon. It, or rather she (*la lune*), looks down as the characters look up, and she holds occult knowledge dispensed gradually as the action unfolds. But whether she is an agent of events, bringing things to pass, or whether she, herself luminous with reflected light, is simply a mirror to reflect the portentous apprehensions of the characters, remains indeterminate. 'Only in mirrors should one look, for mirrors do but show us masks,' says Herod (Works, 601). Wilde pushes the conventional lunar associations of feminine caprice, changefulness and chastity to violent extremes in the play, setting them in conflict with one another. In so doing, he emphasises the oxymoron contained by these associations. The action takes place by moonlight, so an everyday, sunlit consciousness of common sense and rationality is banished, giving place to a lunatic, irrational expression of subconscious desires and fears.

Only Herodias, the embittered and 'sterile' Queen, refuses to participate in the collective dream. She wants to get out of the moonlight and looks forward to daylight, 'But it is late. Let us go within. Do not forget that we hunt at sunrise' (Works, 598). The squabbling Jews, Sadducees, Pharisees and Nazarenes irritate her, and she attributes their 'ridiculous' behaviour to the baneful influence of the moon. 'These men are mad. They have looked too long on the moon' (Works, 595). The word 'ridiculous' echoes through the play, used to signal the incapacity of one to entertain the vision or beliefs of another. Herodias does not believe in very much at all. Her most famous moment of denial is when she refuses to participate in Herod's dangerous mood. His intoxication masks more than simple lechery:

> *Herod*: The moon has a strange look to-night. Has she not a strange look? She is like a mad woman, a mad woman who is seeking everywhere for lovers. She is naked, too. She is quite naked. The clouds are seeking to clothe her nakedness, but she will not let them. She shows herself naked in the sky. She reels through the clouds like a drunken woman . . . I am sure she is looking for lovers. Does she not reel like a drunken woman? She is like a mad woman, is she not?

> *Herodias*: No; the moon is like the moon, that is all. Let us go within . . . You have nothing to do here.

> (Works, 592)

Puncturing the mood with her tart irony, Herodias sets the trance-like behaviour of the other characters into relief. She is the one character in the play most easily linked to those in the social comedies. Like, for instance, a Mrs Allonby, she has an answer for everything and is also prepared to gain by a young girl's seductive encounter. If Salome gets the Baptist's head, at least the prophet will be silenced, his wearing vilification of her over, and Herod may recover his ragged senses. But Salome is no Hester, and Herod no Illingworth.

The other characters are helpless under what the lunar influence represents. Salome and the Baptist are so entranced, so locked in desire and repulsion, love and hate, that they do not notice the young Syrian fall dead between them. The Page of Herodias has to point to the corpse, but still all that Salome can say is: 'Let me kiss thy mouth, Jokanaan' (Works, 591). Herod does try to free himself from the dreadful aura of doom-irradiating events. Having promised Salome up to half his kingdom to dance for him, he is overcome by a Maeterlinckian chill of death – and then immediately by burning fever. The impending convulsions of the spiritual world are manifest in the Tetrarch's reeling mood:

It is my garland that hurts me, my garland of roses. The flowers
are like fire. They have burned my forehead. (*He tears the wreath
from his head and throws it on the table.*) Ah! I can breathe now. How
red those petals are! They are like stains of blood on the cloth.
That does not matter. You must not find symbols in everything
you see. It makes life impossible. It were better to say that stains
of blood are as lovely as rose petals.

(Works, 599)

We have seen Wilde elsewhere ridiculing the egotistic tendency to
draw false conclusions from unjustified allegory. Herod is here struggling to gain some purchase on rationality, to beat off the phantoms
of fear that crowd out common sense. He exhibits a degree of self-
consciousness that is utterly foreign to the theatre of Maeterlinck in
which the play has its roots. Herod, sensitive to the subjective nature
of interpretation, realising that similes are interchangeable, that value
is a matter of perspective and mood, is a creature from an altogether
new kind of drama. He even tries to stifle one of the principal
methods of communication deployed by Symbolism: the use of symbols to point towards a spiritual realm of apprehension. But even his
insight of relative value is, in this context, to submit to the meretri-
cious moon. He cannot sustain his lucidity. He recovers it only in
the closing moments of the play. Charged by the monstrosity of
Salome's song to the Baptist's head, he thunders: 'Hide the moon!
Hide the stars!', as if to end the nightmare. Then the *'great black cloud
crosses the moon and conceals it completely'* (Works, 604–5). His powers of
command return. He uses them to annihilate. 'Kill that woman!' are
the last words of the play. They respond to Salome's last utterance
in triumph, 'I have kissed thy mouth, Jokanaan' (Works, 605).

The journey that Salome makes from 'Princess' to 'woman' is the
passage of the whole drama. It is the rite of passage by romance
to realism – and it ends tragically, not for those who die but for
those who live. Salome achieves the desired apotheosis of her lust.
Jokanaan is sacrificed for his God. Both have a death wish that is
fulfilled. But Herod's world of strategy and power politics is left
empty by Salome's loss, broken by what her emotional extremity has
revealed, threatened by the divine force unleashed by the prophet's
death. The range of human emotion and experience represented by
Salome in the course of the play is astonishing. She begins as a
frightened girl, running away from Herod's banquet, seeking solitude
and sweet air to breathe. Her virginity of mind and body is told by
the way she sees the moon: 'The moon is cold and chaste. I am sure
she is a virgin' (Works, 586). This is an aspect of her nature that she
never loses; even her anguished questioning of the head, 'But where-
fore dost thou not look at me, Jokanaan?' (Works, 604) has a naïve

145

bewildered innocence coupled with monstrosity. Wilful, petulant, spoiled, she becomes intrigued by the 'strange voice' (Works, 587) of the prophet and exercises her status as daughter of Herodias to command his presence. She is cunning, too, manipulating the besotted Young Syrian with the promise of a look and a 'little green flower' to make him do what she wants, just as later she will manipulate Herod. At first she is shy and fearful of the savage holy man – 'he is terrible' (Works, 589) – but soon she is delighted by his vilification of her mother and then intoxicated, perhaps by the power which the Prophet attributes to womankind, perhaps by the ravishing sound of his voice – 'Thy voice is wine to me' (Works, 589) – or perhaps by what she discovers in herself through the presence of the Prophet. From here there is no return: she is carried forward by a primal experience of desire that yearns for the body as for the vision of Herod's vatic prisoner. Through displaced carnal knowledge she acquires transfiguring divine knowledge.

Salome's rapturous end, cradling the head, biting his mouth with her teeth 'as one bites a ripe fruit' (Works, 604) shows her as a monster: a vengeful vampire spirit stripped of humanity in the literal cannibalism and necrophilia in which she engages. But less than human, she is also more than human. The extremity and purity of her desire transfigure an ordinary, or even profane, human state into something holy, untouchable, ecstatic, terrible to behold which only the union of a chaste virgin with a divine man could achieve. 'Did she put on his knowledge with his power?' as Yeats asked of 'Leda and the Swan'. The echo of the Song of Songs in her final speech holds good, both in earnest and in parody. Here is an extract from Salome's last speech (or aria), addressing the severed head, in the French as Wilde wrote it:

Ah! tu n'as pas voulu me laisser baiser ta bouche. Iokanaan. Eh bien! je la baiserai maintenant. Je la mordrai avec mes dents comme on mord un fruit mûr. Oui, je baiserai ta bouche, Iokanaan . . . Ah! Iokanaan, Iokanaan, tu as été le seul homme que j'aie aimé . . . Ton corps était une colonne d'ivoire sur un socle d'argent. C'était un jardin plein de colombes et de lis d'argent. C'était une tour d'argent ornée de boucliers d'ivoire. Il n'y avait rien au monde d'aussi blanc que ton corps. Il n'y avait rien au monde aussi noir que tes cheveux. Dans le monde tout entier il n'y avait rien d'aussi rouge que ta bouche. Ta voix était un encensoir qui répandait d'étranges parfums, et quand je te regardais j'entendais une musique étrange! . . . J'ai soif de ta beauté. J'ai faim de ton corps. Et ni le vin, ni les fruits ne peuvent apaiser mon désir . . . J'étais une Princesse, tu m'as dédaignée. J'étais une vierge, tu m'as déflorée. J'étais chaste, tu as rempli mes veines de feu.[18]

The action of the play is tightly structured and, for all its broad canvas of characters and political context, it is built around three major duologues: the first between Salome and Jokanaan, the second between Herod and Salome, the third between the Princess and the severed head. We begin with the minor characters – pawns in Herod's court – who set the scene and make us curious about the major players, Salome, Herod and Herodias. They start in a minor key the music of the great refrains and leitmotifs to come. Into their talk the voice of the Prophet erupts, like a chthonic force, a disruptive Dionysian power from his cistern-prison beneath the earth. The Soldiers and the Page cannot guard against something so insubstantial as a voice. The sectarian pagan world is pitted against the not-yet-achieved but apprehended monolith of Christian order. Salome enters, in a great rush, seeking solace from the oppression of Herod's feast. The duologue between Salome and Jokanaan takes shape. At first it is between the ravishing beauty of the visible world and the threatening sound of the invisible. It culminates in Salome's inspection of the Prophet, as she usurps his verbal medium and forces him into the light. The Prophet retreats and Herod enters with his Court, seeking Salome. The Tetrarch woos the Princess. Squabbles break out between Herod and Herodias, and among the Jewish factions, before the baleful voice of Jokanaan focuses the noise. Herod seeks relief from Salome and pleads with her to dance. The final sustained couplet of duologues emerges from her dance: Herod's desperate offer to placate Salome with something less than the Prophet, and Salome's last ecstatic address to the severed head.

Within this tight organization of the legendary material Wilde varies the pace of action, the pace of revelation, and the tone. He eschews altogether the 'monotone' of Maeterlinckian theatre. While the drama accelerates with the inevitable rush of tragedy towards the mutual transfiguration of Salome and Jokanaan, the tone is sharpened by satire and the foreseen tragedy is not enacted without delay. The character of Herodias is one bitterly comic device he uses to alter the mood; this is counterpointed by the little tragedy of the Young Syrian who loves Salome unrequitedly and kills himself to divert her from the Prophet. The Page of Herodias, who was in love with the Young Syrian, adds his distinctive voice to the choral expression of unfulfilled and forbidden desire. The chorus of squabbling Jews, discussing the nature of religion in terms of what can be seen and what cannot be seen, provides another kind of comic counterpoint. They make the petty politics in the context of which revelation takes place yet can be overlooked. But the main variations of pace take place within the dialogue of the central characters, Salome and Herod. The distracted urgency of Herod's speech before the dance gives way to the desperate leisure of his temptation speech to Salome, a monumental effort to put off the inevitable which raises his stature as Tetrarch but diminishes it in his defeat. Salome's song of frustrated desire to the body, the hair and the mouth of Jokanaan when first she sets illicit eyes on the holy man, gives way to her song of monstrous rapture at her absolute and legitimate possession of him at the end. The ultimate form of duologue within the play is the dialogue between self and soul, between lover and beloved, between Salome and her mirror, Jokanaan.

The play has sustained innumerable and often contradictory critical interpretations. For Ellmann, Wilde was dramatising the conflicting claims of Ruskin and Pater on his developing maturity. The prophet Jokanaan represents the rigorous claims of Christian conscience associated with Ruskin, Salome yields to the world of sensuous experience advocated by Pater. Herod, swayed by both, yields to neither and emerges triumphant. Others have applied to the play terms of criticism akin to those deployed in the interpretation of Wilde's social comedies and found critiques of gender roles and stereotypes. They have seen in Salome a picture of the *femme fatale*, a beautiful and insensible agent of death. Alternatively she has been presented as a New Woman, using her unchastened sexuality to challenge a patriarchal political order, courting her man, choosing her lover, anatomising and praising his parts as the male sonneteers since Petrarch had done for their female Muses – and finally taking him literally to pieces. She reverses the traditional power structure between the female dancer and her male audience, turning the 'male gaze' back on itself. Or does her pursuit of the forbidden lover mask a male homosexual desire, profane love which requires sacred expression? Does the play dramatise the psyche at war with itself, a battle between what Freud would soon call the id (Salome), the ego (Herod), and the super-ego (Jokanaan)? Other Freudian interpretations turn on investigations of 'scopophilia' (love of seeing) and fetishism as perversions of 'normal' sexual desire in the play.

When Beardsley's pictures were interleaved with the first English text of *Salome*, they provided its first visualisation, a gloss which, in the absence of theatrical production, fixed an interpretation. That Wilde complained of the 'Japanese' style of Beardsley's black and white illustrations seems churlish, given the deliberate striving for Japanese effect in which he had engaged with Ricketts for the set design. Nevertheless, he insisted that Beardsley had misconstrued the 'Byzantine' nature of his play. Consensus about the illustrations is as vexed as the questions of textual interpretation. Some argue that Beardsley was faithful to the spirit of the play; others that his illustrations distort the text and must necessarily remain parodic. His task as illustrator was not enviable. The dialogue and the inscribed action of the play appeal most dominantly to the sense of sight, and the correlative higher powers of vision and apprehension. The reader is compelled to see with the mind's eye, to apprehend something beyond the merely visible. And whenever a character points to something seen, often using simile or metaphor to extend the range of literal vision in keeping with the symbolist enterprise of the piece, we see into the character's mind, while the object ostensibly identified is in fact obscured by the subjectivity of vision. To offer an acceptable concrete articulation of this would seem a virtually impossible task. One way in which Beardsley approaches the arousing imperatives 'to look' and 'not to look' that resonate through the text is to present pictures of characters themselves engaged in the act of looking, often accompanied with a pointing hand, finger, candle flame, or phallus, which picks up the deictic (or 'pointing') function of the dialogue. But already the mischief of his style is apparent.

Three of Beardsley's pictures were withdrawn in their original form: the 'Titlepage', 'The Man in the Moon' (Frontispiece) and 'The Toilette of Salome'. His first attempt at a title page represented a naked, horned hermaphrodite figure, with eyes to represent navel and nipples, multiplying and eroticising the bodily organs of vision. It shocks with disingenuous candour. He replaced it with a dressed figure, her back turned to the spectator, glancing back at us over her shoulder. Immediately the business of dressing and undressing, of veiling and exposing, of seeing and being seen – all central and related motifs of the play – are forced to our attention. In the text Salome makes the most peremptory demands to see the desired body of her beloved on to which she projects her *blazon* of fantasies. The erotic charge of her wish is so apparent that her omitted mention of his genitalia is important only in so far as their named absence intensifies the sense of their apprehended presence. The suppressed frontispiece, to accompany the conversation about the moon by the Young Syrian and the Page of Herodias, was renamed 'The Woman in the Moon' and became acceptable. Beardsley retained the caricature of Wilde's face in the moon, which had motivated his title, rather than the opening dialogue which likens the moon to a woman. Beardsley thereby altered the gender of the author of the piece, and gave fodder to those critics who wish to see the play as an exercise in gender politics, homoeroticism and disguised autobiography. The one picture that was totally altered in design represented the 'Toilette of Salome', an event which is mentioned by the stage directions when she prepares to dance: '*Slaves bring perfumes and the seven veils, and take off the sandals of* SALOME' (Works, 599). Salome sits draped but naked in front of her mirror. She is perfumed by a masked figure, attended by a hermaphrodite and watched by two others who appear to be

masturbating. It was replaced by the representation of an exaggeratedly gowned and hatted Salome, being powdered by the same
masked figure. The other figures are absent, but prominent on her
dressing-table are books of dubious reputation from which she has
dressed her imagination: Zola's *Nana*, *Fêtes Gallantes*, *Manon Lescaut*,
The Golden Ass, and de Sade.

Beardsley's willingness to embellish the text, here with a location
not given and an event described by the stage directions as taking
place in full view of the court, makes the fact that he made no
attempt to picture Salome's dance at first surprising. Instead he
represented Herod watching, pointing with his gaze to an off-stage
spectacle. Wilde wrote in Beardsley's copy of the first edition: 'For
the only artist who, besides myself, knows what the dance of the
seven veils is, and can see that invisible dance' (Letters, 348). The
two men collude about the limits of painterly representation, pointing up the inadequacy of illustration to stand for performance:

> The painter is so far limited that it is only through the mask of
> the body that he can show us the mystery of the soul; only through
> conventional images that he can handle ideas; only through its
> physical equivalents that he can deal with psychology.

Wilde had written this in 'The Critic as Artist' (Works, 1128). But the
way in which Beardsley used the 'mask of the body' at his disposal
gave rise to a sequence of pictures far from conventional, and often
surprising as 'illustrations'. Unconstrained by the period setting of
Wilde's play, Beardsley worked with visual anachronisms. Pagan
fawns and Judaic angels sit side by side with human figures gowned
in chitons (a dress of antiquity revived by the arts and crafts movement), eighteenth-century or Victorian dress (as in the 'Toilette of
Salome'), or pierrot costume; the books on Salome's dressing-table
also span the centuries from Roman decadence through eighteenth-
century France to the contemporary period. Exterior locations are
given by a variety of thorned roses, *fleurs du mal*, heralding the crown
of thorns, and remain suggestive of a perverse mental landscape. All
kinds of fantastically deformed human shapes inhabit Herod's court:
an aging foetus, a wizened dwarf (The Page of Herodias), hermaph-
rodites and eunuchs. The repeated appearance of Wilde's face insists
on the continuous presence of the author. Particularly unconventional, in terms of illustration, was the bold display of erotic nakedness
which problematises the elaborate strategies of concealment and
displacement in which the text engages. Beardsley emphasised sexual
display often by making his figures partially clothed, exposing breasts
and navel, concealing the rest. In 'Enter Herodias' the bare-breasted
Queen, her foetal page whose gown drapes a giant erection, and

the male slave holding simply a mask and a powder puff, partially concealed by the theatrical curtain he seems to draw, gain an erotic charge from the presence, not the absence, of dress. The figure, helmeted with the owl of Athena and holding the staff of Apollo, sits at the footlights of the performance, points indirectly to the erection – and it is Wilde's face that gazes out at the spectator.

The representation of 'John and Salome' on their first encounter toys similarly with display and concealment. The Princess exposes her breasts and navel to the spectator; the prophet, turning away, hides all except a shoulder and an arm. The relationship between Jokanaan and Salome is consistently shown as that between a figure and its mirror image (see 'John and Salome', 'The Dancer's Reward', 'The Climax'). They are of equal height and build, their faces impossible to distinguish. The psychological and erotic interpretation is disturbing, but entirely legitimated by the text. One consequence is a homoeroticism, in which the gender of both Salome and Jokanaan becomes ambiguous. The traditionally masculine literary style in which Salome approaches her beloved justifies the representational shift of her gender, while the Prophet's tantalising urge for falsely modest concealment justifies his corresponding shift towards the feminine. The painting by Leonardo da Vinci of *Saint John the Baptist,* described by Pater as a figure of ambiguous sex, lies behind the iconography of the Prophet as deployed by both Wilde and Beardsley.[19] Beardsley was capable of remaining faithful to the prescriptions of the text, while also indulging in fantastic and interpretive embellishment. One example of this is provided by 'The Dancer's Reward'. The stage direction reads '*A huge black arm, the arm of* THE EXECUTIONER, *comes forth from the cistern, bearing on a silver shield the head of* JOKANAAN. SALOME *seizes it*' (Works, 603). In its very literal quality – a disembodied arm bearing a disembodied head – the picture reifies and extends the text. The distorted phallic shape of the arm and shield reflects Salome's desires, while the neat detail of her slippers removed, faithful to the stage directions about her dance with naked feet, also suggests the fetishisation of the severed head, its metonymic substitution for the sexual body of the Baptist.

That Wilde chose to publish the English text of the play with such embellishments shows him driving home a point he made when the French production of the play was banned:

> I care very little about the refusal of the Lord Chamberlain's to allow my play to be produced. What I do care about is this – that the Censorship apparently regards the stage as the lowest of all the arts, and looks on acting as a vulgar thing. The painter is

151

allowed to take his subjects as he chooses . . . Nobody says, 'Painting is such a vulgar art that you must not paint sacred things.'
The sculptor is equally free . . . And the writer, the poet – he is
also quite free. I can write about any subject I choose. For me
there is no Censorship . . . The insult in the suppression of *Salome*,
is an insult to the stage as a form of art and not to me.

(Mikhail, I, 187)

Wilde's voice contributed to one of growing protest among dramatists and theatre critics against State intervention in the theatre.
A Select Committee of the House of Commons had just been called,
in May 1892, to hear evidence about stage censorship, at which
William Archer was the only person who spoke in favour of its
abolition. Soon the Committee would sit again, with William Archer,
Bernard Shaw, Harley Granville Barker and Henry Arthur Jones
arguing more vigorously for freedom of expression, in line with
Wilde's view that 'there would be little pleasure in criticising an art
where the artist was not free' (Letters, 319). The campaign was not
successful until 1968. Wilde could inveigh against the 'contemptible
official tyranny' (Letters, 319) which invoked a statute passed during the sixteenth century forbidding the representation of Biblical
characters on stage to prohibit his play, but the theatre-going
public would also have to be re-educated if they were to tolerate
such a play as *Salome*. Henry Arthur Jones had fallen foul of conservative intolerance from the auditorium, not the State, in 1885.
Booing and hissing from the audience had been the response to the
use of Biblical phrases in the mouth of a religious hypocrite in Jones'
play *Saints and Sinners* (1884). Jones was provoked to defend himself
in an article 'Religion and the Stage' in the *Nineteenth Century* in
January 1885.

The course of drama has been diverted and hopelessly cut off
from the main current of modern intellectual life. While the companion arts . . . are allowed to present every aspect of human life,
on stage only the narrow, ordinary, convenient, respectable,
superficial contemplation and presentation of human affairs is
allowed.[20]

Jones was addressing a problem which came from the public, not
the legislation of the country. William Archer had followed with a
defence of Jones in an article 'The Duties of Dramatic Critics' the
following month. He claimed that:

the hisses were the result of nothing more respectable than an
unreasoning tradition, which, regarding the theatre as a place

profane, deems sacred phrases as inappropriate within its walls as
a crucifix at a witches' sabbath. Here was an occasion on which
the critics should have come resolutely forward to denounce and
ridicule an absurdity of ignorant and thoughtless habit on the part
of the public whom they address. Unfortunately they missed their
opportunity.[21]

Jones returned to the subject in 1895 with 'The Bible on Stage' in
which again his criticism was equally of the 'virtuous dwellers in
Peckham and Camberwell' as of the office of the Lord Chamberlain.[22]
In the midst of this, Wilde could hardly have expected *Salome* to find
favour with either the public or the censor. As Kerry Powell argues,
only the allure of Bernhardt, and the veil of French, might have
saved him.

Major performances of *Salome,* few though they are, have always
been something of an event. Strauss set the play to music in 1905
and as an opera *Salome* has enjoyed considerable publicity. In 1977
Lindsay Kemp performed cross-dressed in the title role in New York
and London, drawing out the homoerotic dimensions of the play.
Steven Berkoff's 1989 production for the Royal National Theatre in
London took much inspiration from the symbolist origins of the play
and from the design of Beardsley's pictures. The tone of the production is given by Berkoff's account of the style adopted for Salome's
dance:

> Salome's dance became yet another problem to be dealt with
> since it is so talked about, and begged for such a mythic image,
> that who or what could possibly live up to its reputation? What
> does it mean? Is it a stripping off of all our vanities and preten-
> sions? Is it just a dance? It usually means some erotic striptease
> where a poor singer or actress bares all and grits her teeth in the
> alleged name of art. We decided that like everything else it had
> to be an illusion.[23]

The play remains one of the most rewarding challenges in Wilde's
corpus, for reader and performer alike. To Edmund Gosse who was
sent a copy of the 'Tyrian' play, Wilde wrote that he hoped *Salome*
would find a place in his library:

> Should she try to dance, a stern look from a single tome by an
> eighteenth-century writer will quell her, for common sense she
> has none, and reason, a faculty which I am glad to say is rapidly
> dying out, affrights her terribly.

(Letters, 331)

The Dancer's Reward, *by Aubrey Beardsley, in the first English edition of* Salome *(London: John Lane, 1894)*
By permission of the British Library (shelfmark: TC497)

Notes

1 Charles Ricketts, *Oscar Wilde. Recollections by Jean Paul Raymond & Charles Ricketts* (London: The Nonesuch Press, 1932) 53.
2 Cited in Kerry Powell, *Oscar Wilde and the Theatre of the 1890s* (Cambridge: Cambridge University Press, 1990) 45.
3 Robert Fizdale and Arthur Gold, *The Divine Sarah. A Life of Sarah Bernhardt* (London: Harper Collins, 1992) 248.
4 Pater, *The Renaissance*, 99.
5 *Pall Mall Budget*, 30 September 1886.

6   *Men and Memories: Recollections of William Rothenstein,* vol. I: 1872–1900, new edn (London: Faber & Faber, 1934) 184.

7   Herbert Beerbohm Tree, *Some Interesting Fallacies of the Modern Stage. An Address.* 6 December 1891 (London: Heinemann, 1892) 36.

8   *The Poet and the Puppets,* 8.

9   Ibid., 11.

10 Cited in Worth, *The Irish Theatre of Europe,* 77.

11 Arthur Symons, *The Symbolist Movement in Literature* (London: Heinemann, 1899) 146.

12 Graham Robertson, *Time Was: The Reminiscences of W. Graham Robertson* (London: Hamish Hamilton, 1931) 136.

13 See John A. Henderson, *The First Avant-Garde (1887–1894) Sources of the Modern French Theatre* (London, George Harrap, 1971) 98–9.

14 Powell, 35.

15 R. A. Cave, 'Wilde Designs: Some Thoughts about Recent British Productions of His Plays', *Modern Drama,* 37 (1994) 175.

16 Charles Ricketts, *Oscar Wilde. Recollections,* 53.

17 *Recollections,* 53.

18 Oscar Wilde, *Salomé. Drame en un acte* (Paris: librairie de l'art indépendant, 1893; Londres; Elkin Mathews et John Lane, 1893) 80–2.

19 Pater, *Renaissance,* 93–4.

20 H. A. Jones, *Nineteenth Century,* January 1885, 155.

21 William Archer, *Nineteenth Century,* February 1885, 258.

22 Powell, 33.

23 Berkoff, 'Introduction', *Salome* (London: Faber & Faber, 1989) xiii.

8 *The social comedies*

Lady Windermere's Fan. A Play about a Good Woman

The play was first produced by George Alexander, the 34-year-old actor-manager at the St James's Theatre, London, on 20 February 1892 where it ran until 29 July before embarking on a provincial tour from 22 August to 29 October. It was immediately revived in London and ran from 31 October to 30 November. During this time it grossed a profit for Alexander's company of £5570.0.11, and Wilde, being paid a percentage of the box, earned £7000 from the play in its first year. His celebrity status was assured. *Lady Windermere's Fan* was published in 1893. The published version differs from the script that was performed on the first press night, although it is in line with the play that was performed within a week of its opening. The major alteration which Wilde effected early was to bring forward the revelation of Mrs Erlynne's identity as the mother of Lady Windermere. On the first night this information was withheld until the 'very end of the play' (Critical Heritage, 121). Subsequently the audience became privy to this knowledge at the end of Act 2. Reviewing the first night, A. B. Walkley argued:

> If we were told at the outset, I, for one, should not view her conduct and Lord Windermere's in forcing her upon his wife with half the interest which these things afford me while still in the dark.
>
> (Critical Heritage, 121)

This indeed was Wilde's thinking on the matter of delayed revelation, but already during rehearsals Alexander had been pressuring him to change the sequential release of information to the audience – and Wilde, at further advice from his friends, eventually gave in.

The row goes to the heart of Wilde's artistic enterprise with this play. Towards the end of the rehearsal process Wilde wrote a passionate defence of his structure to Alexander:

> With regard to your ... suggestion about the disclosure of the secret of the play in the second act, had I intended to let out the secret, which is the element of suspense and curiosity, a quality so essentially dramatic, I would have written my play on entirely different lines. I would have made Mrs Erlynne a vulgar horrid woman and struck out the incident of the fan. The audience must not know till the last Act that the woman Lady Windermere proposed to strike with her fan was her own mother. The note would

be too harsh, too horrible. When they learn it, it is after Lady Windermere has left her husband's house to seek the protection of another man, and their interest is concentrated on Mrs Erlynne, to whom dramatically speaking belongs the last Act. Also it would destroy the dramatic wonder excited by the incident of Mrs Erlynne taking the letter and opening it and sacrificing herself in the third Act. If they knew Mrs Erlynne was the mother there would be no surprise in her sacrifice – it would be expected. But in my play the sacrifice is dramatic and unexpected. The cry with which Mrs Erlynne flies into the other room on hearing Lord Augustus's voice, the wild pathetic cry of self-preservation, 'Then it is I who am lost!' would be repulsive coming from the lips of one known to be the mother by the audience. It seems natural and is very dramatic coming from one who seems to be an adventuress, and who while anxious to save Lady Windermere thinks of her own safety when a crisis comes. Also it would destroy the last act: and the chief merit of my last act is to me the fact that it does not contain, as most plays do, the explanation of what the audience knows already, but that it is the sudden explanation of what the audience desires to know, followed immediately by the revelation of a character as yet untouched by literature.

(Letters, 308–9)

An ardent defence, but crucially untested in performance. The elaborate justification for the aborted version shows how ambitious Wilde was to alter dramatic convention, to evade predictable melodramatic morality, and to manipulate his audience with unexpected emotions. But the final version fulfils these ambitions more successfully than the first proposal, and the biographer of George Alexander, A. E. W. Mason, attributes the success to the intervention of the actor-manager in charge of the production:

It is impossible . . . to read the letters which during the rehearsals passed between the author and the manager – very feudal and lordly letters from Wilde and purely practical ones from Alexander – without realising that it was the manager at this time who was the more conscious of the two of the creaking conventions, the clever twists, the impossible transitions of character which were making the drama of the day a by-word; who was the more anxious of the two to discard them. The worn out machinery was still rumbling, the fan in fact was still fluttering. At the end of the second Act, as Wilde designed it, Mrs Erlynne was to tear off the stage in a tempest of words, the man to whom they were addressed was for the moment to cease to be, the audience was to be carried away by the acting of the leading lady. It was to be the conventional act-drop of a hundred sensational plays. Alexander

. . . wanted the Act to end not upon a tirade by the leading lady but upon a humorous and apposite comment by the man. The scene was to end on a stroke of comedy rather than on a blare of sensation.[1]

Wilde in fact lost nothing of his dual purpose which was to maintain the focus of interest on Mrs Erlynne and to avoid stereotype. The revision enhances the psychological complexity of the adventuress, and the audience is freed from atavistic curiosity about her identity. It is able to consider at greater leisure the exposure of immovable conventions of social etiquette, which would damn Mrs Erlynne without reprieve, as artificial and corrupting in themselves. And it is able to see her as a 'type untouched by literature', by which Wilde meant more than simply the positive portrayal of an 'unmotherly mother': he constructed Mrs Erlynne to fulfil his vision of the 'individualist', the ideal human type unique to Wilde's work, which dominates 'The Critic as Artist' and 'The Soul of Man Under Socialism'. As Wilde stated, 'Those who have seen *Lady Windermere's Fan* will see that if there is one particular doctrine contained in it, it is that of sheer individualism' (Ellmann, 347–8).

The revised plot is as tightly constructed as a Platonic dialogue to interrogate assumed values and moral positions. Not least among these questioned absolutes are the notions, so dear to Ibsen, that sincerity, truth-telling and honesty are of paramount importance to the moral health of society. Three secrets are left at the end of the play, to which only the audience has access. All of them are in the gift of Mrs Erlynne. Lady Windermere never knows that Mrs Erlynne is her mother; Lord Windermere never hears about his wife's escapade with Lord Darlington; Lord Augustus is duped by Mrs Erlynne about what she was doing in Darlington's rooms. As Ellmann puts it, the play 'concludes with collusive concealment instead of collective disclosure. Society profits from deception' (Ellmann, 344).

Wilde used a topical and conventional dramatic theme – that of the fallen woman or the 'woman with a past' – as a vehicle to carry his radical philosophy of 'individualism' set out in 'The Soul of Man Under Socialism'. He also used the popular dramatic form inherited from the French playwrights, Eugene Scribe and Victorien Sardou, of the 'well-made play' with its four-Act structure comprising exposition, complication, obligatory crisis scene and dénouement. In *Lady Windermere's Fan* these units correspond with the Act divisions. The 'exposition' sets the society scene at the Windermeres' London home and introduces the occasion of Lady Windermere's twenty-first birthday ball. All the major characters are brought on, if not in person then in discussion. The entry of Mrs Erlynne is delayed until Act II. The threat posed by this mysterious woman to the stability of the public order and the private harmony between the Windermeres is a refrain in the dialogue throughout the exposition. The 'complication' concerns the arrival of Mrs Erlynne at Lady Windermere's birthday celebration, Lady Windermere's unfulfilled threat to strike Mrs Erlynne with her fan and her decision instead to abandon her husband in favour of Lord Darlington. This unit begins with a broad social canvas – the picture of the ball – and it becomes ever more focused, leading through a duologue between Mrs Erlynne and Lord Windermere, to a soliloquy by Mrs Erlynne towards the closing moments in which her identity is revealed. The canvas opens up again at the very end as Lord Augustus, Mrs Erlynne's prospective husband, intrudes on her soliloquy and is left in sole possession of the stage at the end.

The obligatory crisis scene takes place in Lord Darlington's rooms. Lady Windermere has fled there, believing her husband to be unfaithful and determined to revenge herself by reciprocation. Mrs Erlynne pursues her daughter there, to stop her from absconding with Darlington. When the men arrive, the women hide behind the curtains. When some form of revelation is forced on them by the fan, conspicuous on the sofa, Mrs Erlynne steps out, creating a diversion which allows her daughter to escape unnoticed. The structure of the scene borrows from Sheridan's *School for Scandal*, revived in London during the 1880s. With the dénouement the scene returns to the Windermeres' house, and the explanations are delivered by Mrs Erlynne who has to talk her way out of a number of difficult positions in order to establish a new equilibrium after the night's events. That the 'fallen woman' effects a constructive resolution of her own drama represents a major departure from the conventional handling of the dénouement. Traditionally, a restoration of order is brought about by the *raisonneur*, one of the stock characters of the well-made play formula. Usually a male of respectable social position – doctor, lawyer, priest – the *raisonneur*'s job is to explain any remaining mysteries, to eject or chasten the intruder, and to restore the social balance that existed at the start of the play. Because Wilde places Mrs Erlynne in this unique position of knowledge, authority and power, the outcome is technically unconventional and thematically unpredictable.

Instead of using the well-made play formula as a conservative form tending towards the restoration of a *status quo* only temporarily disrupted by the appearance of the outsider figure, Wilde sends his female characters on journeys of self-discovery and change. Consequently the order established at the end of the play does not resemble the patriarchy which structured the society we meet at its start. There is a widespread coming of age celebrated in the course of Lady Windermere's twenty-first birthday ball, but it is not enjoyed by any of the male characters. Lord Windermere's status as protector of his 'child' wife is usurped by Mrs Erlynne in Act III; Lord Darlington as alternative lover for Lady Windermere is banished from her mind and from the stage by Mrs Erlynne in Act III; Cecil Graham's role as the wise spectating dandy who restores order by his wit is appropriated by Mrs Erlynne in Act IV. Lord Augustus, a fop from the start, is tricked by Mrs Erlynne in Act IV into performing the right deed (of marrying the fallen woman) for the wrong reason (believing her innocent). All the traditionally male roles, in drama and in society, accrue to Mrs Erlynne who ends as protector, wit and *raisonneur*, restored to her wrongful place in established society.

The discourse of her dialogue matches her appropriation of masculine territory, as the aphoristic rhetoric she uses in public displays the witty superiority and intellectual poise normally reserved for the male dandy. This can be judged within the play by contrasting the rhetorical style of the scenes devoted to the portrayal of exclusively female society with those of exclusively male company. Mrs Erlynne's public discourse matches that of the men returning from their club to Lord Darlington's rooms and it is antithetical to the style deployed by the ladies in Act I after Darlington's departure. It is Mrs Erlynne who acts on the philosophy of individualism mooted by Lord Darlington in his seduction of Lady Windermere when he says: 'there are moments when one has to choose between living one's own life, fully, entirely, completely – or dragging out some false, shallow, degrading existence that the world in its hypocrisy demands' (Works, 439). His departure, after Lady Windermere's ultimate rejection of him, and of this philosophy (because Mrs Erlynne persuades her that her duty is to stay with her child, however badly her husband might treat her) displays nothing of the self-control and dispassionate attitude to deeply felt emotion that characterises Mrs Erlynne's decision to see the action through, before departing for a new life on the Continent. It is the 'adventuress' who acts on Wilde's aphorism in 'The Soul of Man Under Socialism' that '[s]elfishness is not living as one wishes to live, it is asking others to live as one wishes to live. And unselfishness is letting other people's lives alone, not interfering with them' (Works, 1194–5).

Mrs Erlynne begins the play as a victim of this kind of social selfishness which, as Wilde states in the 'Soul of Man', 'always aims at creating around it an absolute uniformity of type'. She has been classified as the fallen woman, and wants to 'get back', to circulate in established society. To do this she must conform, she must live selfishly at the dictates of a selfish society. Wilde's rejection of stereotype in the structuring of her character does not reflect a desire on his part for sheer novelty, but is a step in his cohesive and comprehensive social philosophy. She arrives in London with the sole aim of interfering in the lives of the Windermeres, just as society interfered in hers. She begins with an old-fashioned selfish motive and ends with a radically unselfish one, refraining from revealing herself to her daughter and therefore removing herself from interference in the Windermeres' life. Her arrival in London is precipitated by information about her daughter gleaned from reading the Society newspapers abroad. It is timed to coincide with the birth of the Windermeres' son, named Gerard after Margaret Windermere's 'dead' father, and Mrs Erlynne's husband. The older woman is more than a delinquent mother, she is a delinquent grandmother too. This occasion also coincides with Lady Windermere's twenty-first birthday, so that the birth of Gerard rhymes precisely with Mrs Erlynne's age at the time of giving birth to Margaret. Lord Windermere's susceptibility to blackmail by Mrs Erlynne is motivated not just by the wish to preserve the innocence of his wife, but by the desire to maintain the respectability of his family line. Mrs Erlynne is, as Lord Windermere allows in his last line of the play, 'a very clever woman', capable of manipulating as powerfully as she has been manipulated.

She is led to a more intimate form of interference when she reads her daughter's letter to her husband announcing her decision to abscond with Darlington:

> *Mrs Erlynne . . . (Goes over to bureau and looks at letter. Takes it up and lays it down again with a shudder of fear.)* No, no! It would be impossible! Life doesn't repeat its tragedies like that! Oh, why does this horrible fancy come across me? Why do I remember now the one moment of my life I most wish to forget? Does life repeat its tragedies? *(Tears letter open and reads it, then sinks down into a chair with a gesture of anguish.)* Oh, how terrible! The same words that twenty years ago I wrote to her father! and how bitterly I have been punished for it! No; my punishment, my real punishment is tonight, is now!
>
> (Works, 443)

This is Mrs Erlynne's moment of self-discovery, for she experiences a quickening of the maternal instinct. 'Only once in my life have I known a mother's feelings. That was last night. They were terrible – they made me suffer – they made me suffer too much. For twenty years . . . I have lived childless – I want to live childless still' (Works, 459–60). Not the 'unmotherly mother' she thought she was, Mrs Erlynne wants to protect her daughter. To do this she must wrestle with the terrible spectre of heredity, to free her daughter from the constraints of determinism. Only then can Lady Windermere be liberated from the horrible fate of the outcast which fell to her mother. The rhetoric which Wilde deploys here displays its literary heredity just as powerfully as Mrs Erlynne seeks to evade domination by the laws of natural inheritance. Ibsen is at the forefront. *Ghosts*, with Mrs Alving's anguish at finding her son no less dissolute than her husband in the repetition of the past in the present, and *Hedda Gabler* with its refrain of 'people don't do things like that', play into Wilde's phrasing of Mrs Erlynne's self-revelation to compound the sense of impending inevitability and to heighten the drama of the mother's battle against fate to save her daughter. Wilde's assertion of his philosophy of individualism allows him to evade the constraints of naturalist theatre. Mrs Erlynne succeeds where unconventional women in drama before her had failed.

The price of the mother's punishment, her transitory experience of an emotion which makes her wish to conform with dominant social mores, is the conformity of her daughter. At Darlington's rooms she pleads with Lady Windermere to honour her obligations as a mother:

> You have a child, Lady Windermere. Go back to that child who even now, in pain or in joy, may be calling to you. (*Lady Windermere rises.*) God gave you that child. He will require from you that you make his life fine, that you watch over him. What answer will you make to God if his life is ruined through you? Back to your house, Lady Windermere – your husband loves you! . . . But even if he had a thousand loves, you must stay with your child. If he was harsh to you, you must stay with your child. If he ill-treated you, you must stay with your child. If he abandoned you, your place is with your child.

> (*Lady Windermere bursts into tears and buries her face in her hands.*)
> (Works, 448)

Reconciliation between mother and daughter is effected, the lost parent finds the lost child. But instead of being placed at the end of the drama, it is embedded in the centre of the play. And instead of releasing tension, the emotional charge of the scene is heightened by the fact that Mrs Erlynne reveals neither her identity nor her personal motive. She also refrains from the clinching dramatic gesture, which would have set the sentimental seal on the encounter. There is no embrace:

> (*rushing to her*): Lady Windermere!

> Lady Windermere (*holding out her hands to her, helplessly, as a child might do*): Take me home. Take me home.

> Mrs Erlynne (*is about to embrace her. Then restrains herself. There is a look of wonderful joy in her face*): Come! Where is your cloak?
> (Works, 448)

163

In delivering this message, couched in terms of the dogmatic morality Lady Windermere will understand, Mrs Erlynne overturns the
emancipatory message of *The Doll's House* which was that a woman's
primary responsibility was to herself, and that the definition of her
identity was not to be achieved in relation to others, such as husband
or child. Mrs Erlynne is freed from the charge of hypocrisy, preaching what she would not practise herself, on rather flimsy grounds.
She believes her daughter to be internally weaker than herself, less
able to withstand the assaults of intolerant society than herself, and
there is no doubt that Lady Windermere is set up as a naïve puritan
in Act I to make this interpretation of her character plausible. 'You
haven't got the kind of brains that enables a woman to get back.
You have neither the wit nor the courage. You couldn't stand dis-
honour' (Works, 448). But Lady Windermere confirms this herself
during the sober light of day, when Mrs Erlynne is probing to find
out whether revelation would be safe. 'We all have ideals in life. At
least we all should have. Mine is my mother . . . If I lost my ideals,
I should lose everything' (Works, 461). Mrs Erlynne's act of self-
sacrifice, in presenting herself to the men at Lord Darlington's rooms
to let Lady Windermere escape, has the effect of ameliorating Lady
Windermere's puritanism, opening a more complex ethical code to
her understanding. To be an individualist of Wilde's school in a
society which itself rejects such a type is virtually impossible – and
certainly not for the faint-hearted. Lady Windermere seems to have
inherited her mother's vices without her virtues.

The alteration of her ethical understanding, Lady Windermere's
matured classification of Mrs Erlynne as 'good' (Works, 464) rather
than 'infamous' (Works, 428), is a small step on the road to the
conversion of the conventional into the radical. But a coded gesture
of hope is held out for Lady Windermere's further development
towards individualism in the line which describes the place of her
country retreat from London following the trauma of her birthday.
She asserts her desire for reconciliation with her husband: 'Oh Arthur,
don't love me less, and I will trust you more. I will trust you absolutely. Let us go to Selby. In the Rose Garden at Selby the roses are
white and red' (Works, 463). Wilde closed 'The Soul of Man Under
Socialism' with the statement that 'The new Individualism is the
new Hellenism', and we have seen how his construction of Hellenism drew inspiration from Pater's Hellenism described in the essay
'Winckelmann': 'a perfect world, if the gods could have seemed for
ever only fleet and fair, white and red!'.[2] Just as Dorian Gray met his
moment of conversion at his country estate called Selby (although
revelation rather than redemption was to be effected by this), so
there is hope that Lady Windermere at Selby will encounter the
'white and red' gods that inform the spirit of her mother's behaviour.

Mrs Erlynne's experience of the turbulent emotions of motherhood, which she was only just able to contain, confirm her individualist stance. She decides to withdraw from her interference in the Windermeres' life. 'I am going to pass entirely out of your two lives. My coming into them has been a mistake – I discovered that last night' (Works, 460) she admits to Lord Windermere, turning the sentiments of the unmotherly mother into a principled rejection of the family as the unit of social foundation. 'Socialism annihilates family life . . . Jesus knew this . . . "Who is my mother? Who are my brothers?" he said . . . He would allow no claim whatsoever to be made on personality' (Works, 1181). And just as Mrs Erlynne's flight into the trap of conventional behaviour was marked by the knowing echo in her discourse of dramatic precedent, so her final passing out of it recognises the determining literary convention rejected by Wilde's manipulation of her character:

> I suppose, Windermere, you would like me to retire into a convent, or become a hospital nurse, or something of that kind, as people do in silly modern novels. That is stupid of you, Arthur; in real life we don't do such things – not as long as we have any good looks left, at any rate. No – what consoles one nowadays is not repentance, but pleasure. Repentance is quite out of date.
>
> (Works, 460)

The echo of the last line of *Hedda Gabler*, which Wilde saw on its first English staging in the spring of 1891, is there again. 'People don't do such things,' says Judge Brack as the curtain falls on Hedda's suicide. And the references to the conventional fate of delinquent mothers in literature of the period are there, too, as Kerry Powell has demonstrated. Wilde departs explicitly from the punishment doled out to the repenting wayward mother in plays such as Sardou's *Odette* (staged at the Haymarket in 1882), Sydney Grundy's *The Glass of Fashion* (1883), Arthur Shirley's *Saved: or a Wife's Peril* (1885), Pierre Leclerq's *Illusion* (staged at the Strand Theatre in 1890), or the dramatisations of *East Lynne* (staged in London throughout the 1880s).[3] These are the rejected moralities. An equally powerful echo comes from the last paragraph of 'The Soul of Man Under Socialism', in which Wilde stated 'Pleasure is Nature's test, her sign of approval. When man is happy, he is in harmony with himself and his environment' (Works, 1197). Even if this philosophy goes unrecognised in the last Act of the play, the affectiveness of the drama is enormously enhanced by the dramatic irony of Mrs Erlynne's maintained disguise in relation to her daughter. Wilde tantalises his audience, exploits an intolerable tension, throughout the farewell scene between mother and daughter in which Mrs Erlynne asks for a photograph of Lady Windermere ('Margaret', 'What a wonderful chance our names being the same!'), and her son Gerard. Mrs Erlynne steps outside the evolutionary cycle and the progress of generations. The photographic method of 'realism' is exposed as an instrument in the construction of idealism. 'I like to think of you as a mother. I like you to think of yourself as one' (Works, 462) she says to Lady Windermere, surrendering her maternal responsibility to the next generation. She begins and ends the play as an outsider. The individualist cannot be assimilated.

Wilde's sense that theatre was a visual medium meant that he was as careful about the use of stage directions as about dialogue. His wish to maintain Mrs Erlynne's status as an outsider to the last, and his wish to maintain the visual focus on her character in the fourth Act, is inscribed in the pictorial effect he sought to achieve even through the disposition of stage furniture for the last Act of the play, although little of this found its way into the printed stage directions of the 1893 edition. Act IV, in the published version, is set in the same room – Lady Windermere's morning-room – as that in which the play began: but this is not how Wilde first envisaged its setting. It represents a compromise struck with Alexander. Wilde had wanted the last scene to be played out in Lady Windermere's boudoir, a more intimate, feminine setting for the last encounter between the two central women. Just as the action that intervenes between the first and last scenes has changed the world-views of Lady Windermere and Mrs Erlynne, Wilde wanted to avoid a visual repetition of the initial setting which would be shadowed by an inappropriate recollection of the exposition scene. He described the way in which he wanted to situate the furniture, and the characters' negotiation of it, in a detailed letter to Alexander:

> I heard by chance in the theatre today ... that you intended using the first scene a second time – in the last Act ... [M]ore than four weeks ago you agreed to have what is directed in the book of the play, namely Lady Windermere's boudoir, a scene which I consider very essential from a dramatic point of view ...
>
> If through pressure of time, or for reasons of economy, you are unable to give the play its full scenic mounting, the scene that has to be repeated should be *the second, not the first*. Lady Windermere may be in her drawing-room in the fourth Act. *She should not be in her husband's library*. This is a very important point.
>
> Now, from the point of view of stage-management, the advantages of using Scene II are these:
>
> In Act 2 the scene is night. The ballroom is open, and so is the terrace. In Act 4, the scene being day, the ballroom is closed, the window shut, and the furniture can be differently arranged. Rooms

are cleared out of some of their contents for a reception. These contents are restored the next day. That is to say, the repetition of the library would have to be an exact replica: the repetition of the drawing-room would not have this disadvantage.

And the disadvantage is a great one, because the scene – a vital one in the play – between the Duchess and Lady Windermere takes place on the sofa on the right of the stage. Now Mrs Erlynne should not have her scene in the same place. It impoverishes the effect. I want you to arrange Mrs Erlynne on a sofa more in the centre of the stage and towards the left side. In my own rough draft of the stage-setting of this Act, made when I was writing the piece, I placed Mrs Erlynne on a high-backed Louis Seize sofa so:

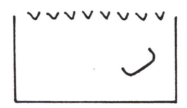

She would then be, what she should be, in full view of the audience. She should not be at the side. The situation is too important. The sofa is of course not parallel with the foot-lights. It is placed like this $\smile$ and Mrs Erlynne sits on the upper side naturally ... The use of the second Act, instead of the first, enables us to give Mrs Erlynne a very much better position on the stage. There are only three people in the last Act (setting aside the servants) till the arrival of Lord Augustus, and the play should not go on in a corner. Mrs Erlynne should hold the centre of the stage, and be its central figure.

(More Letters, 109–110)

Wilde was determined to avoid any sense that Mrs Erlynne might be assimilated with the Society she chooses to leave. This, he feared, would be the visually communicated statement were she to occupy the same seat at the end as the Duchess of Bewick, a caricature creature of fashion, had occupied at the beginning. Furthermore, if any set is to be reused, Wilde prefers it to be that of the ball-room, the social territory which Mrs Erlynne sought to conquer and succeeded in appropriating when she attended her daughter's birthday celebration, and in which she can move with relative ease the next morning. The change in social structure effected by Mrs Erlynne's behaviour is to be made apparent by the change in the physical appearance of the room and her negotiation of the space.

That Wilde was exploiting a form of drama in which stage properties held important functions within the plot is already manifest in the title of the play. But *Lady Windermere's Fan* puns on the signification of 'fan' as 'admirer' (abbreviated from 'fanatic' as early as 1682): Lord Darlington and Mrs Erlynne fulfil this role, like Lord Windermere whose birthday gift is the fan. All of them are devoted to Lady Windermere in different ways. Equally ambiguous is the referent of the 'good woman' in the title. Is this the naïvely puritanical Lady Windermere who must be educated to a maturer understanding of goodness in the course of the play, or is it Mrs Erlynne, the agent of change in her daughter, who acquits herself decently in Society after the disastrous mistakes of her youth which brought about her expulsion? Even the professional personality of actors could have a stage value equivalent with properties, and the first reviewers commented in this way on the casting of Marion Terry, normally 'the embodiment of dramatic innocence and theatrical guilelessness'[4] in the role of Mrs Erlynne. 'When did good woman ever play bad woman so well?'.[5]

Despite his dextrous handling of the three episodes centring on the fan (Lady Windermere's unfulfilled threat to strike the unwelcome guest at her ball; its discovery at Lord Darlington's rooms leading to the disclosure of Mrs Erlynne and the escape of Lady Windermere; Mrs Erlynne's return of the property to the newly matured Lady Windermere the next morning), Wilde can otherwise be seen negotiating certain stage conventions of the day which permitted the unrealistic use of properties in the motivation of behaviour or the disclosure of secrets with varied degrees of sophistication. Letters are the main culprits: a device used commonly in the well-made play and typified by Scribe's *Scrap of Paper*. Mrs Erlynne finds, reads and destroys Lady Windermere's letter to her husband explaining her departure; Lord Darlington removes himself temporarily from the conversation of the men in his rooms on the pretext of having to write some letters occasioned by his departure from England the next day. This anticipates the critically ridiculed first act of Pinero's *The Second Mrs Tanqueray* (1893; it shared Alexander's bill with *Lady Windermere's Fan* during 1893 and made twice as much profit) in which the hero leaves his invited guests alone because he has to write letters, permitting them to get on with the ironically loaded exposition.

The difference between these two letter-writing hosts is that Wilde does not actually need to remove Darlington from the action in order to proceed with the drama, but Pinero does have to engineer his protagonist off stage in order to establish the required exposition for the ensuing drama. Wilde motivates Lady Windermere's departure from the stage more plausibly in Act IV, when she leaves to find the photograph for Mrs Erlynne, allowing the adventuress and Lord Windermere to be alone on stage for their final confrontation. Even so, Wilde takes advantage of the old-fashioned convention of the soliloquy or aside to permit the revelation of inner thoughts. The construction of Lady Windermere – the most transparent character of the play – depends most heavily on this: Acts III and IV both begin with her extended soliloquies, while the first and second Acts also focus on the heroine's inner turmoil in this way. Wilde's deployment of soliloquy in relation to Mrs Erlynne is judiciously sparing. It reflects the older woman's maintenance of an impenetrable social front which drops only once: the consequence of reading her daughter's letter and discovering 'I feel a passion awakening within me that I never felt before' (Works, 444).

> It is no use telling me of the constructive faults, the flimsy plot, the unreasonable conduct of the characters. My answer is, 'I know all that; but the great thing is, that the play never bores me; and when a dramatist gives me such a perpetual flow of brilliant talk as Mr. Wilde gives, I am willing to forgive him all the sins in the dramatic Decalogue, and the rest.'
>
> (Critical Heritage, 123)

So A. B. Walkley rounded off his applauding review of the play, and set the tone that would dominate the reception of the three subsequent comedies Wilde wrote.

Notes

1   A. E. W. Mason, 33–4.
2   Pater, *The Renaissance*, 166.
3   Powell, 14–21.
4   *Truth*, Vol. XXXI, February 1892, 386.
5   *Daily Telegraph*, 22 February 1892.

A Woman of No Importance

A Woman of No Importance was commissioned by Herbert Beerbohm Tree, actor-manager at the Haymarket Theatre, after witnessing the success of *Lady Windermere's Fan* at the St James's. Wilde began to write the play, with the working title 'Mrs Arbuthnot', during the summer of 1892, and he presented it to Beerbohm Tree in October 1892. Rehearsals began in late March the following year and it opened on 19 April 1893 with the actor-manager in the role of Lord Illingworth.

The circumstances in which Wilde wrote the play have some bearing on the world it represents. He was at the height of his affair with Lord Alfred Douglas and leading a separate life from his wife, Constance. She and the boys spent the late summer months at the elegant pre-Raphaelite home of her relation, Lady Mount-Temple, at Babbacombe Cliff in Devon, while Wilde rented a farmhouse near Cromer in Norfolk during August and September to concentrate on writing and entertaining Bosie. During the winter Wilde moved to Babbacombe, with Bosie in tow, and Constance went to Italy with her aunt. Wilde announced to a friend that he had established 'Babbacombe School', Lord Alfred Douglas was the only 'Boy' and Wilde himself was the Headmaster of the institution which combined 'the advantages of a public school with those of the private lunatic asylum' (Letters, 333).

A Woman of No Importance has a provincial, country-house setting and includes the use of Norfolk place names in its 'actual' location at Hunstanton Chase; it represents a society that is sexually segregated with the men operating in one sphere and the women in another; it also toys with the suggestion that Lord Illingworth's interest in Gerald is sexually motivated. This aspect of the play was modified during the initial writing process, but became conspicuous again after Wilde's trial in 1895, so that Lytton Strachey could write of its revival in 1907 that: 'Mr Tree is a wicked Lord, staying in a country house, who has made up his mind to bugger one of the other guests – a handsome young man of twenty' (Ellmann, 357).

But the latently illicit sexual passions which fuel the plot are by no means the most audacious features of this extraordinary play. William Archer hailed it as the apotheosis of modernity upon the stage: a claim he justifies by discussing certain scenes which display 'keenness of intellect, the individuality of [Wilde's] point of view, the excellence of his verbal style, and . . . the genuinely dramatic quality of his inspirations'. He points to the scene 'between Lord Illingworth and Mrs Arbuthnot at the end of the second Act of this play' as 'the most virile and intelligent . . . piece of English dramatic writing of our day . . . There is no situation-hunting, no posturing . . . There is nothing conventional about it, nothing insincere' (Critical Heritage, 145).

This is the scene in which the two estranged lovers confront each other for the first time since Lord Illingworth deserted Mrs Arbuthnot after the birth of their son, Gerald. The verbal exchange is sober, rational and controlled; there is none of the melodramatic hysteria that an audience would have been trained to expect from such an encounter. Wilde succeeds with a double audacity. The subject matter was daring: two mature people admit their participation in the breach of great Victorian pieties. Not only did their illicit sexual encounter produce a child, but also neither party agreed to be beholden to the other as a consequence. Illingworth refused to marry his lover and she refused his offer of financial support as substitute. The dramatic handling of the situation in which these facts are revealed to the audience is the second bold feature of the scene. The cool rationality of the discussion in which both parties maintain their poise departs from all conventional expectation – both dramatic and social – about what kind of moral evaluation should be meted out to confessions such as these.

The 'modern' quality of this scene is central to the dramatic experiment Wilde undertook with the way in which *A Woman of No Importance* is structured. It reveals the core of Wilde's post-naturalist theatre and the theoretical principles, outlined in 'The Critic as Artist', Wilde here put into practice:

> By revealing to us the absolute mechanism of all action, and so freeing us from the self-imposed and trammelling burden of moral responsibility, the scientific principle of Heredity has become, as it were, the warrant for the contemplative life.
>
> (Works, 1137)

The application of this insight, Wilde argued, was the way 'to make ourselves absolutely modern' (Works, 1137). In the scene Archer isolates for praise, the characters operate at a contemplative level. They talk about past action. The only stage direction inscribed in the printed text throughout the entire episode is that '*Lord Illingworth shrugs his shoulders*' (Works, 490). It was to perform this kind of dramatic interaction that Wilde primed Beerbohm Tree on the way to play the character of Lord Illingworth:

> Before you can successfully impersonate the character I have in mind, you must forget that you ever played Hamlet; you must forget that you ever played Falstaff; above all, you must forget that you ever played a duke in a melodrama by Henry Arthur Jones . . . I think you had better forget that you ever acted at all

171

> ... Because this witty aristocrat whom you wish to assume in
> my play is quite unlike anyone who has been seen on the stage
> before ... He is a figure of art. Indeed, if you can bear the truth,
> he is MYSELF.
>
> (Ellmann, 359)

Wilde was further offended when the play was praised by Beerbohm
Tree for its 'plot'. 'Plots are tedious. Anyone can invent them. Life
is full of them' (Ellmann, 359). Instead, he viewed the first Act of
the play as the most accomplished, because 'there was absolutely no
action at all. It was a perfect Act.'[1]

At times Wilde honoured his century's faith in 'the absolute mechanism of all action', if only to express the superiority of thought over
action; at other times he set out to subvert the distinction. 'What is
really dramatic is not necessarily that which is fitting for presentation
in a theatre. The theatre is an accident of the dramatic form. It is
not essential to it. We have been deluded by the name of action. To
think is to act,' he wrote in the *Woman's World* in May 1889. Couple
with this Wilde's trivialising of causal narrative and his preferred
emphasis on tone and rhythm, and we can look forward to T. S.
Eliot's dismissal of the reductive quest for the 'meaning' of a poem:

> The chief use of 'meaning' ... may be ... to satisfy one habit of
> the reader, to keep his mind diverted and quiet, while the poem
> does its work upon him: much as the imaginary burglar is always
> provided with a piece of nice meat for the house-dog.[2]

With the construction of *A Woman of No Importance* Wilde attempted
to find a dramatic method for the presentation of thought as action,
to challenge the century's theatrical 'accidents'. A consequence of this
radical experiment is that the play suffers from apparent inconsist-
encies of style and it has been consistently underrated in Wilde's canon.
The first Act of the play, which Wilde admired so much because it
seemed to evade the constraints of conventional drama, draws a
leisurely picture of a leisured society. The characters simply talk:
they do nothing. What they say, where, when and to whom, carries
the full burden of the dramatic action: 'all conversation and no action.
I can't describe action: my people sit in chairs and chatter' (Letters,
255), as Wilde said of *The Picture of Dorian Gray*.

A Woman of No Importance is the dramatic partner of Wilde's novel,
for reasons more profound than the simple repetition of dialogue
from the novel in the play. Also concerned with the consequences of
heredity on the freedom of the individual, *Dorian Gray* sets up a dichotomy between action and thought: it exposes the moral poisoning
that occurs when the dichotomy collapses and the liberty of thought
influences libertine action. And just as that novel was packed

with sensational incident, so too the play has its moments of high melodrama:

> How different is the 'He is your father!' tableau at the end of Act III from the strong and simple conclusion of Act II – how different and how inferior! It would be just retribution if Mr Wilde were presently to be confronted with this tableau in all the horrors of chromolithography, on every hoarding in London, with the legend, 'Stay, Gerald! He is your father!' in crinkly letters at the corner.
>
> (Critical Heritage, 146)

This is how Archer objected to the apparent uneven quality of writing and tone in the play which would seem to confirm Wilde's self-criticism that the description of action was beyond him. The conventional extremity of this tableau is so marked as to suggest that Wilde was simply not interested in it. For him, the focus and interest of the play lay elsewhere and the blazing melodrama of this scenario matches the perfunctory handling of action and sensation in *The Picture of Dorian Gray*. The justice in Archer's view is that he implicitly acknowledges the transitional nature of the play, both in Wilde's corpus and in the larger context of the evolution of British drama.

The breaches in tone and style maintained by the structure of the play can, however, be justified in other terms, perhaps more aesthetically satisfying. When Philip Prowse, the director of *A Woman of No Importance* in its successful revival at the RSC in 1991, was asked how seriously he thought Wilde took this tableau, he responded:

> What he must have taken seriously was that sort of terrifying revelation – really rather awkward – at an English country house. The social embarrassment of it must have struck him very acutely. The morality less so. Although I'm sure he would have paid it lip service in dealing with his actors, just as I had to.[3]

Prowse's interpretation offers a way of understanding Wilde's deployment of melodrama at this point in the play as a deliberate strategy to heighten the interest in how society deals with indiscretion. How far can its rules be broken before the game breaks down completely? The scene shifts immediately to Mrs Arbuthnot's sitting-room for the beginning of Act IV, which takes place the following morning. Wilde has inscribed a silence into the tempo of the play, a chance for the audience to draw breath and be fired with curiosity to watch the action to its dénouement, while 'society' regroups off stage. Lady Hunstanton, and Mrs Allonby are invited in to the sitting-room, having come to inquire after Mrs Arbuthnot. 'I hope she is better?' asks Lady Hunstanton of Gerald. The dictum of *Dorian Gray* – 'If one doesn't talk about a thing, it has never happened' (Works, 85) – comes into operation. Lady Hunstanton offers three explanations for Mrs Arbuthnot's sudden departure the previous night, all them respectably feminine: 'I'm afraid the heat was too much for her last night. I think there must have been thunder in the air. Or perhaps it was the music' (Works, 503–4).

The narrative voice of *Dorian Gray* affords an account of Lady Hunstanton's behaviour:

> Society, civilized society at least . . . feels instinctively that manners are of more importance than morals . . . the canons of good society are, or should be, the same as the canons of art. Form is absolutely essential to it. It should have the dignity of a ceremony, as well as its unreality, and should combine the insincere character of a romantic play with the wit and beauty that make such plays delightful to us.
>
> (Works, 107)

Wilde breaks the form of the drama he established in the first two Acts with the melodramatic tableau in order to reflect the compound breaches of social etiquette which force private behaviour into public view at the end of Act III, and then to examine how society recovers from them. Gerald is the living proof of his parents' indiscretion; Hester, a New World outsider ignorant of any 'form' to be maintained in the Old World, triggers the revelation of Illingworth's identity to Gerald by exposing his persistent private abuse of social form. Wilde's use of the much criticised tableau in juxtaposition with more sophisticated forms of dramatic writing can therefore be seen as integrally strategic to his satire. He inscribes the collision between old and new morality into the conventional fabric of the play. Prowse overcame the potential stylistic problems of reconciling the 'melodrama of Mrs Arbuthnot with the urbanity of her seducer' by focusing on the accommodations of impropriety sustainable within polite society. 'My interest lay in Illingworth and Mrs Arbuthnot *both* finding themselves in the middle of this exquisitely embarrassing social dilemma, rather a public one. I was interested in how they resolved it, socially as well as morally.'[4]

As if to emphasise that *A Woman of No Importance* was not a play of 'action', a traditionally male preserve, Wilde stated that this was 'a woman's play' (Letters, 335). Female characters dominate the play and three types of 'new woman' are delineated in the characters of Hester, Mrs Allonby and Mrs Arbuthnot. Together they act out a confrontation between the moral values of the New World and the Old.

While much has been made of Hester's literary ancestry,[5] the origins of this character and the conflicts generated when she is transplanted to England may also be found in the flesh and blood of Lady Wilde's journalism. In an article for the *Home Journal* on 2 May 1883, 'American Traits. Women and Society in the States' (no doubt culled from her son's accounts of America), Lady Wilde described the differences between the two types of women:

> The English girl never stares, nor asks questions with obtrusive curiosity. She is trained to seem and be a negation – a dormant soul without volition or an opinion on any subject, felt or expressed. Her American cousin, however, has an aggressive frankness, based chiefly upon interrogatories and bold personalities. Her gaze is clear and direct; not the 'stony British stare,' but with the large, truthful eyes of childhood – the eager, inquiring glance of a candid nature. Truth is in all her words. This Puritan virtue has indeed remained an heirloom in the American family. They have none of the subtle evasions and graceful mendacities of high life in Europe – the delicate flatteries, so charming and so false. These are stamped out at once by the frank, fearless candour of the American girl. Yet one trembles a little before a candour so uncompromising; for we all shrink from the downright expression of the actual, and the glare of the unshadowed truth makes one nervous. But the Americans have no mercy. Nature meant them for a nation of interviewers.

Lady Wilde is clearly fond of Old World 'mendacities', and prefers charm to candour. Feeling uncomfortable at the exposure of decadence, she dismisses New World ethics with the charge of vulgarity: a move that is made against Hester in the play more than once. 'In my young days, Miss Worsley, one never met anyone in society who worked for their living. It was not considered the thing' (Works, 466) says Lady Caroline to her young guest. Later Lady Caroline exercises one of Lady Wilde's 'subtle evasions' in response to Hester's denunciation of English double standards. The 'Don't have one law for men and another for women' speech, steeped in the brimstone rhetoric of the Old Testament, meets with: 'Might I, dear Miss Worsley, as you are standing up, ask you for my cotton that is just behind you? Thank you' (Works, 483–4). It is a moment of carefully poised hilarity – but laughter is only rescued from unease at one of Wilde's favourite arguments by the absurd language in which Hester couches her argument.

Hester begins the play with all her Puritan heirlooms on show and it is not just Lady Wilde who thinks discretion about such an inheritance in order. Mrs Allonby, the most consummate player of the social games to which Lady Wilde alludes, is the most threatened by Hester. 'What is that dreadful girl talking about?' she asks Lady Stutfield. 'She is painfully natural, is she not?' is the rejoinder (Works,

482). Lord Illingworth allows his mistress, Mrs Allonby, to set him up to re-educate 'the Puritan', but Wilde, holding to the notion that this is 'a woman's play', allots the task to Mrs Arbuthnot, another woman who quails at Hester's fierce morality.

Wilde himself published an article about American women in *Court and Society* on 23 March 1887, called 'The American Invasion', the tone of which is in striking contrast to that of his mother's piece. 'They take their dresses from Paris and their manners from Piccadilly, and wear both charmingly ... [T]he chief secret of their charm is that they never talk seriously' (Works, 964, 965). Compare this with the echo in the dialogue of the play: 'All Americans do dress well. They get their clothes in Paris' as Lady Hunstanton pronounces (Works, 470). But in his article Wilde allows a spectre to loom: 'They have, however, one grave fault – their mothers ... The Pilgrim Mothers ... dull, dowdy or dyspeptic' (Works, 965). Illingworth's quip 'All women become like their mothers. That is their tragedy' (Works, 487) has its roots in this observation – and it is certainly from Hester's Pilgrim maternity that he wishes to rescue her.

The plot of the play also has designs on Hester and the Puritanism she represents. The character is constructed to be deeply ambiguous. An orphan but a wealthy heiress, a guest but thoroughly ungrateful to her hosts, voicing 'truths' about social intercourse that are proved to be false, she condemns herself by her own words and actions. At a light-hearted level, her protestation that 'a friendship ... between a young man and a young girl' (Works, 466) can be innocent of romance proves disingenuous as the only such liaison in which she engages, with Gerald, quickly reveals all the symptoms the older generation suspect. This detail, incidentally, contradicts one of Lady Wilde's observations that 'their general camaraderie with the other sex is often much more allied to friendship than to love'. More seriously, Hester's morality, like that of all her Puritan sisters in Wilde's plays, is exposed as an insufficient light by which to guide her life.

> *Hester*: ... When you came into the Drawing-room this evening, somehow you brought with you a sense of what is good and pure in life ... A woman who has sinned should be punished, shouldn't she?
> *Mrs Arbuthnot*: Yes.
> *Hester*: She shouldn't be allowed to come into the society of good men and women?
> *Mrs Arbuthnot*: She should not.
> *Hester*: And the man should be punished in the same way?
> *Mrs Arbuthnot*: In the same way. And the children, if there are children, in the same way also?

Hester: Yes, it is right that the sins of the parents should be visited on the children. It is a just law. It is God's law.

Mrs Arbuthnot: It is one of God's terrible laws.

(*Moves away to fireplace*)

(Works, 499–500)

Hester may be a woman of the New World but she has inherited from her Pilgrim Mothers the ethics of the Old Testament, and Mrs Arbuthnot tests just how thoroughgoing these are. Only after she has inquired about Hester's views on the offspring of 'sinful' encounters, as if reeling off a catechism in which questions take the grammatical form of statements, does she submit, temporarily, to Gerald's departure with Illingworth. Marriage to Hester is apparently hopeless, since he is branded with his mother's shame. When this conversation takes place the audience is in full possession of the facts about Gerald's parentage and the dramatic irony of the situation manipulates the audience into rejecting Hester's unquestioning appropriation of old-fashioned moral law. Wisdom lies, after all, with Lady Hunstanton's advice to Hester that 'you mustn't believe everything that was said' (Works, 482). Just as Hester mistakes the penitential bearing of Mrs Arbuthnot to signal 'purity', so she mistakes the applicability of moral law to life. She does not command the 'relative spirit', which Wilde himself had learned to value from Pater.

Illingworth's attempted seduction of Hester triggers the melodramatic climax on which Act III concludes.

Gerald (*he is quite beside himself with rage and indignation*): Lord Illingworth, you have insulted the purest thing on God's earth, a thing as pure as my own mother ... As there is a God in Heaven, I will kill you! ...

Mrs Arbuthnot: Stop, Gerald, stop! He is your own father!

Gerald clutches his mother's hands and looks into her face. She sinks slowly on the ground in shame. Hester steals towards the door. Lord Illingworth frowns and bites his lip. After a time Gerald raises his mother up, puts his arm round her, and leads her from the room.

(Works, 503)

The assault on Hester links her inextricably with Mrs Arbuthnot as one of Illingworth's victims, and the reality behind the appearance of Mrs Arbuthnot's demeanour is revealed to her. Experience teaches the injustice of her inflexible righteousness.

Mrs Arbuthnot: ... We rank among the outcasts. Gerald is nameless. The sins of the parents should be visited on the children. It is God's law.

Hester: I was wrong. God's only law is Love.

(Works, 510)

177

It now remains for Gerald to learn that fulfilment of the letter of the law is no measure of its spirit, as he is talked out of the grotesquely funny determination to make his parents marry; there is no better illustration in Wilde's plays of his dictum that 'to be conventional is to be a comedian' (Ellmann, 349). It is, finally, Mrs Arbuthnot and not Hester who strikes Illingworth across the face with his glove, despite Mrs Allonby's jesting prediction. The conclusion of the play sketches a future for the new family – Hester, Gerald and Mrs Arbuthnot – in America. Hester will take back to the New World a chastened and more experienced spirit of forgiveness and regeneration, learned in the Old.

The character of Mrs Arbuthnot displays the features of an old world dying and a new one struggling to be born. The nature of the relationship she once entered into with her lover, and the subsequent independence with which she chose to raise the illegitimate offspring of that alliance, suggest the life-style of a 'new woman' determined to make her way alone and against all odds. This is confirmed by the self-possession with which she addresses Illingworth at the end of Act II and by her confession to Gerald that she refuses to repent of her 'sin'. 'How could I repent of my sin when you, my love, were its fruit' (Works, 508). But she also fits a quite different stereotype: that of the self-negating, guilty 'woman with a past' who conforms with the social mores that condemn her. She sets herself apart from other women by dressing in lugubrious black, making herself officially unattractive. This creates for the audience a visual statement of the kind Wilde observed in his letter to the Editor of the *Daily Telegraph* in 1891 about men's dress: 'the uniform black that is worn now, though valuable at a dinner-party, where it serves to isolate and separate women's dresses, to frame them as it were, still is dull and tedious and depressing in itself' (Letters, 283). Mrs Arbuthnot is therefore not simply distinguished from the bright display of the other women at the house-party, she also asserts certain conventionally masculine qualities of her character. She spends her days shunning society as she believes it shuns her, doing charitable work for the Church because 'God's house is the only house where sinners are made welcome' (Works, 508). Similarly there is an inscrutability about her refusal to part with Gerald. Is she possessive to the point of overriding her son's welfare for her own? Does she harbour, as some critics have suggested, an incestuous desire for him ('you were always in my heart, Gerald, too much in my heart' (Works, 508))? Or is it that she cannot bear the emotional humiliation of raising her son alone, only for him to be championed by the man she most resents? However the audience interprets her wilfulness, it is selfish. And it is therefore at odds with the prevailing Victorian view that women should be selfless servants of their maternal respons ibilities and at odds with her own hymn to motherhood and her protestation of self-denial which she delivers to Gerald in Act IV (Works, 508).

And just as there is inconsistency between Mrs Arbuthnot's behaviour at the end of Acts II and III, so there is ambiguity in her actions at the end of Act IV. She strikes Illingworth across the face with his glove as a response to his 'It's been an amusing experience to have met amongst people of one's own rank, and treated quite seriously too, one's mistress, and one's – '(Works, 514). She displays both self-assurance and self-respect here, but as soon as he has left she '(*falls sobbing on the sofa*): He would have said it. He would have said it.' What would he have said? 'Whore'? And why does she weep? In grief, or in rage, with regret or with relief? The text leaves these issues unresolved, bringing the ambiguities of her character to finely balanced rest and inviting interpretation from performance. Mrs Arbuthnot's monologues exhibit the same two faces of the new woman defying convention and the guilty one bowed down by it. When she tells Gerald why she objects to his working for Illingworth, she describes her past as though it were a kind of dystopic fairy tale: 'There was a girl once . . .' She begins dispassionately, using simple diction. But as she moves into the present tense to describe herself in the present, her discourse reverts to the ghoulishness of punitive morality: 'She is a woman who drags a chain like a guilty thing. She is a woman who wears a mask, like a thing that is a leper . . . No anodyne can give her sleep! No poppies forgetfulness! . . . She is lost' (Works, 502).

The monologue moves from compassionate contemplation of past mistakes to overwhelming expressions of self-pity and self-hatred in the present, all couched in the third person functioning both as useful disguise and accurate index of her alienated identity. The new woman cannot shed the skin of the old morality, while the conventional woman cannot tolerate the injustice of her position. To create a protagonist caught in this double bind Wilde has used a generically mixed dramatic style, which is neither melodrama nor new drama but a purposeful fusion of the two.

The third species of New Woman is represented by Mrs Allonby. She is a mistress of mendacity and evasion, who finds perfect freedom in the service of convention. She is also the mistress of Lord Illingworth, enjoying a relationship that thrives on evasion, 'infinite expectation' (Works, 482) and public display. Her challenge to him to seduce Hester is apparently as much to stimulate her own excitement as to authorise his likely waywardness. Rhetorically his match, she frequently trumps his epigrams with her own. This gives her a verbal androgyneity. Just as Wilde had argued that 'there is no such thing as a definitely feminine garment',[6] so he challenges the notion that there is such a thing as 'womanly' discourse. It is more appropriate, in these terms, to look on her as a woman of the future speaking a language that, like the apparel of the future, 'belongs equally to both sexes'. This is true of her even when she is expressing, in exclusively female company, an awareness of the social segregation between the sexes. 'We have a much better time than they have. There are far more things forbidden to us than are forbidden to them' (Works, 468). Mrs Allonby, like all of Lady Hunstanton's guests unconnected with Mrs Arbuthnot, makes no moral journey through the play. She remains manipulative and self-assured to the end, not heedful of what her lover has done to 'the Puritan' and incurring no penalty by it. Her ethical sensibility is outwardly atrophied; she is a true decadent and dandy, both trapped and liberated by her quest for 'exquisite moments' (Works, 479). But her inner life is hinted at by the malice she bears Hester and by her clear sense that some pleasures are forbidden not just by social convention but by a deeper ethical law which at their best these conventions can represent.

The social context in which these women move is fully drawn, far more so than the Society context of *Lady Windermere's Fan*. Wilde's skill in delineating the variegated inhabitants of this world is extraordinary. Each minor character presents a precisely and individually drawn face, solely through the deployment of dialogue. Two of these are purely off-stage creations: the long-suffering Mrs Kelvil, wife of the dreadfully earnest MP, Mr Kelvil, who is preparing his speech on 'the usual subject', 'Purity' (Works, 469). He is full of noble *sententiae* about the role of women in society and his wife, who has borne him eight children (Works, 473), appears, especially in her absence, to epitomise these female virtues. The second invisible wife is the ailing Mrs Daubeny, married to the Archdeacon. 'Dear Mrs Daubeny's hearing is a little defective, is it not? . . . Her deafness is a great privation to her . . . The eyesight is rapidly going. But she's never morbid, never morbid' (Works, 488). After more detailed accounts of Mrs Daubeny's moribund pastimes, the character rallies suddenly as the Archdeacon announces his departure: 'Tuesday is always one of Mrs Daubeny's bad nights' as though her illness were a convenient tool. But she flags again at her last mention, which cannot even muster grammatically complete expression, 'Lives entirely on jellies' (Works, 498). These, too, are women of 'no' importance.

Notes

1 Cited in Katherine Worth, *Oscar Wilde* (London: Macmillan, 1983) 99.
2 T. S. Eliot, *The Use of Criticism and the Use of Poetry* (London: Faber & Faber, 1933) 151.
3 Interview with Joel H. Kaplan, *Modern Drama*, 37 (1994) 198.
4 Ibid., 198.
5 Powell, 59–72.
6 *Pall Mall Gazette*, 11 November 1884.

An Ideal Husband

The knowing women of *A Woman of No Importance* had toyed with the fantasy of 'the Ideal Husband'. Mrs Allonby dismisses the notion: 'The Ideal Husband? There couldn't be such a thing. The institution is wrong' (Works, 480). Instead she teases the company with the idea of 'the Ideal Man': a lover, dandy and flirt who keeps consummation deferred and indulges every insincere posture of desire woman can manufacture. Her grounds for banishing the notion of the ideal husband from discussion stem from the radical social philosophy Wilde put forward in 'The Soul of Man Under Socialism'. There Wilde explained that the institution of marriage was founded iniquitously on ethics of ownership, possession and property, and that in an ideal communist state marriage, as the nineteenth century recognised it, would be an intolerable anachronism. In his penultimate play *An Ideal Husband*, Wilde explores the mutual folly of husband and wife in pursuing belief in ideal partnership founded more conspicuously than most on the possession of property and high social status. By making the 'ideal husband' an ambitiously successful politician, Wilde links his vision of the corrupt and corrupting institution of marriage with the more general legislative government of the State. In exposing the moral vacuum of the one he infers the bankruptcy of the other.

An Ideal Husband was commissioned by John Hare for the Garrick Theatre, but when he rejected it before the writing was completed, Wilde took the play to the Haymarket Theatre where it opened on 3 January 1895, directed by the matinée idol Lewis Waller who also played the part of the 'ideal husband', Sir Robert Chiltern. Although it received a rather cool response in the press, it was still playing to full houses in April when, on the day of Wilde's arrest for 'gross indecency', 6 April 1895, his name was removed from the advertising hoardings shortly before the production closed down altogether. The script of *An Ideal Husband* was revised by Wilde after his release from prison, and published by Leonard Smithers in 1899. Wilde thought then that it 'reads the best of all my plays' (More Letters, 181). He added unusually elaborate stage directions and introductory character notes as if to assert control over subsequent productions. This kind of detail sets the text apart from his other published plays, which are sparing in their delineation of set, character and action. Act I opens on a grand reception held at the Grosvenor Square home of Sir Robert and Lady Chiltern:

The room is brilliantly lighted and full of guests.

At the top of the staircase stands LADY CHILTERN, *a woman of grave Greek beauty, about twenty-seven years of age. She receives the guests as they come up. Over the well of the staircase hangs a great chandelier with wax lights,*

which illumine a large eighteenth-century French tapestry – representing the
Triumph of Love, from a design by Boucher – that is stretched on the staircase
wall. On the right is the entrance to the music room. The sound of a string
quartet is faintly heard. The entrance on the left leads to other reception rooms.
MRS MARCHMONT *and* LADY BASILDON, *two very pretty women, are seated*
together on a Louis Seize sofa. They are types of exquisite fragility. Their
affectation of manner has a delicate charm. Watteau would have loved to
paint them.

(Works, 515)

The references to Boucher (1703–1770) and to Watteau (1684–1721)
set the aesthetic tone of the Chilterns' home and the ambience of
the Society party taking place there. Watteau, the costumes of whose
characters were never out of the fashion pages of the ladies' papers
during the 1880s, had been the subject of an *Imaginary Portrait* by
Pater in 1887, 'A Prince of Court Painters'. He was best known as
the painter of elegant *fêtes champêtres* (on view to the London public at
exhibitions of the Hertford House Collection, later called the Wallace
Collection in Fitzrovia) in which masked characters engage in erotic
pastoral play, overlooked by sinisterly brooding statues. There is no
single work in Boucher's corpus with the title *Triumph of Love*, but
Love, either as Venus or Amour, was one of his major subjects (also
in the Hertford House collection from the 1890s), and his style is to
tease the spectator with representations of erotic desire played out
in a heavenly sphere among nude gods and goddesses. On Wilde's
set the tapestry functions in a way analogous with the ironic commentary established within Watteau's paintings by his statues. The way
in which Wilde consistently likens his characters to works of art
suggests the cultivated artifice of their behaviour. The whole composition puts into practice the vision for the expressive potential of set
design which Wilde learned from Godwin, and seems to illustrate the
principles of decorative art attributed to Whistler:

> The fundamental principles of decorative art with which Whistler
> impressed me, related to the necessity of applying scientific methods
> to the treatment of all decorative work; that to produce harmonious
> effects in line and 'colour-groupings', the whole plan or scheme
> should have to be thought out so as to be *finished* before it was
> practically begun.[1]

The character note included in the description of Mrs Cheveley on
her entrance to the ball indicates this woman's breach of the carefully established harmony of composition achieved by the Chilterns
and their guests, by describing her as 'a work of art . . . but showing
the influence of too many schools'. Aesthetic promiscuity stands in
for a multitude of conventional sins:

183

Costume sketches for An Ideal Husband *reviewed in* Queen, *12 January 1895. Mrs Cheveley's Act I ball gown is depicted lower right, showing three swallows on the back and hem*
By permission of the British Library (shelfmark: LD45)

MRS CHEVELEY . . . *is tall and rather slight. Lips very thin and highly coloured, a line of scarlet on a pallid face. Venetian red hair, aquiline nose, and long throat. Rouge accentuates the natural paleness of her complexion. Gray-green eyes that move restlessly. She is in heliotrope, with diamonds. She looks rather like an orchid, and makes great demands on one's curiosity. In all her movements she is extremely graceful. A work of art, on the whole, but showing the influence of too many schools.*

(Works, 517)

Wilde's description of her costume differs from that which the character wore in Waller's production which the *Sketch* evoked for its readers as an 'evening-dress of emerald-green satin decorated with a sextet of dead swallows'.[2] Wilde's choice of the term 'heliotrope' to describe the colour of her dress for the published text constituted a clever pun, while leaving the costume designer some freedom to choose an interpretation. Originally used to describe flowers that follow the sun, like the sunflower or marigold (just as Mrs Cheveley follows the social sun of wealth and success), 'heliotrope' also denotes a specific genus of plants with purple flowers, therefore suggesting that her dress be a kind of mauve. The word also describes a quartz, which is green and streaked with red, also known as the bloodstone, to which are attributed magic powers such as rendering the wearer invisible, just as Mrs Cheveley seeks to carry her malevolence towards Sir Robert Chiltern in such a way that only he can see it. Her threat of blackmail will expose him, and conceal her, permitting her continued indulgence in the pleasures of decadent Society.

The plot of *An Ideal Husband* turns on the exposure of discrepancies between the public role and the private reality of a distinguished politician in the Conservative Party. The pressure of high-minded public opinion, exercised by the press, threatens to topple the career of Sir Robert Chiltern, who is blackmailed by the unscrupulous Mrs Cheveley, for the corruption in which he engaged to launch his career 18 years earlier. With uncanny accuracy, the complications of the plot chart the journey into opprobrium which Wilde himself would make within four months of the opening night.

Two immediate models among the politicians of Wilde's day present themselves for the character of Sir Robert Chiltern. Sir Charles Dilke (1843–1911), a dining friend of Wilde, was the Liberal Party's Under-Secretary for Foreign Affairs from 1880 to 1882 and President of the Local Government Board from 1882 to 1885. His career came to an abrupt end in 1885 when he appeared as the co-respondent in a divorce case. A more contemporary model for the victimised public figure, who has committed a crime to which he cannot confess, was

185

the leader of the Irish campaign for Home Rule, Charles Stuart Parnell. In 1889 Parnell found himself accused of condoning political murder in an assault on his reputation spearheaded by *The Times* which printed a number of 'Parnell's' letters to prove his guilt. A public inquiry, itself the subject of much publicity, acquitted him by exposing the fact that the letters had all been forged by one Pigott. Wilde followed these proceedings carefully. He attended meetings of the inquiring commission, while his brother wrote influentially to support Parnell in the *Daily Chronicle*. The politician's tribulations did not end with acquittal; shortly afterwards he was named as the co-respondent of divorce proceedings by O'Shea, husband of Parnell's mistress. This time he could not contest the allegation and withdrew from public life. He died in 1891. In the sordid attempt to end the career of the man who seemed about to secure Home Rule for Ireland, that well-worn prop of the well-made play, the misappropriated letter, played an unfortunately crucial role. *An Ideal Husband*, itself structured according to the rules of this popular form, deploys the device unashamedly. Not once, but twice, are letters stolen by the greedy Mrs Cheveley, who forges not these but her own reputation. And the threat posed to Chiltern by her use of the letters would first topple him by means of political scandal; that failing, it would compromise the sanctity of his marriage.

Structurally, *An Ideal Husband* is a formulaic well-made play. The four Act drama unfolds in an orderly fashion, beginning with exposition through Society gossip, moving to the 'complication' when the woman with a past turns up, building to the climactic *scène à faire* in Lord Goring's rooms where misunderstanding and malevolence peak, before settling it all in a dénouement that restores the political and domestic *status quo*. Sir Robert Chiltern's career and his marriage are not just saved but enhanced by the end of the play; the wicked woman, Mrs Cheveley, has been hounded out; the dandy, philosopher and *raisonneur* Lord Goring, is to be married into the fold. What could be more reactionary? What better justification for Shaw's dismissal of the form as 'Sardooledum'? But the terms on which resolution is based are in fact radical, pointing to far-reaching social and moral change, while the exaggerated manner in which Wilde fulfils the demands of the well-made play suggests a burlesque of the very form deployed.

The moral centre of the play is voiced by Lord Goring, the dandy who is given added authority by the character notes which emphasise his attention to the decorum of dress. Wilde goes so far as to equip the character with his own Inverness cape and Louis Seize cane. At the start of Act III the dandy enters:

in evening dress with a buttonhole. He is wearing a silk hat and Inverness cape. White-gloved, he carries a Louis Seize cane. His are all the delicate fopperies of Fashion. One sees that he stands in immediate relation to modern life, makes it indeed, and so masters it. He is the first well-dressed philosopher in the history of thought.

(Works, 553)

Lord Goring is a stage version of the author. Wilde had claimed for himself in 'De Profundis', written before these stage directions, that 'I stood in symbolic relation to art and culture of my age'. Revising the play for publication, he invests Lord Goring with the same 'symbolic relation'. In Act II, seeing crisis approaching, Lord Goring promises help to Lady Chiltern:

All I do know is that life cannot be understood without much charity, cannot be lived without much charity. It is love, and not German Philosophy, that is the true explanation of this world, whatever may be the explanation of the next. And if you are ever in trouble, Lady Chiltern, trust me absolutely, and I will help you in every way I can. If you ever want me, come to me for my assistance, and you shall have it. Come at once to me.

(Works, 543)

The speech makes sense of the subject of Boucher's *Triumph of Love*, the fictional backdrop for Act I which Wilde was careful to evoke, and which in its opening context had seemed to represent simply a display of opulence and fashionable taste. Lord Goring's words ironise the setting, pointing up a deeper significance of the tapestry, unperceived by the party guests. He utters the speech without selfish motive, unlike its echo by Sir Robert Chiltern when he begs for his wife's unconditional affection: 'All lives, save loveless lives, true Love should pardon' (Works, 552). Chiltern's speech has been prepared for by what Lord Goring had previously said, and while the politician's desperate plea to save his marriage is the crux of the drama, it exposes him as still too deeply flawed and ignorant of the real import of what he says to function as the moral core of the play. Lord Goring's earlier speech drops the dandy's mask, in order to reveal a Christ figure beneath. 'Love your neighbour like yourself'; 'Come unto me those who are weary and heavy laden and I will give you rest' are the *dicta* of the Gospels which he puts into action.

Goring's exchange with Lady Chiltern is a sentimental moment, the claims sound grandiose. But Wilde toys with the lapse in tone, turning it to his purposes in a number of ways. The first is immediately to undercut the speech with pragmatism, for Lady Chiltern's response is that it is a pleasant surprise to hear Lord Goring talk out of character, with seriousness and sincerity. This sweeps emotion aside, while it signals the importance of the speech to the audience. The second means of undercutting while underscoring what Lord Goring says is the twist in the plot that arises as a result of his offer. Lady Chiltern, discovering how things really stand with her husband, writes the ambiguous letter to Lord Goring announcing her arrival, but then it is stolen for further blackmail purposes by Mrs Cheveley. While the involvement of the gospel of charity in a smear campaign seems reductive, the fate of Lady Chiltern's 'I trust you. I want you. I am coming to you' (Works, 558) at least keeps Lord Goring's role as Christian sanctuary firmly in the audience's mind. And this is important because, in human terms, he turns out to have promised Lady Chiltern neither more nor less than he can deliver. Having proof of Mrs Cheveley's felonious past in his possession in the shape of the ruby and diamond brooch, he knew, when he uttered his words of succour to Lady Chiltern, that he could, if necessary, bring the adventuress down. Paradoxically a thorough-going assent to the doctrine of charity would equally prevent him from doing just that. And it nearly does, for when in the final moments of the play Sir Robert forbids Lord Goring's marriage to Mabel on the grounds that he is having an affair with Mrs Cheveley, the dandy withdraws his request: 'I have nothing more to say' (Works, 581). Only Lady Chiltern can intervene to 'explain' appearances. Lord Goring himself would sacrifice his own needs rather than disrupt the delicate harmony between the Chilterns. He emerges as the ideal husband. Lady Chiltern's final line of the play, 'Love, and only love. For both of us a new life is beginning' (Works, 582) signals how the formulaic resolution of the play depends rather on an evolution of moral sentiment than the restoration of existing positions.

Wilde refashions New Testament philosophy to make it an appropriate instrument for the dandy. In 'The Soul of Man Under Socialism' he had represented Christ as a dandy, an individualist who preached: 'Don't imagine that your perfection lies in accumulating or possessing external things. Your [perfection] is inside of you . . . In the treasury-house of your soul, there are infinitely precious things, that may not be taken from you' (Works, 1180). In *An Ideal Husband* he represents the dandy as Christ, at the heart of whose preaching is forgiveness and moral generosity, a New Law to replace the Old. With it will come freedom from hypocrisy, freedom from double moral standards and freedom from the other evils of property-based morality that Wilde, no less than his fellow playwrights Ibsen and, later, Shaw, battled against. Even Lady Chiltern, whose writing has '[t]he ten commandments in every stroke of the pen' (Works, 558), must learn a new hand. When Sir Robert informs Lord Goring that 'every man of ambition has to fight his century with its own weapons' and that the god of this century is 'wealth', he reveals his weakness (Works, 536). Compelling though Chiltern's assertion is, and long though the radical Victorian sages such as Carlyle, Ruskin and Morris had been disputing prevailing capitalist ethics, in being of the times he is behind the times, at least according to the values that lie implicit in the convolutions and convulsions of the plot of *An Ideal Husband*.

Love, not wealth, is the god Wilde promotes. The plot turning on the thoroughly contemporary exercise of power by the media ('the tyranny of the weak over the strong'), illustrates how intimately power is dependent not on wealth, but on knowledge. Wilde, having constructed his own fame and arranged his own ascent in the 1880s by manipulating newspaper reporting and society gossip – continuing to control this form of broadcast by holding interviews – knew well how little money had to do with power. Equally, having watched how seriously Parnell was damaged by press allegations, only to withdraw without even attempting a fight when the accusation was true, Wilde knew that the press could make or break a career. It is Mrs Cheveley, in Act I, who points this out to Sir Robert, in a line which clinches her efforts at blackmail: 'Even you are not rich enough, Sir Robert, to buy back your past. No man is' (Works, 529). In possessing the secret of his past, in having intimate knowledge about him, she effectively disempowers the MP:

> Remember to what a point your Puritanism in England has brought you . . . Nowadays, with our modern mania for morality, everyone has to pose as a paragon of purity . . . the result? You all go over like ninepins . . . Not a year passes in England without somebody disappearing . . . Sir Robert, you know what your English newspapers are like.
>
> (Works, 528–9)

Mrs Cheveley is the enemy, her weapon is the press and her aim is to control the business of the House of Commons. No mean ambition for a woman in a heliotrope dress wearing too much rouge. After his first encounter with this woman, at no point in the play is Sir Robert ever in possession of sufficient or accurate information to recover his initial status. Furthermore, he misinterprets events because he is only partially informed. Discovering Mrs Cheveley at Goring's rooms, he wrongly concludes that the two are conspiring against him; receiving the letter Mrs Cheveley redirected from Goring, he assumes it is a love letter to himself. The first of these incidents heightens the climactic passion of the *scène à faire*, while the second frustrates audience expectations and creates an anti-climactic effect, comic at Sir Robert's self-preoccupied expense, and deferring the dénouement.

He is beholden to Lord Goring for divesting Mrs Cheveley of the letter which threatens his career, and Goring achieves this because he knows more about her past than she anticipates. Ultimately Wilde handles the link between knowledge and power to confirm the Christian doctrine that to know everything is to forgive everything. And from forgiveness follows the triumph of love.

The audience is placed throughout in a position of superior knowledge, and therefore moral power to judge, by the liberal use of dramatic irony. We are constantly better informed of circumstances than all characters in the play except Lord Goring who possesses the secret of the diamond brooch. The plot encourages the audience to suspend judgement and condemnation and, instead, to exercise charity. In a magnificent set piece, Mrs Cheveley is trapped by her own past. A wonderful reversal, brought about by the *deus ex machina* Lord Goring, indicates that even she is not knowledgeable enough to control how her past will affect her future. On her entry to Lord Goring's rooms in Act III she is transformed from a ruthlessly opportunist dandy to a stereotyped villain as she creeps about, stealing and eavesdropping, before she is trapped in the bracelet. Powerless to remove it from her arm because she does not know how the clasp works, anger renders her inarticulate and she loses every shred of poise. The 'Lamia'-like bracelet is both the insignia and fetter of the *femme fatale*. She is forced to leave Lord Goring's rooms wearing evidence of her theft which is equally evidence of the life she has led. The expression of her character in Act III is constructed visually, contrasting strongly with the verbal articulations of her character in Act 1 which had lent her an androgynous quality despite her dress. Lord Goring, the real dandy, fights the god of the present with the god of the future. He fights wealth with knowledge linked to love – and he wins.

Lord Goring's particular victory in the play is the reassembly of the Chilterns' marriage and the maintenance of his friend's political career. He achieves this by using his wisdom as a means to an end, not always telling the truth, but dispensing contingent 'truths' according to the lights of his interlocutor. This is the situation when he encourages Lady Chiltern to forgive her husband, and to support him in his newly offered cabinet seat, rather than requiring of him the absolute renunciation of public life. The terms in which he puts the course of future events to Lady Chiltern are fashioned for her character, its strengths and weaknesses, and not as absolute social truths. He tells her:

> A man's life is of more value than a woman's. It has larger issues, wider scope, greater ambitions. A woman's life revolves in curves of emotions. It is upon lines of intellect that a man's life progresses.

Don't make any terrible mistake, Lady Chiltern. A woman who can keep a man's love, and love him in return, has done all the world wants of women, or should want of them.

(Works, 579)

His words are lent apparent authority by their extra-textual resemblance to Ruskin's account of the separate nature of men's and women's lives in *Sesame and Lilies* (1865). But Lord Goring offers this to Lady Chiltern as a way of securing the development of her 'personality', the fulfilment of self, that is the basis of Wilde's philosophy in 'The Soul of Man Under Socialism'. Sir Robert will only be fulfilled by a career in politics and Lady Chiltern will be fulfilled through a life of loving support. Neither partner will find happiness, or exercise self-development in the punitive future she proposes. For this reason Lord Goring modifies his political and philosophical beliefs – at least as Wilde expresses them elsewhere – and offers Lady Chiltern a 'truth' on which to anchor her life and by which to justify her actions. By the end of the play the audience, granted plenary vision, can judge the worth of a 'relative spirit' in ethics and the gospel of charity it supports.

Notes

1 Letter from Lady Archibald Campbell to E. R. Pennell and J. Pennell, *The Life of Whistler* (London: W. Heinemann, 1908) 222.
2 *Sketch*, 9 January 1895.

The Importance of Being Earnest

'It must be like a pistol shot' Wilde stated about the playing style of his only farce and most famous play (Mikhail, II, 269): the success of *The Importance of Being Earnest* continues to be informed by surprise, resonance and, above all, consummate marksmanship both in the timing of comic delivery and in hitting the targets of its social satire. The first production opened at the St James's Theatre on 14 February 1895 with George Alexander, the actor-manager, in the role of Jack Worthing. 'What sort of play are we to expect?' asked Robert Ross of Wilde: 'It is exquisitely trivial, a delicate bubble of fancy, and it has its philosophy ... That we should treat all the trivial things of life very seriously, and all the serious things with sincere and studied triviality' (Mikhail, I, 250).

Just as Wilde had manipulated the form of the well-made play to suit innovatory practice in his earlier society comedies, so with *The Importance of Being Earnest* he adapts the popular genre of farce to find theatrical expression for the subversive philosophy previously stated in the critical dialogues. Arthur Wing Pinero was the reigning London master of farce, with his commercial successes *The Magistrate* (1885), *The Schoolmistress* (1886) and *Dandy Dick* (1887). Brandon Thomas' *Charley's Aunt* (1892) also enjoyed conspicuous success with this form, as had W. S. Gilbert's *Engaged* (1877). A host of forgotten Victorian farces have been discussed by Kerry Powell to elucidate Wilde's deployment of the genre and its contemporary kinships.[1] These dramatists had used the complexity of fast-moving plot and a succession of unlikely coincidences, accidents and lost identities for the construction of their farces, to which Pinero in particular had added detailed character portraiture as a source of humour. *The Magistrate*, for example, plunges the protagonist into a sequence of compromising situations that derive comic piquancy from his respectable social status. But the resolution of the plot simply restores characters to an orderly middle-class existence, temporarily disrupted by saturnalia. Although governesses and reverends feature in *The Importance of Being Earnest*, Wilde represents an aristocratic society rather than the middle class, and the play neither begins nor ends with respectability or obvious order. Wilde's characters are not, ultimately, compromised by what others know about them, but by what they discover about themselves. While the plots of his earlier comedies had turned on a central character seeking to evade an overwhelming past, here the plot muses on what happens when a character without a past rushes to embrace one. Inverting the traditional values of 'the serious' and 'the trivial', Wilde makes farce into an instrument for political subversion and sets the tone for the way this genre would be deployed by twentieth-century exponents such as Dario Fo and Joe

Orton. In adopting this form, Wilde was availing himself of the 'very great freedom' permitted by censorship laws and an indulgent public to 'work produced under burlesque or farcical conditions' which he had noted in 'The Soul of Man Under Socialism' (Works, 1185).

Wilde did not publish the text of the play until 1899, after he had lost all his possessions, including manuscripts, in the course of his conviction and bankruptcy in 1895. To recover the script of *The Importance of Being Earnest*, he sent for Alexander's acting copy, from the St James's Theatre, and entered his revisions on this, which the printer for the publisher Leonard Smithers copied. Unlike his preparation of the text of *An Ideal Husband*, Wilde kept his stage directions and character notes to a minimum. Other drafts of the play did survive, and the consequence of this is that the script of the play is notoriously variable and unstable. Later editors have drawn alternative scenarios into the script and its scholarly annotations.

The first scenario for *The Importance of Being Earnest* was sketched by Wilde in a letter to Alexander in July 1894. 'The real charm of the play . . . must be in the dialogue. The plot is slight, but, I think, adequate' (Letters, 359). He aims for an 'amusing thing with lots of fun and wit'. By September 1894 he had finished the first draft, which had a four-Act structure and the working title 'Lady Lancing'. Writing again to Alexander from The Esplanade, Worthing, where he had rented accommodation for the summer, Wilde referred to the play as a 'farcical comedy', with dialogue of 'sheer comedy . . . the best I have ever written'. Although in the same letter Wilde states that 'I would like to have my play done by you,' and clearly had Alexander in mind as the performer of either male lead '(I must tell you candidly that the two young men's parts are equally good)' (Letters, 369), later that year it was accepted for production at the Criterion Theatre by Charles Wyndham. It was only the spectacular failure of Henry James' play *Guy Domville* at the St James's Theatre in January 1895 that made Wilde retrieve the play from Wyndham so that Alexander could have something new to put into production after the early closure of *Guy Domville*. There then began extensive and delicate negotiation between author and manager about the tailoring of the script for performance. Just as Alexander had influence over the script of *Lady Windermere's Fan*, so again his editorial and managerial skills helped to fashion the script of the play which has come down to us. The major alteration Alexander insisted on was the change from four Acts to three, setting Wilde's work in line with the three-Act structure of farce then traditional for the genre. This involved the conflation of Acts II and III and, in the process, what is now known as the 'Gribsby' episode was cut.

The elimination of this scene shows how Alexander was tightening the structure of the plot by excising diversions. The 'Gribsby'

episode concerns the arrival of a solicitor (Gribsby) at Jack's Hert-
fordshire house to arrest 'Mr Ernest Worthing' for unpaid supper
bills at the Savoy, amounting to the fantastic sum of £762.14.2.
(Works, 385). The confusion over who is answerable extends the
farce since both men have assumed the same cognomen. Jack is
Ernest Worthing in town and Algy has just introduced himself to
Cecily as Jack's brother Ernest. Gribsby's threatened removal of
Ernest Worthing (taken by all except Algy to be himself) to Holloway
Prison throws a further impediment in the way of Cecily's engagement to him. Finally, after Jack has agreed to pay the bill for his
'brother' (the net tightening around their real family relationship
(Works, 387)), although the two men and the audience know that the
debt is his own, Wilde pulls off a coup that toys with the numerous
false doubles on which the plot depends. The solicitor's card had
announced 'Parker and Gribsby, Solicitors'; it emerges that they are
one and the same individual, 'Gribsby when I am on unpleasant
business, Parker on occasions of a less severe kind'.[2] Wilde's purpose
in writing the scene at all was to amplify the themes of the play.
Appetite, identity, propriety and extravagance are all foregrounded
by the episode, and the dialogue is as insouciantly comic here as
elsewhere in the play. He eventually gave way to the call for cuts
and the result is a play with clear, precise lines of plot development
and a little less diverting dialogue than Wilde envisaged.[3]

As Wilde stated at the very start of composition, the plot is 'slight'.
Two men fall in love with two women and, after various impediments to the happy conclusion are overcome, their marriages are
announced. Wilde throws in a third marriage, between Miss Prism
and Canon Chasuble, for good measure. Only Lady Bracknell, the
outsider and major source of impediment, remains unchanged by
events. The complications in the plot concern the nature of the
difficulties that must be overcome before the matches can be made.
Both men, Jack and Algernon, have invented *alter egos* to facilitate
their social mobility. Jack Worthing, whose home is in the country,
goes under the name of Ernest in town and has informed his household that he is constantly called away in order to help his notorious
'brother'. Algernon Moncrieff has invented an ailing relative,
Bunbury, whose invalidity requires frequent attention, so insuring
his unquestioned departure to the country. When Jack, known as
Ernest, proposes to Algernon's cousin Gwendolen, Algernon takes
advantage of Jack's alias to visit Jack's ward, Cecily. Suddenly there
are two men masquerading as Ernest Worthing and two women
determined to marry a man called Ernest. The proliferation of
'Ernests' coincides with Jack's decision to kill off his fictitious brother.
Wilde's trick is to have devised an absurd plot in which, as he
argued in 'The Decay of Lying', life comes to imitate art. Not only

has Cecily been conducting a fictitious affair with 'Ernest Worthing' in her diary, which Algernon's appearance under this name seems simply to consummate, but both men find themselves encumbered with the brother they thought they never had in the shape of each other, as it emerges finally that Jack – not Worthing but Moncrieff – really was christened Ernest before Miss Prism lost him in her handbag.

There are many sources, ancient and contemporary, that may have served Wilde in the construction of this plot. But from Shakespeare's *Comedy of Errors* and *Twelfth Night*, to *The Foundling* (1894) by W. Lestocq and E. M. Robertson, the protagonists who lose and then recover their identities do not find that their own artful plot-making is simply a replication of a 'real-life' plot which finally traps them. The interchangeable relationship between fact and fiction is Wilde's unique contribution to the literary history of reunited siblings and lost identities. One hitherto overlooked source, a magazine story from the *Woman's World*, 'A Christmas Comedy' by Miles Bradford (January 1887) which Wilde would have read in preparation for his innovatory editorship of the journal, comes close to Wilde's use of 'fiction' to solve the mounting problems of 'fact'. It also illustrates Victorian sentiment for family reunions which Wilde burlesques in the play. There are two brothers: Donald betrothed to Nora, and David to Frances. The brothers become separated on their way to a house-party. David gets lost and Donald, arriving first, is mistaken for his brother and deliberately assumes his identity. He proposes that the company play a charade, based on an Eastern story about the magic transformation of one brother into the shape of his banished brother. Just as the charade has reached the moment at which the banished brother returns, David walks into the room. Not realising that he has walked into a play, Nora addresses her rehearsed lines to him which exactly fit his real situation, 'I had begun to think you would not come':

> Seeing that the crisis had come, Donald came from his hiding-place.
> 'My friends,' said Donald, 'allow me to finish the play. The wanderer has returned, and, instead of supplanting his brother, he is only too happy to explain that he is but an impostor.'
> 'Donald!' cried David, in a stentorian voice, and the two brothers clasped hands.

Here fiction anticipates fact and life resembles art. 'Life is Art's best, Art's only pupil', as Wilde stated in 'The Decay of Lying' (*Works*, 1083) and as he illustrated in *The Importance of Being Earnest* by concealing one fiction about 'Ernest' within another and finally revealing all. He puts a new spin on the dictum from *A Woman of No Importance*:

it is perfectly monstrous 'that people go about saying things behind one's back which are absolutely true'. The major and compelling source for his last play is the collective body of Wilde's previous work.

The political targets of the farce are manifold, but they centre on the exposure of the moral bankruptcy of the rules governing Society. Instead of addressing this question by an engagement in political argument, as he did in 'The Soul of Man Under Socialism', Wilde adopts an indirect method of attack. In the drama he caricatures the rules of social etiquette by depicting characters so harnessed by the inflexibility of the system that their attempts both to fulfil the requirements of propriety and to depart from them result in deception ('Bunburying'), self-deception (Cecily and her diary), tyranny (Lady Bracknell) and aggression (Cecily and Gwendolen at tea). '[T]he canons of good society are, or should be, the same as the canons of art. Form is absolutely essential to it. It should have the dignity of a ceremony, as well as its unreality,' Wilde had written in *The Picture of Dorian Gray* (Works, 107). Throughout his career as a journalist – and indeed throughout his celebrated circulation in the houses of the great – Wilde had ample opportunity to gauge the dignity of social ceremony and measure what dictated it. The play itself has the perfection of form which the rules of Society fell short of establishing.

Marriage is the driving motive of the plot. It is first mentioned in the exposition between Algernon and Lane, his butler:

> *Algernon*: Why is it that at a bachelor's establishment the servants invariably drink the champagne? I ask merely for information.
> *Lane*: I attribute it to the superior quality of the wine, sir. I have often observed that in married households the champagne is rarely of a first-rate brand.
> *Algernon*: Good heavens! Is marriage so demoralizing as that?
> *Lane*: I believe it *is* a very pleasant state, sir . . .
>
> (Works, 357)

Algernon conflates two meanings of the word 'demoralizing', using it to indicate both 'morale sapping' and 'morally corrupting'. Both invert the values traditionally associated with marriage. Lane's rejoinder picks up Algernon's second meaning – but instead of rejecting corruption he assents to it, asserting his superiority over the system of moral values of those he serves. The marriage market of the Season had been a constant subject of satire in Wilde's earlier comedies; with this play he turns satire into mirth.

But it is hilarity which accommodates all the serious utterances Wilde had previously made about marriage. Under the headline 'A Handbook to Marriage' he had reviewed a book in 1885 called *How To Be Happy Though Married. Being a Handbook to Marriage. By a Graduate in the University of Matrimony*. 'In spite of its somewhat alarming title this book may be highly recommended to every one . . . In our day it is best for a man to be married, and men must give up the tyranny in married life which was once so dear to them' (Works, 957). Politically correct, Wilde is acknowledging the influence on married life of the higher education of women (Cambridge University opened its doors to women in 1869), and the legislative effects of the Married Woman's Property Act of 1882. But by the time he came to write 'The Soul of Man Under Socialism' his views on marriage had become radically subversive, precisely because he observed how deeply the institution was embroiled in property and commerce. 'With the abolition of private property, marriage in its present form must disappear,' he stated, having noted how 'demoralizing' is 'the industry necessary for the making of money' (Works, 1181, 1178). The term 'demoralizing' echoes through the essay, as Wilde discovers again and again institutions which sap the spirit of the individual and foster ethical corruption.

In *The Importance of Being Earnest* Lady Bracknell is erected as the monstrous pillar of institutionalised vice ('When I married Lord Bracknell I had no fortune of any kind. But I never dreamed for a moment of allowing that to stand in my way' (Works, 409)), aghast at the prospect that her daughter might 'marry into a cloak-room, and form an alliance with a parcel' (Works, 370). She is also determined to prohibit the marriage of her nephew Algernon to Cecily Cardew until she learns that the girl has 'a hundred and thirty thousand pounds! And in the Funds!' (Works, 409). Jack uses this as a bargaining tool. 'The moment you consent to my marriage with Gwendolen, I will most gladly allow your nephew to form an alliance with my ward' (Works, 412). But Lady Bracknell will not be bought so readily. Only when Miss Prism arrives, and Jack's lineage attains familial respectability, can the comedy move to its formal resolution: marriage.

Much of the stage business of the comedy is occupied with activities of polite hospitality. Act I begins with the preparation of tea with cucumber sandwiches for Lady Bracknell and ends with the two men drinking sherry together. The confusions of Act II peak at the table, when Cecily and Gwendolen, competing for 'Ernest', must accommodate their hostilities to the taking of tea and cake; the curtain falls on the two men eating muffins with Algernon's line 'I haven't quite finished my tea yet! and there is still one muffin left' (Works, 405). The Victorians had strict codes for how social visits were to be made, cards left, and for how tea was to be served and consumed. There were numerous handbooks on etiquette and the problem pages of the ladies' papers were crowded with questions about how to deal with social niceties. An article by Lucie Armstrong in the *Woman's World* (September 1890), 'Persistent Delusions in

Etiquette', set out to deal with these questions firmly, announcing 'It is extraordinary to find how long a custom will continue amongst the middle classes after the upper classes have altogether given it up.'

Wilde inverts this at the start of the play with Algernon's lines 'if the lower orders don't set us a good example, what on earth is the use of them? They seem, as a class, to have absolutely no sense of moral responsibility' (Works, 358). Alternatively, *Cassell's Domestic Dictionary: An Encyclopaedia for the Household* ([1877–79]) is filled with advice about how to manage every domestic occasion. 'It is scarcely possible to be too particular in laying a table . . . The tea is brought into the drawing-room, placed on a small table over which an em-broidered white cloth is previously laid, and brought in front of the hostess. If visitors are in the room they are invited to partake. It is not usual to take a second cup at this tea'.[4] Just as such handbooks can today offer information on the acting style of the play, so Wilde's first audience would have recognised how Algernon and Jack persist-ently breach the codes of convention, and how polite constraint is exploited by Cecily as the hostess of Gwendolen's undrinkably sugared tea in their battle for possession.

The way in which such prescription tends to exert a levelling influence on behaviour, manufacturing a uniform social surface, is caricatured by Wilde, both in the farcical duplication of 'Ernest', character and situation, and in the way the four lovers seek to extricate themselves from the predicament. At the start of Act III the women, having discovered that there are two men to be had, if not two Ernests, form an instant sisterly alliance in the face of gross duplicity by their lovers. The men also offer a united front against feminine outrage. They enter 'arm in arm', and Wilde's stage direction in an early draft indicates just how united the men had become:

> *Jack and Algy both move together like Siamese twins in every movement until both say 'christened this afternoon'. First to front of sofa, then fold hands together, then raise eyes to ceiling, then sit on sofa, unfold hands, lean back, tilting up legs with both feet off the ground, then twitch trousers above knee à la dude, so as not to crease them, then both feet on ground, fold hands together, on knee and look perfectly unconcerned.*[5]

This dance-like business was designed to overlap with the decision by Cecily and Gwendolen to 'speak at the same time':

> *Gwendolen beats time with uplifted finger*
> *Gwendolen and Cecily (speaking together):* Your Christian names are still an insuperable barrier. That is all!
> *Jack and Algernon (speaking together):* Our Christian names! Is that all? But we are going to be christened this afternoon.
>
> (Works, 406)

Wilde cut the stage direction from later drafts, and Alexander's acting copy retained only the first clause, deleting everything after 'movement'. The sheer pleasure in visually created mirth still retains a serious political motivation: to ridicule the veneer of manners concealing moral atrophy. George Bernard Shaw, reviewing the production, was one of the few critics who had not enjoyed his evening at the theatre because he found himself overwhelmed by 'miserable mechanical laughter' (Critical Heritage, 195). If his laughter was mechanical, it was because Wilde was burlesquing the effects of inflexible codes of decorum that automate rather than vivify its adherents.

The comic climax of the play is the scene in Act II when Jack enters dressed in mourning to announce the death of his brother, Ernest, ignorant of the fact that Algernon, masquerading as Ernest, has just entered the house with Cecily. '*Enter* JACK *slowly from the back of the garden. He is dressed in the deepest mourning, with crêpe hatband and black gloves*' (Works, 380).

> *Chasuble*: Mr. Worthing, I trust this garb of woe does not betoken some terrible calamity?
> *Jack*: My brother.
> *Miss Prism*: More shameful debts and extravagance?
> *Chasuble*: Still leading his life of pleasure?
> *Jack* (*shaking his head*): Dead!
> *Chasuble*: Your brother Ernest dead?
> *Jack*: Quite dead.
> *Miss Prism*: What a lesson for him! I trust he will profit by it.
>
> (Works, 381)

Here too Wilde was mocking the elaborately codified behaviour of the Victorian response to death. Jack, haloed in dramatic irony, illustrates the fact that for many families 'the sense of loss is almost overlooked and forgotten in questions of millinery and trimmings', as the author of 'Mourning Clothes and Customs' in the *Woman's World* for June 1889 warned. Like everything else in *The Importance of Being Earnest*, the joke is double. Not only does Jack's display of grief relate to a figment, and therefore emphasises the theatricality of Victorian mourning practice, but the audience also knows that within minutes his ruse will be tumbled by the entrance of another masquerader. 'And how they laughed, when dignified George Alexander arrived on the stage in the deepest mourning,' Ada Leverson remembers about the first night (Mikhail, II, 269). William Archer, reviewing the production, described how the comedy was achieved:

> Monsieur Sarcey himself (if Mr. Wilde will forgive my saying so) would 'chortle in his joy' over John Worthing's entrance in deep

Jack (George Alexander) announces the 'death' of his brother to Miss Prism (Alice Beet) and Canon Chasuble (Vivian Reynolds) in The Importance of Being Earnest, *St James's Theatre, London, 1909, from* Playgoer and Society Illustrated, *Vol. 11, p. 207 (1909) By permission of the British Library (shelfmark: PP5224AB)*

mourning even down to his cane to announce the death of his brother Ernest, when we know that Ernest in the flesh – a false but undeniable Ernest – is at that moment in the house making love to Cecily. The audience does not instantly awaken to the meaning of his inky suit, but even as he marches solemnly down the stage before a word is spoken, you can feel the idea kindling from row to row, until a 'sudden glory' of laughter fills the theatre.

(Critical Heritage, 190)

Alexander was clearly not to be hurried into dialogue, allowing hilarious lugubriety to fill the silence in anticipation of the explanations to follow. 'Dead!', and then absurdly intensified, 'Quite dead'. It is met with the nonsense of censoriousness from Miss Prism, illustrating the tenacious myopia of her moral creed, and the lazy accommodations of Canon Chasuble's versatile sermon.

The resolution of the farce parodies conventional scenes of family reunion. Lady Bracknell's role as the director of proceedings, which hitherto everyone had sought to evade, is transfigured to that of *raisonneur* and *deus ex machina*. Only she can recognise the Prism of former years and demand an explanation for the unfinished business between them. Only she can point to the source which reveals Jack's magic Christian name and restore his identity. This conventionally 'happy' ending contains a further parodic twist, for although 'The good ended happily, and the bad unhappily. That is what Fiction means' (Works, 376), as Governess Prism had instructed Cecily, the criteria by which any of the characters can be termed 'good' remain elusive:

Lady Bracknell: . . . Prism! Where is that baby? . . .
Miss Prism: . . . In a moment of mental abstraction, for which I never can forgive myself, I deposited the manuscript in the basinette, and placed the baby in the handbag.

(Works, 413).

The confusion of baby with manuscript is a laughing allusion to Ibsen's *Hedda Gabler* in which the manuscript of Lovborg's great work is more valuable to Hedda than her own unborn child – and consistently likened to a child throughout the play. But aside from this glancing reference, Wilde is also toying with meta-fiction in the creation of his own yarn, illustrating again that Life imitates Art. The lost baby (frozen in time in the imaginations of Lady Bracknell and Miss Prism) grew up without knowledge of the parentage which so crucially informs his identity. ' "Who is my mother? Who are my brothers?" ' Wilde quotes his idealised Jesus in 'The Soul of Man Under Socialism' (Works, 1181). Not only was Jack's growing-up constructed along fabricated lines, according to the family which took him in, but he also constructed a further fictional identity for himself which replicated the 'true' state of affairs more closely than he could guess. The life of Jack Worthing and his *alter ego* turn out to have been like the work of fiction which Miss Prism authored, therefore appropriately mistaking one for the other. The whole emphasis on lineage as the only indicator of identity and social worth (Jack Worthing's last name is not accidental and could not be replaced by Margate or any other seaside resort favoured by farces of the period), mocks at the exaggerated Victorian respect for breeding and the appeal to heredity for scientific explanation throughout the nineteenth century.

The light-hearted treatment of issues which Wilde had investigated so seriously in previous work is characteristic of the play and he takes the opportunity to parody his own work as much as that of others. When Jack gives the missing handbag back to the delighted Miss Prism, he jumps to the conclusion that she must be his mother:

> *Jack*: Unmarried! I do not deny that is a serious blow. But after all, who has the right to cast a stone against one who has suffered? Cannot repentance wipe out an act of folly? Why should there be one law for men, and another for women? Mother, I forgive you. (*Tries to embrace her again.*)
>
> (Works, 415)

This speech, and the lightening speed at which it moves, is a pastiche not simply on Victorian literary convention, but also on Wilde's own ponderous treatment of the same theme in *A Woman of No Importance*. The puritan Hester moralises 'Set a mark, if you wish, on each, but don't punish the one and let the other go free. Don't have one law for men and another for women' (Works, 483); and the behaviour of the illegitimate Gerald could not be more different from Jack's. One newspaper parody of *A Woman of No Importance* had made a lame attempt at what Wilde achieves in his last play:

> Wilde: Several plays have been written lately that deal with the monstrous injustice of the social code of morality at the present time. It is indeed a burning shame that there should be one law for men and another law for women. I think that there should be no law for anybody.[6]

The heavy-handed reference to Wilde's anarchist politics ('The form of government that is most suitable to the artist is no government at all', Works, 1192), falls far short of its celebration in *The Importance of Being Earnest*.

Reference to Wilde's revolutionary sympathies are scattered through the play, embodied principally by Lady Bracknell's hostility.

As the valkyrie guardian of the foundations of aristocratic mores, she interviews Jack about his eligibility for her daughter's hand. In the course of this she voices fierce rejection of social change: 'The whole theory of modern education is radically unsound. Fortunately in England, at any rate, education produces no effect whatsoever. If it did, it would prove a serious danger to the upper classes, and probably lead to acts of violence in Grosvenor Square' (Works, 368). Here Wilde alludes to contemporary agitation for change, which had indeed deployed a bombing campaign in the heart of London. Those with the most to lose – the upper class – were the fiercest enemies. Inveighing against Jack's contemptible parentage, Lady Bracknell reaches for an historical analogy: 'To be born, or at any rate bred, in a handbag, whether it had handles or not, seems to me to display a contempt for the ordinary decencies of family life that reminds one of the worst excesses of the French Revolution. And I presume you know what that unfortunate movement led to?' (Works, 369–70).

'Liberty, Equality, Fraternity' could serve as a caption for the final tableau of the play. But Wilde had expressed himself seriously on the subject of the French Revolution in 'The Soul of Man Under Socialism':

> The only thing that one really knows about human nature is that it changes. Change is the one quality we can predict of it. The systems that fail are those that rely on the permanency of human nature, and not on its growth and development. The error of Louis XIV was that he thought human nature would always be the same. The result of his error was the French Revolution. It was an admirable result.
>
> (Works, 1194)

Lady Bracknell, a newcomer to the most privileged class when she married, is the epitome of inflexibility, and its representative in the upper classes. As Jack says after his introductory interrogation by her, 'she is a monster, without being a myth' (Works, 370), underlining the lively danger to civilisation represented by her politics while heralding her as an emblem of a failing system. In the course of this interview Jack's politics are scrutinised:

> *Lady Bracknell*: . . . What are your politics?
> *Jack*: Well, I am afraid I really have none. I am a Liberal Unionist.
> *Lady Bracknell*: Oh, they count as Tories. They dine with us. Or come in the evening, at any rate.
>
> (Works, 369)

Jack names the Liberal Unionists to indicate an indifference to political affairs, but for Wilde the power held by this group was of vital concern. They were Liberals who splintered from Gladstone's Party in 1886 in order to vote against his Bill to introduce Home Rule for Ireland. They therefore voted with the Conservative opposition and helped to bring down Gladstone's parliament as well as frustrating the efforts to bring about what Wilde viewed as a just government for his Irish compatriots. Like Lady Bracknell, they opposed change.

Wilde is so thoroughly determined to expose the preposterous aspect of Lady Bracknell's ideology of inertia that even on the one subject where Jack and his prospective mother-in-law find accord, he allows misunderstanding to rule:

> *Lady Bracknell*: . . . Do you smoke?
> *Jack*: Well, yes, I must admit I smoke.
> *Lady Bracknell*: I am glad to hear it. A man should always have an occupation of some kind. There are far too many idle men in London as it is.
>
> (Works, 368)

The revelation of Jack's cognomen had come about early in the play by the loss of his engraved cigarette case in Algernon's rooms. The frequent references to cigarettes in Wilde's work, as an emblem of leisure enjoyed in male company (notwithstanding the new woman who smokes at a dinner party in *Dorian Gray*), shows that Wilde thought of smoking as an exquisite pleasure which released the mind to engage in the free play of the intellect. 'Where are the cigarettes? Thanks,' says Gilbert to Ernest at the start of the dialogue first called 'The True Function and Value of Criticism; with some Remarks on the Importance of Doing Nothing' before revision as 'The Critic as Artist' (Works, 1109–10). This early title is revised to the jocularly punning name of his last play, in which the participants enjoy the ease of leisured life to pursue their ideals and incidentally provide a subversive gloss on contemporary values, just as Gilbert and Ernest, in the dialogue, had pursued revolutionary aesthetic ideas. Towards the end of Act I the men are left alone together and they return to the prospect of their common pursuits:

> *Algernon*: Well, what shall we do?
> *Jack*: Nothing!
> *Algernon*: It is awfully hard work doing nothing. However, I don't mind hard work where there is no definite object of any kind . . .
>
> (Works, 373)

The play is a fantasia on the 'Importance of Doing Nothing'. 'Ernest' is not 'earnest' except in name, just as his prototype and namesake, Mrs Allonby's husband in *A Woman of No Importance*, exists only as a figmentary off-stage character (Works, 479). The two men who are intermittently known as Ernest provide a joking illustration of the principle Wilde puts forward in 'The Critic as Artist': 'to do nothing at all is the most difficult thing in the whole world, the most difficult and the most intellectual. To Plato, with his passion for wisdom, this was the noblest form of energy . . . It is to do nothing that the elect exist' (Works, 1136).

So Gilbert informs his justly named partner, Ernest. As farce, escapism, the bank holiday of propriety and theatre of ideas, *The Importance of Being Earnest* triumphantly defies utilitarian values in a utilitarian age. The absurdly decorous existential question with which Wilde caps the hilarity of revelations about the provenance of Jack's handbag, 'Lady Bracknell, I hate to seem inquisitive, but would you kindly inform me who I am?' (Works, 415), is framed by farce, but founded in Wilde's deeper conviction that 'Yes, Ernest: the contemplative life, the life that has for its aim not *doing* but *being*, and not *being* merely, but *becoming* – that is what the critical spirit can give us' (Works, 1138–9). In its deployment of comedy to air serious critical and existential ideas, and in the complexity of its stage language, this play, more emphatically than any other by Wilde, has served as a model for some of the most innovatory theatre work of the twentieth century.

While *The Importance of Being Earnest* was generally well-received by press and public alike, critical responses were mixed. William Archer, usually one of Wilde's most perceptive critics and loyal admirers, distinguished between the visual richness of the production and what he understood as its intellectual vacuity:

> It is delightful to see, it sends wave after wave of laughter curling and foaming round the theatre; but as a text for criticism it is barren and delusive . . . What can a poor critic do with a play which raises no principle, whether of art or morals, creates its own canons and conventions, and is nothing but an absolutely wilful expression of an irrepressibly witty personality?
>
> (Critical Heritage, 189–90)

Subsequent critics have overturned this view, while often appealing to the notion that the play is difficult to classify and unique in kind. It is Wilde's consummate ability to combine intellectual play with theatrical play that makes *The Importance of Being Earnest* such an astonishing achievement. But the sensation it created among the theatre-going public of its day was soon overshadowed by the author's precipitate fall. On Wilde's arrest, his name was immediately removed from the programme of the play. The production itself closed shortly afterwards. It was not to be revived until late 1901, a year after his death.

Notes

1 Powell, 107–38.
2 *The Importance of Being Earnest*, ed. Russell Jackson (New Mermaids, 1980) 112.
3 Commentary on the structure of the play in this chapter refers to the play in three acts as it has been most frequently performed and printed since 1895. To maintain uniformity with the rest of this study, page references are to the *Complete Works* (1994). It must be noted, however, that Merlin Holland's edition has printed a four-act version of *The Importance of Being Earnest*.
4 'Tea, Five o'clock', *Cassell's Domestic Dictionary* (London: Cassell, Petter & Galpin, [1877–79]) 1141–2, cited in *The Importance of Being Earnest. The First Production*, ed. Joseph Donohue (Gerrards Cross: Colin Smythe, 1995) 274.
5 *Importance*, 84.
6 *The Theatre*, June 1893, cited in Hesketh Pearson, *The Life of Oscar Wilde* (London: Methuen, 1946) 251.

9   *Letters*

Wilde was a superb and prolific correspondent. There are two major collections of his letters, *The Letters of Oscar Wilde* (1962) and *More Letters of Oscar Wilde* (1985), both edited by Rupert Hart-Davis. They provide a major source of biographical information, valuable for the insights they give into Wilde's complex construction of his persona for his friends and the press and for more factual details about the business side of his activity. Writing to friends, his warmth, wit and intellectual play with ideas radiate delight in conversational companionship and engagement with the cultural topics of the day. Writing to the press in self-defence, acid contempt shimmers beneath the veneer of perfectly controlled politeness and rigorously logical argument. Unfortunately most of the letters he wrote to his wife, Constance, during the early years of their marriage were destroyed by her or by her family in the aftermath of Wilde's imprisonment and their divorce. But many of the intimate letters Wilde wrote to Lord Alfred Douglas during the last eight years of his life, from 1892 to 1900, have survived. With malicious irresponsibility Douglas had allowed some of these letters to stray into the hands of blackmailers, putting Wilde at risk and providing evidence for the Crown prosecution against Wilde when they were produced in court during April and May 1895. These documents, which Wilde himself wished at one time to retrieve and destroy, reveal the passion, exhilaration and playfulness of their relationship, as well as the torment of cruelty and betrayal Wilde experienced at the hands of Douglas.

On the day when the jury was to deliver its verdict on Wilde, and the judge his sentence, Wilde wrote to console his lover in the face of inevitable separation:

> be happy to have filled with an immortal love the soul of a man who now weeps in hell, and yet carries heaven in his heart. I love you, I love you, my heart is a rose which your love has brought to bloom, my life is a desert fanned by the delicious breeze of your breath, and whose cool springs are your eyes; the imprint of your little feet makes valleys of shade for me, the odour of your hair is like myrrh, and wherever you go you exhale the perfumes of the cassia tree.
>
> (Letters, 398)

Here Wilde articulates his love on the model of the Song of Songs. In another letter written during the same period he had described his emotional involvement with Douglas according to the model of a different ancient religious text about love: Plato's *Symposium*. 'Our souls were made for one another, and by knowing yours through love, mine has transcended many evils, understood perfection, and entered into the divine essence of things' (Letters, 397).

'De Profundis'

Wilde's most famous letter to Lord Alfred Douglas, written from Reading Gaol between January and March 1897, was published under a religious title by Robert Ross to whom Wilde entrusted its delivery: 'De Profundis'. During the years of bitter emotional pain and physical privation which Wilde suffered in prison, he confronted the nature of his relationship with Douglas candidly and without the ennobling or infatuated masks of religious iconography. 'When you have read the letter you will see the psychological explanation of a course of conduct that from the outside seems a combination of absolute idiocy and vulgar bravado' (Letters, 512) he wrote to Ross, explaining how he wished the long letter to Douglas to be treated and read. Wilde was prevented by the prison authority from sending the work directly to Douglas; on his release from gaol he handed the manuscript to Ross, having already instructed him on what to do with it. He asked for two copies to be made, one to be retained by Ross, another for Wilde himself, and the original to be sent to Douglas. He wished not only his lover but eventually also the world at large to have access to the 'explanation' he discovered in prison. 'Some day the truth will have to be known: not necessarily in my lifetime or in Douglas's: but I am not prepared to sit in the grotesque pillory they put me into, for all time' (Letters, 512). Since Wilde subjected Douglas's behaviour to the same ruthless scrutiny with which he beheld his own, Douglas could neither be trusted to preserve the letter nor to make it public. Indeed Douglas denied ever receiving the copy (not the original, as Wilde had instructed) which Ross sent to him in 1897. Wilde, for the sake of his parents' reputation, and to boost his sons' inheritance from him, wished the letter to be published and sold. As the complete text gradually emerged in successive publications, the letter has assumed the stature of a major exercise in literary autobiography, unique in form and the conditions of its production, but ranking with other nineteenth-century achievements in the genre such as John Cardinal Newman's *Apologia Pro Vita Sua* (1864), and John Stuart Mill's *Autobiography* (1873).

In 1905 Robert Ross edited the work, excluding every reference to Douglas, and so reducing the letter to less than half its original length. This was published as 'De Profundis'; a slightly fuller version was printed in Ross' *Collected Edition* of Wilde's work in 1908. It was not until 1962 that Rupert Hart-Davis published the complete text of what Wilde had written on the 'twenty folio sheets . . . of blue ruled prison paper' (Letters, 424) which Ross had lodged in the British Museum in 1909 with the injunction that no one should read it for 50 years. Douglas himself claims that although he reviewed the 1905 'De Profundis' for a journal called *The Candid Friend*, he did so without 'the slightest idea' that he was reading parts of a letter addressed to himself. It was not until 1912 that he was obliged to acknowledge a full copy of the text which was to be used by Arthur Ransome's defence counsel against Douglas' libel suit. He was claiming defamation by Ransome's 1912 study, *Oscar Wilde*. Even then Douglas refused to confront the contents of the letter publicly, leaving the courtroom when it was read out as evidence against him (Ellmann, 552). Referring to the work in 1925, Douglas pronounced, '[m]ost of the letter is simply incomprehensible to me. He invents the maddest fictions,'[1] safe in the knowledge that the author was dead, and that he had moreover written to the *Daily Chronicle* in 1898 to argue for the alleviation of the British prison conditions that induce insanity among the inmates.

An example of the kind of material Douglas refused to recognise can be given by Wilde's recollection of how Douglas neglected him during a bout of influenza while writing *The Importance of Being Earnest*. Douglas was bored in Worthing and persuaded Wilde to move to Brighton. On arrival Douglas fell ill, to be nursed lavishly for a few days before Wilde himself succumbed:

> It was not a question of grapes, flowers, and charming gifts: it was a question of mere necessaries: I could not even get the milk the doctor had ordered for me . . . All the while you are of course living at my expense, driving about, dining at the Grand Hotel, and indeed only appearing in my room for money . . . At three in the morning, unable to sleep, and tortured with thirst, I made my way, in the dark and cold, down to the sitting-room in the hopes of finding some water there. I found *you*. You fell on me with every hideous word an intemperate mood, an undisciplined and untutored nature could suggest . . . You accused me of selfishness in expecting you to be with me when I was ill; of standing between you and your amusements . . . In the morning . . . you began to repeat the same scene with renewed emphasis and more violent assertion. I told you at length to leave the room: you pretended to do so, but when I lifted my head from the pillow in which I had buried it, you were still there, and with brutality of laughter and hysteria of rage you moved suddenly towards me. A sense of horror came over me . . . I got out of my bed at once, and bare-footed and just as I was, made my way down the two flights of stairs to the sitting

room, which I did not leave till the owner of the lodgings . . . had
assured me that you had left my bedroom.

(Letters, 436–7)

'De Profundis' was motivated by Douglas' neglect of Wilde in prison:
'What I must know from you is why you have never made any
attempt to write to me, since the August of the year before last'
(Letters, 512) he asks, drawing to a close and telling Douglas how to
send word via the Prison Governor. Wilde began the letter by con-
structing a monologue to his absent lover, a conversation met with
silence, which picks painfully over the sorry details of their romance
and Wilde's entanglement in the feud between Queensberry father
and son. 'Hate blinds people. You were not aware of that. Love can
read the writing on the remotest star, but Hate so blinded you that
you could see no further than the narrow walled-in, and already lust-
withered garden of your common desires' (Letters, 445). This opening
section is a lengthy catalogue of indulgences and, in hindsight,
mistakes of weakness, committed by Wilde in relation to Douglas'
treatment of him. He relives the life of extravagant pleasure from
the perspective of the pain it brought him.

Gradually the subject changes. Wilde soars above the sordid and
banal details of tormented passion and begins to converse with himself. He acts as his own confessor, purging his conscience without
ever assuming the role of penitent. Far from it:

> I see quite clearly what I have got to do . . . And when I use such
> a phrase as that, I need not tell you that I am not alluding to any
> external sanction or command. I admit none. I am far more of an
> Individualist than I ever was. Nothing seems to me of the smallest
> value except what one gets out of oneself. My nature is seeking a
> fresh mode of self-realisation.

(Letters, 467)

Wilde admits no guilt before the 'unjust laws' which have placed
him in gaol. 'I am a born antinomian. I am one of those who are
made for exceptions, not for laws' (Letters, 468). Instead he uses the
extreme experiences of suffering undergone to construct another
self, 'a new life, a *Vita Nuova* for me', for which his new understanding of 'Humility' will be the starting point (Letters, 467).

Charting his mental development in prison, Wilde begins the new
section of the letter with an astonishing, but not unjust, review of his
position:

> I was a man who stood in symbolic relation to the art and culture
> of my age. I had realised this for myself at the very dawn of my
> manhood, and had forced my age to realise it afterwards. Few
> men hold such a position in their own lifetime and have it so

acknowledged. It is usually discerned, if discerned at all, by the historian, or the critic, long after both the man and his age have passed away. With me it was different. I felt it myself, and made others feel it. Byron was a symbolic figure, but his relations were to the passion of his age and its weariness of passion. Mine were to something more noble, more permanent, of more vital issue, of larger scope.

The gods had given me almost everything. I had genius, a distinguished name, high social position, brilliancy, intellectual daring: I made art a philosophy, and philosophy an art: I altered the minds of men and the colours of things: there was nothing I said or did that did not make people wonder: I took the drama, the most objective form known to art, and made it as personal a mode of expression as the lyric or the sonnet, at the same time that I widened its range and enriched its characterisation: drama, novel, poem in rhyme, poem in prose, subtle or fantastic dialogue, whatever I touched I made beautiful in a new mode of beauty: to truth itself I gave what is false no less than what is true as its rightful province, and showed that the false and the true are merely forms of intellectual existence. I treated Art as the supreme reality, and life as a mere mode of fiction: I awoke the imagination of my century so that it created myth and legend around me: I summed up all systems in a phrase, and all existence in an epigram.

(Letters, 466)

This may seem a strange way to introduce psychological development arrived at through the knowledge of 'humility', but Wilde is emphasising the individualistic achievements of his career of which public degradation, bankruptcy, the loss of all personal possessions, the loss of his family and the reduction of his name to the prison cypher C.3.3, cannot strip him. He surveys the past in order to move forwards. Freely admitting his own part in the degenerative behaviour that led to his fall, he confesses: 'I let myself be lured into long spells of senseless and sensual ease.' The cardinal sin was that 'I ceased to be Lord over myself. I was no longer the Captain of my Soul, and did not know it. I allowed you to dominate me, and your father to frighten me. I ended in horrible disgrace. There is only one thing for me now, absolute Humility' (Letters, 466). He wishes to inhabit a new world, the world which 'Sorrow' reveals to him, leaving behind the paths of 'Pleasure' which led him to abandon himself to others (Letters, 472).

Picturing himself as destitute and homeless, but possessed with magnificent inner strength, Wilde proceeds to construct an elaborate and audacious comparison between his own artistic life and the life of Christ:

I see a far more intimate and immediate connection between the true life of Christ and the true life of the artist, and I take a keen pleasure in the reflection that long before Sorrow had made my days her own and bound me to her wheel I had written in The Soul of Man that he who would lead a Christ-like life must be entirely and absolutely himself, and had taken as my types not merely the shepherd on the hillside and the prisoner in his cell but also the painter to whom the world is a pageant and the poet for whom the world is a song.

(Letters, 476)

Christ becomes the 'true precursor of the romantic movement'; the archetype for the artist, 'Christ's place indeed is with the poets. His whole conception of Humanity sprang right out of the imagination and can only be realised by it'; and the 'supreme of Individualists' (Letters, 476, 477, 479). In developing these ideas Wilde sets out a radically poetic interpretation of the life of Christ, taking it beyond the historiographically controversial *Vie de Jésus* by Renan (1863), a copy of which Wilde was permitted to have in his cell in 1896, appropriating the Gospels as 'prose-poems' (Letters, 483) to serve his own aesthetic and political philosophy. He seeks to make Christ his contemporary, just as Pater had brought Plato to life as a nineteenth-century figure in *Plato and Platonism*.

Wilde makes the culture which Christ rebelled against rhyme with that of his own era, 'the Jew of Jerusalem in Christ's day was the exact counterpart of the British philistine of our own' (Letters, 486). He is assisted by the vocabulary which Matthew Arnold deployed in *Culture and Anarchy*, in which he labelled contemporary English classes with New Testament names, 'Philistine' and 'Barbarian', according to his judgement of the cultural type represented. In *Dorian Gray*, the artist Basil Hallward described revolutionary moments in the history of art when new media of expression were discovered, so in 'De Profundis' Wilde argues that Christ made precisely such an innovation to the life of humanity, permitting what had previously been formless and inarticulate to take shape and discover a voice:

To the artist, expression is the only mode under which he can conceive life at all. To him what is dumb is dead. But to Christ it was not so. With a width and wonder of imagination, that fills one almost with awe, he took the entire world of the inarticulate, the voiceless world of pain, as his kingdom, and made of himself its eternal mouthpiece ... And feeling, with the artistic nature of one to whom Sorrow and Suffering were modes through which he could realise his conception of the Beautiful, that an idea is of no value till it becomes incarnate and is made an image, he makes of himself the image of the Man of Sorrows, and as such has fascinated and dominated Art as no Greek god ever succeeded in doing.

(Letters, 481)

New definitions in cultural life are coupled with innovation in morality and law. As for Wilde, so for Christ 'there were no laws: there were exceptions merely'. Like Wilde in his revolt against the Philistine mechanics of English Society, so Christ 'had no patience with the dull lifeless mechanical systems that treat people as if they were things' (Letters, 485). Like Wilde, Christ is represented as consorting with sinners and criminals, preaching a celebration of Beauty and a rejection of the life devoted to the accumulation of possessions. Even the lily, the emblem of effete aestheticism for which Wilde in his twenties was so ridiculed, is given a new dignity in the context of Wilde's refashioning of Christian doctrine. 'He was the first person who ever said to people that they should live "flower-like" lives. He fixed the phrase.' Wilde quotes in Greek from Matthew, vi, 28, 'Consider the lilies of the field, how they grow; they toil not, neither do they spin', to justify the claim (Letters, 484, 483). Pater's aesthetic philosophy contained in the 'Conclusion' to *The Renaissance* receives its beatification here too, as Wilde, interpreting Christ's response to Mary Magdalene's lavish gift of 'odorous spices', argues that Christ himself taught that '*every* moment should be beautiful' (Letters, 486). Most important of all for Wilde was his view 'that to Christ imagination was simply a form of Love, and that to him Love was Lord in the fullest meaning of the phrase'. Just as in *An Ideal Husband*, Lady Chiltern has to learn from the dandy Lord Goring that earned love is no love at all, so Wilde asserts again 'Nobody is worthy to be loved' (Letters, 484) – and this is what makes it sacramental. Throughout this section of the letter, Wilde manipulates his interpretation of the Gospels to criticise the social inhumanity of his era, to sanctify aestheticism as a way of life, and to establish himself as a martyr in an age of artistic unbelief and imaginative atrophy.

Wilde announces that if he should ever produce artistic work again, there are only two subjects on which he wishes to express himself: 'Christ, as the precursor of the Romantic Movement in life', and 'The artistic life considered in its relation to Conduct' (Letters, 484). In fact he is in the midst of composing both these works in the course of the letter. He develops these ideas further there and then. The two proposed pieces shade into one another as Wilde argues that the conduct of the artist, like that of Christ and like that of the criminal, must always necessarily stand in conflict with the established mores of the day. He illustrates this with an autobiographical example:

People thought it dreadful of me to have entertained at dinner the evil things of life, and to have found pleasure in their company. But they, from the point of view through which I, as an artist in life, approached them, were delightfully suggestive and stimulating. It was like feasting with panthers. The danger was half the excitement ... Their poison was part of their perfection ... I don't feel at all ashamed of having known them ... What I do feel ashamed of is the horrible Philistine atmosphere into which you brought me. My business as an artist was with Ariel. You set me to wrestle with Caliban.

(Letters, 492)

Finally Wilde turns once more to the gnawing troubles of his affair with Douglas and the appalling consequences it has had for his own life and the lives of his children. Still he craves attention from Douglas and he concludes by imagining an idyllic reunion when 'the June roses are in all their wanton opulence ... in some quite foreign town'. There the two men will meet with changed names and changed natures (Letters, 510). His engagement with Douglas throughout the composition had been so vivid that he hoped to have taken his lover with him on his journey through purgatory to beatification, teaching him humility, forgiveness and love to match his own and to permit their meeting on restored terms.

On prison reform

Two letters which Wilde wrote to the *Daily Chronicle* following his release from gaol reflect the changed nature of his enterprise. Both of them participate in a wider campaign to reform the British penal system and the management of prison life.[2] Voicing fierce criticism of the treatment of both children and adults in prison, they expose and indict the barbarity of the penal system and represent Wilde's most direct efforts to influence political events. Few prisoners could articulate the realities of their prison experience as eloquently as Wilde, and none could share the political philosophy, evolved through 'The Soul of Man Under Socialism' and 'De Profundis', which informed his perspective. 'The Case of Warder Martin: Some Cruelties of Prison Life', published on 28 May 1897, and 'Prison Reform', published 24 March 1898, share the epigrammatic style and flawless logic which characterise his earlier letters to the press on matters of aesthetic concern, but they seek to generate immediate pragmatic response in the sphere of legislation and public life.

The first letter is occasioned by the dismissal of Warder Martin from Reading Gaol for having given a sweet biscuit to a distressed and hungry child. Wilde respected Warder Martin for his humane treatment of the inmates. Wilde manipulates the Victorian sentimentality that governed the topos of the poor, lost child, to evoke the horror of systematic brutality. Aphorism directs his anger as he analyses the social forces which subject the criminalised child to intolerable cruelty and he draws general conclusions from a particular case:

> The child's face was like a white wedge of sheer terror. There was in his eyes the terror of a hunted animal. The next morning I heard him at breakfast-time crying, and calling to be let out. His cry was for his parents. From time to time I could hear the deep voice of the warder on duty telling him to keep quiet. Yet he was not even convicted of whatever little offence he had been charged with. He was simply on remand ... Justices and magistrates, an entirely ignorant class as a rule, often remand children for a week, and then perhaps remit whatever sentence they are entitled to pass. They call this 'not sending a child to prison'. It is, of course, a stupid view on their part. To the little child, whether he is in prison on remand or after conviction, is not a subtlety of social position he can comprehend. To him the horrible thing is to be there at all. In the eyes of humanity it should be a horrible thing for him to be there at all.
>
> (Letters, 569)

Wilde proceeds to inveigh against the system of solitary 'cellular confinement', applied to adult and child alike for 23 hours of the day, as itself the criminal treatment of a victim which no law would sanction were a child to be subjected to such treatment outside the prison walls. Wilde objects to this treatment of children not simply because it is cruel in an absolute sense, but more especially because of its relative cruelty to the child who cannot understand the origin or function of this form of punishment: 'to the child to be so treated by a strange abstract force, of whose claims it has no cognisance, is much worse than it would be to receive the same treatment from its father or mother, or some one it knew' (Letters, 570).

Throughout his mature writing Wilde had found various ways of exposing and satirising the stupefying effects of systematically induced behaviour. In observing that 'most warders are very fond of children. But the system prohibits them from rendering the child any assistance' he finds a precise and persuasive illustration for his revolt against Philistinism. In 'De Profundis' he had defined the Philistine as one who 'upholds and aids the heavy, cumbrous, blind mechanical forces of Society, and who does not recognise the dynamic force when he meets it in either man or movement' (Letters, 492). Demonstrating to readers of the *Daily Chronicle* the brutalisation which affects not just inmates but prison warders too, as a consequence of the penal system they are compelled to uphold, Wilde indicts the very foundations of the society which is policed by this legislation, judiciary and prison system. At the same time he affirms the moral health of his own radical politics and the antimonian stance of the individualist.

Wilde's personal correspondence soon recovered its sense of fun with his release from prison. The necessity he experienced of maintaining a disguised persona, which before the trials had led to his celebration of the double life in the form of Bunbury, was now different in motivation but nevertheless a subterfuge required for the preservation of privacy and dignity. He assumed the name 'Sebastian Melmoth' during the last years of his life in exile on the Continent. Saint Sebastian was martyred in the fourth century and his iconography, a favourite in homosexual discourse, had fascinated Wilde ever since he saw Guido Reni's *San Sebastian* in Genoa on his tour of Italy in 1877. 'Melmoth' was adopted from the name of the eponymous hero *Melmoth the Wanderer*, a novel written by the Reverend Charles Maturin, an ancestor of Wilde in his mother's family. Writing from Dieppe to Ada Leverson to explain this, Wilde also added information about the assumed names of his companions there: Reginald Turner and Robert Ross:

> I am staying here as Sebastian Melmoth – not Esquire but Monsieur Sebastien Melmoth. I have thought it better that Robbie should stay here under the name Reginald Turner, and Reggie under the name of R. B. Ross. It is better that they should not have their own names.
>
> (Letters, 566)

Even in 1900 Wilde was still inventing alias names for his friends. From Rome in April 1900 he wrote to Robert Ross telling him that he had persuaded an acquaintance that 'your real name is Edmondo Gosse'. He continued:

> Rome is burning with heat: really terrible: but at 4.30 I am going to the Borghese, to look at daisies, and drink milk: the Borghese milk is as wonderful as the Borghese daisies. I also intend to photograph Arnaldo. By the way, can you photograph cows well? I did one of cows in the Borghese so marvellous that I destroyed it: I was afraid of being called the modern Paul Potter. Cows are very fond of being photographed, and, unlike architecture, don't move.
>
> (Letters, 823–4)

The last months of Wilde's life brought a more serious tone. His last published letter, dated 20 November 1900, was dictated from his sick bed. It was a plea to Frank Harris for money to cover the expenses of his illness. Harris had agreed to pay Wilde a share of profits made by the play *Mr and Mrs Daventry*, for which Wilde had written the treatment and even submitted it to George Alexander in August 1894 (Letters 360–1). Unable to compose further in the genre of Society comedy on release from gaol, Wilde had given the outline to Harris for completion. The play, with Mrs Patrick Campbell as Mrs Daventry, opened at the Royalty Theatre, London, on 25 October 1900 and ran until 23 February 1901. Wilde died a pauper on 30 November 1900.

Notes

1   Frank Harris and Lord Alfred Douglas, *The Life and Confessions of Oscar Wilde* (London: Fortune Press, 1925) 36.
2   See John Stokes, *In The Nineties* (London: Harvester Wheatsheaf, 1989) 95–113.

Part Four
Reference Section

10   *Wilde and his circle*

Wilde had an enormous circle of friends, acquaintances and professional contacts. The following is a small selection:

ALEXANDER, GEORGE (1858–1918)   English actor and manager of the St James's Theatre. He acted with Henry Irving from 1881 to 1889, then managed his own company at the St James's until his death. He was knighted in 1911.

ARCHER, WILLIAM (1856–1924)   Scottish critic, translator and playwright. He was active in introducing knowledge of Ibsen to Britain, translating his plays and publishing critical articles. Theatre critic of *The World* from 1884 to 1905, he was forthcoming in praise for Wilde and he was the only drama critic to protest at the censorship of *Salome* in 1892.

BEARDSLEY, AUBREY (1872–1898)   English artist whose drawings were first published in the *Pall Mall Gazette* in 1893. He became art editor of the *avant-garde* publications the *Yellow Book* (1894–95) and the *Savoy* (1896). He illustrated the first English edition of *Salome* in 1893 and Wilde inscribed his copy with the dedication 'For Aubrey: for the only artist who, besides myself, knows what the dance of the seven veils is, and can see that invisible dance. Oscar.'

BERNHARDT, SARAH (1844–1923)   World-famous French actress, the 'divine Sarah' was an extraordinary performer both on and off stage. Her career began in 1862 at the Comédie Française in Paris. She first visited England in 1879 when Wilde is reputed to have greeted her by strewing lilies in her path as she set foot on English soil. Her performance in the lead of *Salome* in London in 1892 came to nothing when the play was banned shortly before it was due to open. In 1899 Wilde said: 'The three women I have most admired are Queen Victoria, Sarah Bernhardt and Lily Langtry. I would have married any one of them with pleasure' (Letters, 65).

CARSON, EDWARD (1854–1935)   An ardent Irish Unionist who, after reading classics at Trinity College Dublin in the same class as Wilde, took a career in law. He became Solicitor-General for Ireland in 1892 and was called to the English bar in 1893. His judgement over the libel action brought by Wilde against the Marquess of

Queensberry and the subsequent sentencing of Wilde assured his prominence as a respected advocate. He was knighted in 1896.

CARTE, RICHARD D'OYLY (1844–1901)   English entrepreneur in concert agency and theatrical management, he produced the comic operas by Gilbert and Sullivan. From the astonishing wealth generated by these he built the Savoy Theatre in 1881: the first public building in the world to be lit by electricity. He also built the luxurious Savoy Hotel in London in 1889, one of Wilde's favourite haunts. He sponsored Wilde's American lecture tour in 1882 as promotion for the American tour of *Patience*.

DOUGLAS, LORD ALFRED (1870–1945)   English aristocrat, third son of the Marquess of Queensberry, nicknamed 'Bosie'. Educated at Winchester and then at Magdalen College, Oxford, when he met Wilde in 1891 during his second year of reading 'Greats' (Greek and Latin). The tempestuous romance with Wilde that developed from 1892 became one of the most publicly scrutinised love affairs in British history, forced into the public arena not just by the trials undergone by Wilde for 'gross indecency' in 1895 but also by accounts of its progress made subsequently by both parties. Wilde exposed his version of events in 'De Profundis', and Douglas made repeated efforts to clear his reputation with *Oscar Wilde and Myself* (1912; second edition 1919), *Autobiography* (1928) and *Oscar Wilde. A Summing Up* (1940) among others.

GODWIN, EDWARD W. (1833–1886) FSA, FRIBA   English architect, theatrical designer and interior designer. He designed both civic and private buildings, including 'The White House' (1879) for Whistler on Tite Street, next door to the house he designed for Oscar and Constance Wilde, the 'House Beautiful' (1885). He designed scenery and costumes for the Bancrofts' production *The Merchant of Venice* (Prince of Wales, 1875) in which Ellen Terry, who had borne him two children, played Portia. Godwin and Ellen Terry were partners from 1868 to 1875, and their children were Edith Craig who became an actress, and Edward Gordon Craig who extended his father's interests in stage design. Godwin founded The Costume Society in 1881 for the promotion of historical accuracy in stage costume design and he also argued fiercely for architectural accuracy in the production of plays with historical settings.

GREIN, JACK THOMAS (1862–1935)   Dutch theatre critic, playwright and manager, who took British nationality in 1895. Inspired by Antoine's *Théâtre Libre* in Paris, Grein opened the Independent Theatre in London in 1891. This was a private theatre club whose audience members paid a subscription. By this means Grein was able to stage plays which had been censored or which were com mercially unviable. In 1891 Grein produced Ibsen's *Ghosts* and in 1892 Shaw's *Widowers' Houses*.

HARRIS, FRANK (1856–1931)   English writer and editor who grew up mostly in America. On his return to England he became editor of the *Evening News* in 1883 and the *Fortnightly Review* in 1886. Notori- ously unreliable as a factual writer, his biographies, including *Oscar Wilde, His Life and Confessions* (1916) contain much fiction. He was one of Wilde's most loyal friends.

IRVING, HENRY (1838–1905)   Stage name of John Henry Brodribb, one of the most famous English actors of the nineteenth century. His acting career began in 1855; he joined the Lyceum company (Lon- don) in 1871 where he specialised in the portrayal of Shakespeare's tragic heroes. He began his distinguished management of the Lyceum in 1878. Wilde admired Irving's Macbeth in 1876 and he went with John Ruskin to watch him perform Shylock in *The Merchant of Venice* in 1879. Irving rejected Wilde's offer of a production of *The Duchess of Padua* in 1891. He was knighted in 1895.

LANE, JOHN (1854–1925)   English publisher who founded the Bodley Head with Elkin Mathews in 1887. He published *The Sphinx* in 1892. Wilde disliked him, and named the manservant in *The Importance of Being Earnest* after him.

LANGTRY, LILY (1852–1929)   Born in Jersey, her real name was Emily Charlotte Le Breton. In her teens she married the Irish widower, Edward Langtry, who brought her to London where she rapidly became a leading figure in Society. She was of fabled beauty and became mistress of the Prince of Wales. Millais called his por- trait of her *The Jersey Lily* from which her nickname originates. Others who painted her portrait include Burne-Jones, Leighton, Poynter, Watts and Whistler. Wilde paid court to her for a time during the 1870s, acting as her amanuensis. His poem to her, 'The New Helen', was printed in *Time* in July 1879. He inscribed her copy of his *Poems* (1881) 'To Helen, formerly of Troy, now of London'.

LEVERSON, ADA (1862–1933)   Her maiden name was Ada Esther Beddington. She married Ernest Leverson and Wilde nicknamed her 'The Sphinx' throughout their close friendship, which flourished from 1892. She contributed a number of parodies of his work to *Punch*, later publishing novels and a memoir of her friendship with Wilde (*Letters to the Sphinx*) in 1930. She and her husband received Wilde on his release from prison in 1897 and assisted his departure to France.

LUGNÉ-POË, A. M. (1869–1940)   French actor-manager who founded the *avant-garde Théâtre de L'Œuvre* in Paris in 1893. There he mounted the first production of *Salome* on 11 February 1896 with himself as Herod and Lina Munte as Salome.

MAHAFFY, JOHN PENTLAND (1839–1919)   Irish Reverend, in 1869 he was made Professor of Ancient History at Trinity College Dublin when Wilde first met him as a student there in 1871. He was knighted in 1918, having become Provost of Trinity College in 1914. Mahaffy exercised a great influence on his star pupil, taking Wilde to see ancient sites in Italy (1875) and Greece (1877) and restraining Wilde's inclinations towards Catholicism in 1875. Their friendship was ruptured by the unionist politics of Mahaffy's *Greek Life and Thought: From the Age of Alexander to the Roman Conquest* (1887) which Wilde savaged in a review (PMB 17 November 1887) and by Wilde's more satirical review of Mahaffy's *The Principles of the Art of Conversation* (1887) (PMB 16 December 1887). Harmony was restored, and in 1893 Wilde thanked Mahaffy for his praise of *A Woman of No Importance* and called him 'my first and best teacher . . . the scholar who showed me how to love Greek things'.

MALLARMÉ, STEPHANE (1842–1898)   French symbolist poet whose 'salons' at home in the Rue de Rome in Paris offered a centre of intellectual exchange and inspiration for the symbolist movement. Wilde visited Mallarmé's salon twice in 1891, and always addressed him as 'Cher Maître'.

MATHEWS, ELKIN (1851–1921)   English publisher and bookseller, he founded the Bodley Head in London in 1887 with John Lane. He published a number of works by Wilde.

MONACO, PRINCESS ALICE OF (1858–1925)   Her maiden name was Heine and she was grandniece of the German poet, Heinrich Heine. She was the widow of the Duc de Richelieu and married Prince Albert Honoré Charles of Monaco in 1889. She cultivated an artistic circle of friends and was a great patron of the arts. Wilde visited her in Paris in 1891, attended a dinner held for her by Frank Harris at Claridge's in 1891 and dedicated his story 'The Fisherman and His Soul' to the Princess.

MORRIS, WILLIAM (1834–1896)   English poet, artist and manufacturer whose creative endeavours were always linked with his commitment to Socialism. A founder member of the Pre-Raphaelite Brotherhood in Oxford in 1850 and designer for the 'Arts and Crafts' movement in England, his example was an inspiration for Wilde who professed in 1891: 'I have loved your work since boyhood. I shall always love it.'

MOUNT-TEMPLE, LADY (1822–1901) Georgina Tollemache, sister of the first Lord Tollemache and married to William Francis Cowper-Temple (1811–88), first Lord Mount-Temple related to both Lord Melbourne and Lord Palmerston. Lady Mount-Temple was a distant cousin to Constance Wilde and offered her and the two boys generous and unfailing friendship. Wilde leased her home, Babbacombe Cliff in Devon, to write during the winter of 1892–93.

PATER, WALTER (1839–1894) English Fellow and Tutor in classics at Brasenose College, Oxford. He published his first book, *Studies in the History of the Renaissance*, in 1873. The 'Conclusion' to this collection of essays described life as a state of flux and art (its creation or appreciation) as the only means of securing some measure of stability. The account was so vivid that Pater's aesthetic creed exercised an enormous influence on the younger generation of poets, including Wilde, but he himself was forced to withdraw the 'Conclusion' from the subsequent edition of the book. Wilde first met Pater in 1877. Both men maintained lifelong respect for each other's work.

PIGOTT, E. F. S. (1826–1895) Examiner of Plays for the Lord Chamberlain from 1875 to his death in 1895. He was responsible for the censorship of *Salome* in 1892. Wilde said he 'panders to the vulgarity and hypocrisy of the English people'. After his death Shaw called him 'a walking compendium of vulgar insular prejudice'.

PINERO, A. W. (1855–1934) English dramatist, a rival society playwright for Wilde during the 1890s. Distinguished as a writer of farce, he also exploited the well-made play formula for his serious dramas. The most successful of these was *The Second Mrs Tanqueray* (1893), far more reactionary in form and content than any play written by Wilde.

RICKETTS, CHARLES (1866–1931, elected to the Royal Academy in 1928) English artist, writer, book and stage designer. He lived and worked closely with his partner, Charles Shannon (1863–1937, elected R. A. 1921), first at a house in Chelsea known as 'The Vale' from which they issued the privately printed journal the *Dial* (1889–1897). They sent a copy of the first issue of the *Dial* to Wilde in 1889 which occasioned their first meeting, friendship and long-lasting professional collaboration. Ricketts designed the title-page and binding of *The Picture of Dorian Gray* (1891), the limited edition of Wilde's *Poems* (1892), the binding of *Intentions* (1891) and of *Lord Arthur Savile's*

Crime (1891). Rickett's most sustained piece of design for Wilde was his setting and illustration of *The Sphinx* (1894). He also designed the binding for the *Collected Edition* of Wilde's work in 1908. He was at work on the stage design for the London production of *Salome* when the performance was banned in 1892. Ricketts and Shannon together designed and decorated *A House of Pomegranates* (1891) while Shannon designed the binding for the first editions of all four of Wilde's Society comedies. Wilde is reported to have said that Ricketts provided the model for the character Basil Hallward in *The Picture of Dorian Gray*, while Ricketts wrote a fanciful memoir of his friendship with Wilde, *Oscar Wilde: Recollections* (1932), 'co-authored' with a fictional narrator, Jean Paul Raymond.

ROBINS, ELIZABETH (1862–1952)   American actress and writer. Widowed in 1887, she moved to London in 1888 where she met Wilde at the home of Louise Chandler Moulton. He befriended her and exercised his influence among theatre practitioners to get her work. She played the lead in the English premier of Ibsen's *Hedda Gabler* in 1891 and Hilda Wangel in the English premier of *The Master Builder* in 1893. Among her later writings are the suffragette play, *Votes for Women*, and a book about performance, *Ibsen and the Actress*.

ROSS, ROBERT (1869–1918)   Canadian born, raised in England since the age of two, Ross read History at Cambridge University before working in London as a literary journalist and art critic. He met Wilde in 1886 and remained one of Wilde's closest and most loyal friends. Ross attended Wilde during his last illness; when Father Cuthbert Dunne administered the conditional Baptism to Wilde on his deathbed Ross knelt by the bed, answering the responses during Extreme Unction on Wilde's behalf. He made the funeral arrangements in 1900 and oversaw the removal of Wilde's remains to the new site at the Père Lachaise cemetery in 1909. His ashes were buried with Wilde in 1918. Because he introduced Wilde to the practice of homosexuality, Ross felt responsible for his fall and in his capacity as Wilde's literary executor he worked hard to bring Wilde's estate back into credit after his death. He stimulated foreign interest in Wilde's work, which brought in revenue from translations, and he edited the *Collected Edition* of Wilde's work in 1908. He was unfailing in support and friendship towards Wilde's sons, Cyril and Vyvyan.

RUSKIN, JOHN (1819–1900)   English art historian and critic, Slade Professor of Art at Oxford 1869–1879 and 1883–1884. An enormously influential figure with a prolific output to match, Ruskin shaped nineteenth-century debate about the moral purpose of art and defended the dignifying work of artisan and craftsman against encroaching mechanisation. His most famous publications are the five volumes of *Modern Painters* (1843–60), in which he admires Turner and the Pre-Raphaelites, and *Stones of Venice* (1851–53). Wilde also drew on *Sesame and Lilies*, a series of lectures Ruskin gave about education, for the delineation of separate social roles for men and women in *An Ideal Husband*. Wilde first met Ruskin as a student at his lectures on Florentine Art in Oxford in 1874 from which a friendship developed. In 1888 Wilde wrote to Ruskin: 'The dearest memories of my Oxford days are my walks and talks with you, and from you I learned nothing but what was good.' In the same letter Wilde hailed Ruskin 'prophet', 'priest' and 'poet'.

SHAW, GEORGE BERNARD (1856–1950)   Irish journalist, critic and playwright of outspoken Socialist convictions, Shaw was music critic for the *World* when Wilde chose to send him a copy of *Salome* in 1893 as a token of respect for his arguments against stage censorship, and in admiration for Shaw's book on Ibsen, *The Quintessence of Ibsenism* (1891). After this the two men regularly exchanged publications.

SHERARD, R. H. (1861–1943)   English journalist and writer, great-grandson of Wordsworth, he first met Wilde in Paris in 1883 and maintained a lifelong friendship with him. He became Wilde's first biographer, with *Oscar Wilde: The Story of an Unhappy Friendship* (1902), *The Life of Oscar Wilde* (1906), *The Real Oscar Wilde* (1915), and *Bernard Shaw, Frank Harris and Oscar Wilde* (1937). Although Sherard made efforts to be accurate, he scarcely saw Wilde during the busy years of 1889–95 and his knowledge is therefore limited.

SMITHERS, LEONARD (1861–1907)   English solicitor working in Sheffield until 1891 when he moved to London and began business as a publisher and bookseller. Keen to take various risks, he traded in pornography but he also published Wilde's last three books – *The Ballad of Reading Gaol*, *An Ideal Husband*, and *The Importance of Being Earnest* – and a number of other supposedly disreputable works, such as poems by Ernest Dowson and Arthur Symons, pictures by Beardsley, and the *avant-garde* literary journal, the *Savoy*.

SYMONS, ARTHUR (1865–1945)   English poet and critic, pioneering in his introduction of contemporary French literature to the English-speaking world. He was acquainted with Wilde from 1890 onwards and particularly pleased Wilde by his favourable review of *The Ballad of Reading Gaol* in the *Saturday Review* in March 1898. He published *A Study of Oscar Wilde* in 1930.

TERRY, ELLEN (1847–1928)   English actress who made her first stage appearance at the age of nine. She acted with the Keans and the Bancrofts and was engaged by Henry Irving as the 'leading lady' in his company at the Lyceum from 1878 to 1902. She married the painter G. F. Watts but separated from him in 1866. Her next partner was the designer, Edward Godwin (q.v.), with whom she lived in Hertfordshire from 1868 to 1875. They had two children: Edward Gordon and Edith Craig. In 1875 she returned to her career on stage as Portia in *The Merchant of Venice* which Godwin designed for the Bancrofts at The Prince of Wales. Wilde admired her immensely. He sent her a crown of flowers for the first night of her performance as Camma, the lead in Tennyson's verse play *The Cup*, at the Lyceum in 1881, and wrote two sonnets to her.

TREE, HERBERT BEERBOHM (1853–1917)   English actor-manager at the Theatre Royal, Haymarket, London, who produced *A Woman of No Importance*. Half-brother of the artist, Max Beerbohm.

WALLER, LEWIS (1850–1915)   English actor, specialising in romantic leads. He acted in Beerbohm Tree's touring production of *A Woman of No Importance* which opened in Birmingham in 1893. He produced and acted in *An Ideal Husband* in 1895.

WHISTLER, JAMES MCNEILL (1834–1903)   American artist (with Scottish ancestry), he studied in Paris and settled in England in 1862. His abstract style of painting portraits, rural and urban landscapes, was highly controversial and a marked contrast to Pre-Raphaelite style. He sued Ruskin in 1877 for libellous remarks about his paintings exhibited at the Grosvenor Gallery. His nickname was 'The Butterfly', his wit was a ready match for Wilde and they struck a lively friendship nurtured by uneasy rivalry from the late 1870s. When Whistler delivered his 'Ten O'Clock Lecture' in February 1885, much of which ridiculed the aestheticism and social criticism Wilde promoted, his hostility towards Wilde became conspicuous. From about 1888 the two men went their separate ways.

WHITMAN, WALT (1819–1892)   American poet most famous for *Leaves of Grass* (1855), the eighth edition of which was withdrawn by the publishers in 1882 for threatened prosecution for indecency. Wilde met him in Philadelphia in 1882 and claimed: 'There is no one in this great wide world of America whom I love and honour so much.'

WILDE, LADY (Jane Francesca, née Elgee) (1821–1896)   Wilde's mother. An ardent Irish nationalist, she published poems for the Young Ireland movement during the 1840s under the pen name

'Speranza'. She published a number of translations: William Meinhold's *Sidonia the Sorceress* (1849), Alphonse de Lamartine's *Pictures of the First French Revolution* (1850) and *The Wanderer and his Home* (1851), Alexandre Dumas père's *The Glacier Land* (1852), Marcel Schwob's *The First Temptation or 'Ecrits Sicut Deus'* (1863) and Emmanuel Swedenborg's *The Future Life* (1874). She published a volume of *Poems* in 1864 and to make money as a widow living in London from 1879 she wrote *Memoir of Gabriel Beranger* (1880), *Driftwood from Scandinavia* (1884), *Ancient Legends, Mystic Charms, and Superstitions of Ireland* (1888), *Ancient Cures, Charms, and Usages of Ireland* (1890), *Notes on Men, Women, and Books* (1891) and *Social Studies* (1893). Her salons at Merrion Square, Dublin, and at Oakley Street, Chelsea, in London were legendary, as was her extravagant sense of dress. She was a devoted mother to both her sons and Wilde helped to support her financially in her old age.

WILDE, SIR WILLIAM ROBERT (1815–1876)   Wilde's father, knighted in 1864. He practised as a physician, founded St Mark's Hospital in Dublin in 1844 and specialised in the medicine of the ear and the eye. He published pioneering studies in the field: *Aural Surgery* (1851) and *Epidemia Ophthalmia* (1853). For the Irish census of 1851 he was appointed Census Commissioner to collate the medical information and he compiled the first statistical analysis of diseases of the eye and ear in Ireland. He was appointed Surgeon Oculist to the Queen in Ireland in 1863. His politics were nationalist and he cultivated a passionate interest in the history, antiquity and folklore of Ireland. His collection of legends (told to him by his poorer rural patients, often in lieu of a fee), *Irish Popular Superstitions*, was published in 1852 and proved an important inspiration for the poet, Yeats. He published the first of his three-volume *Catalogue of the Antiquities in the Museum of the Royal Irish Academy* in 1857. He wrote accounts of the countryside, *The Beauties of the Boyne and Blackwater* (1849) and *Lough Corrib: Its Shore and Islands* (1867). Among his miscellaneous publications is *The Closing Years of Dean Swift's Life* (1849) in which he argues that Swift died not insane but ill. He married Jane Elgee in 1851, and became the father of three children: William (1852), Oscar (1854) and Isola (1857). He also fathered three illegitimate children before his marriage: Henry Wilson (1838), Emily (1847) and Mary (1849). Henry was raised and educated by William Wilde and then practised as a doctor in his father's surgery. The girls were adopted by William's elder brother, the Reverend Ralph Wilde, and they died tragically in 1871 when their ball gowns caught fire at a party.

WILDE, WILLIAM ROBERT KINGSBURY WILLS (1852–1899)   Wilde's brother, Willie, followed the same educational path as Oscar, at

Portora Royal School and at Trinity College Dublin. But he then went on to practise at the Irish bar for a time before moving with his mother to London in 1879 and making a meagre and desultory living as a journalist (he was dramatic critic for *Vanity Fair*, and wrote for the *Daily Telegraph*). In 1891 he married the wealthy American widow, Miriam Leslie, in New York but he was soon back in London and they divorced in 1893. He married Lily Lees in 1894. Willie suffered by comparison with his brilliant younger brother and developed an alcoholic, idle character. Never close to Oscar, the brothers were at best cordial.

YEATS, W. B. (1865–1939) Irish poet, playwright and critic. He compiled *A Book of Irish Verse* (1895) and chose to represent Wilde by 'Requiescat'; for his later anthology, *The Oxford Book of Modern Verse* (1936) he selected 39 stanzas from *The Ballad of Reading Gaol*.

Gazetteer

Wilde's life can be seen to fall into three phases, each associated with a different principal location: he grew up in Ireland, moved to England at the age of 20 where he spent his fruitful maturity and in 1897, after his release from Reading Gaol, he travelled restlessly on the Continent until his death at the age of 46 in Paris in 1900. The exceptions to this pattern are the years 1882 which Wilde spent constantly on the move in America and Canada delivering lectures at major centres, and 1895–97 when he was in prison, for most of that period in Reading Gaol.

IRELAND. In Dublin Wilde's family lived at 1 Merrion Square. At the age of nine Wilde was sent to Portora Royal School in Enniskillen where he boarded until he was 16. He then moved back to Dublin to study at Trinity College.

ENGLAND. Wilde left Ireland for good when he was 20, returning to Dublin only to give the occasional lecture during the 1880s. He moved first to Magdalen College, Oxford, and in 1879 he settled in London.

London

HOME. Wilde's first lodgings in London were at 13 Salisbury Street which he shared with his friend, the portraitist, Frank Miles, in 1879. Miles had been negotiating with the architect Edward Godwin to have a house specially designed for him. This project was eventually completed in 1880 when Miles and Wilde moved together into the new accommodation at 1 Tite Street in Chelsea, close to the River Thames. In 1885, after Wilde had married, he established his family home a little further down the same road, at 16 Tite Street (now 34, marked with a blue plaque). He and Constance named this house, internally redesigned and furnished by Godwin, the 'House Beautiful'. As his marriage degenerated from the late 1880s Wilde became an ever more infrequent resident here. It was at 16 Tite Street that the dismal scenes of auction took place on 24 April 1895 as part of the bankruptcy proceedings against Wilde. Every last shred of his belongings was sold off, from Thomas Carlyle's writing table which stood in his study, to the boxes of children's toys in the top floor nursery and the rabbit hutch in the back yard.

SOCIAL LIFE. Wilde often socialised in the restaurants, hotels and gentlemen's clubs of London. He was a member of The Albemarle Club, 37 Dover Street in Piccadilly; he stayed at the Albemarle Hotel; he was arrested at the Cadogan Hotel; he dined frequently and lavishly at the Café Royal; he stayed at the Savoy Hotel.

WORK. Wilde's plays were staged at two London theatres: The St James's Theatre and The Theatre Royal, Haymarket. The office of the publishers Cassell & Company which Wilde frequented as the editor of the *Woman's World* was at the Belle Sauvage Yard on Ludgate Hill near Fleet Street.

Provinces

During the 1890s Wilde lodged for significant spells in various parts of the south of England. He named several characters of the plays written during these intervals after places in the region of his accommodation.

He stayed in NORFOLK, at Grove Farm, Felbrigg, near Cromer, during August and September of 1892 to write *A Woman of No Import-ance* (character name: Lady Hunstanton). In November 1892 he moved to south DEVON, to rent Babbacombe Cliff near Torquay where he stayed until February 1893. Babbacombe Cliff was the name of the exquisitely appointed home of Lady Mount-Temple, a distant cousin of Constance Wilde. It was hung with drawings by Rossetti and had a window designed by Burne-Jones. From June to October 1893 Wilde rented The Cottage at Goring-on-Thames, planning *An Ideal Husband* (character name: Lord Goring). The following year he spent August and September on the south coast in Worthing (5 Esplanade) writing *The Importance of Being Earnest* (character name: Jack Worthing) before moving to the Hotel Metropole in Brighton for a brief and tormented stay with Lord Alfred Douglas.

The Continent

Wilde enjoyed travelling and before his exile from Britain in 1895 he was seasoned in European culture.

He toured Italy in 1875, visiting Rome again in 1877 on his way home from Greece. In early 1883 he stayed in Paris at the Hotel Voltaire and visited Paris again for his honeymoon in 1884. In late 1891 he returned to Paris to write *Salome*. He took a cure in Hom-burg, Germany, in July 1892. He visited Florence with Lord Alfred in May 1894 and together they went to Algiers in January 1895. In March 1895 they went Monte Carlo.

On release from prison in May 1897 Wilde settled in Berneval, near Dieppe, before reuniting with Lord Alfred in Rouen in August. In September and October 1897 they travelled in Italy, staying in Naples, Capri and Sicily. In 1898 Wilde returned to Paris, staying in a number of hotels before touring France more widely. In 1899 he travelled in the south of France and Switzerland before settling at the Hotel d'Alsace in Paris. In the spring of 1900 he visited Palermo and Rome, returning to Paris by June. He died in the Hotel d'Alsace.

Grave

Wilde was buried at the Bagneux Cemetery in Paris on 3 December 1900. The simple gravestone read:

> Oscar Wilde
> RIP Oct 16th 1854–Nov 30th 1900
> Job xxix Verbis meis addere nihil audebant et super illos stillebat eloquium meum.

(The translation of the verse from Job reads 'To my words they durst add nothing, and my speech dropped upon them.')

Wilde's remains were removed to the cemetery of Père Lachaise in Paris in 1909 when a commissioned monument by Jacob Epstein was erected in his memory. The stone underneath the angel gives the name OSCAR WILDE, and bears a verse from *The Ballad of Reading Gaol*:

> And alien tears will fill for him
> Pity's long-broken urn
> For his mourners will be outcast men,
> And outcasts always mourn.

Manuscripts

The manuscripts and typescripts of Wilde's work are widely dispersed. Some are in private collections, such as that owned by his grandson, Merlin Holland. Public collections are held across America: the New York Public Library, the Houghton Library at Harvard and the William Andrews Clark Library at the University of California in Los Angeles have significant holdings. In Britain some manuscripts and typescripts can be consulted at the British Library, where, for example, Acts III and IV of *The Importance of Being Earnest* are held in manuscript, as is the Licensing Copy of the play, under the title *Lady Lancing. A Serious Comedy for Trivial People.*

Jacob Epstein's sphinx monument for Oscar Wilde's tomb at the Père Lachaise Cemetery, Paris (photographed after restoration in 1993)
© Merlin Holland 1993

Short glossary of critical terms

AESTHETICISM   A movement in the arts which developed in Britain during the later nineteenth century as a protest against the prevailing industrial emphasis on 'the useful' or utilitarianism. Aestheticism places art in binary opposition to life and values art at the expense of life. It privileges form over content, style over sincerity or 'truth', and prizes ornament, colour, intensity and pleasurable effect. The primary exponent of aestheticism in England was Walter Pater, who learned from the French school of Gautier and Baudelaire. 'Art comes to you proposing frankly to give nothing but the highest quality to your moments as they pass, and simply for those moments' sake,' he wrote in the gospel of British aestheticism, the 'Conclusion' to *The Renaissance* in 1873.

DECADENCE   Closely related to aestheticism, decadence is a morally pejorative term which describes the apparent neglect of moral value which follows from a pleasure-seeking emphasis on beauty. Pater makes no distinction between art and life when he describes the perspective of contemplative disinterest which the aesthetic critic must adopt. 'The function of the aesthetic critic is to distinguish . . . the virtue by which a picture, a landscape, a fair personality in life or in a book, produces this special impression of beauty or pleasure,' he writes in the 'Preface' to *The Renaissance*.

MELODRAMA   In nineteenth-century Britain this was a popular, commercially lucrative and non-literary form of drama, accommodated by newly built theatres of enormous capacity. A simple plot, rich with suspense and danger to be overcome, in which good versus evil and morality is black and white, was narrated by spectacular performance and musical accompaniment. Dialogue was minimal, and the actors' gestures were bold and highly conventional to communicate clearly across the space of the large theatres.

NATURALISM   A movement in literature which responded to the methods and discoveries of early- to mid-nineteenth-century science. In keeping with scientific method, Naturalism sought to explain human behaviour, which is presented as supremely determined. Naturalism focuses principally on three factors which constrain the freedom of the individual: heredity, the environment and the pressure of the present moment. This asserted human kinship with the animal king-dom. As a literary movement it developed first in France, with Zola as a pioneer both in the novel and in drama. He adapted his natural-ist novel *Thérèse Raquin* (1868) for the stage in 1873 and argued with zeal that 'now is the time for a theatre of reality'. The Norwegian playwright, Henrik Ibsen, wrestled with the challenge set by the naturalist movement to re-establish the human capacity for moral choice and a meaningful understanding of good and evil which appears to be eradicated by a scientific interpretation of behaviour. In practical terms for the theatre, naturalism led to an emphasis on the significance of the stage set which provides a living picture of the determining environment in which the characters interact. It introduced characters from humble social backgrounds and altered the conventions of dialogue to permit a more accurate representa-tion of everyday speech – itself a revealing environmental signifier.

SYMBOLISM   There are as many definitions of symbolism as there are symbolists whose artistic manifestos proliferated in Paris throughout 1890. The symbolist poets, playwrights, musicians and artists were united by their rejection of naturalism and their idealistic belief in a realm of spiritual experience available to man that would free him of the sordid trappings of material life. Although this pure and universalising state of spiritual awareness could only be intimated by material things, pointers to a higher realm, the symbolist work of art was itself held to mirror this realm. Consequently, symbolism (its creation and appreciation) became 'a kind of religion, with all the duties and responsibilities of the sacred ritual'. This is how Arthur Symons described it in his book *The Symbolist Movement in Literature* (1899) which introduced French and Belgian practitioners to English readers. Wilde was particularly affected by the symbolist poetry of Mallarmé, the plays of Maeterlinck, the prose of Huysmans and the paintings of Moreau.

WELL-MADE PLAY   A formulaic type of play, defined by its structure. The first major exponents of the form were the French playwrights Eugène Scribe (1791–1861) and his disciple Victorien Sardou (1831–1908). They each developed *la pièce bien faite* (from which the English term 'well-made play' derives) into a method of securing huge com-mercial success, and their plays were copied or translated across Europe and America. The well-made play has a four-part structure: exposition, complication, climax and dénouement. The 'climax', or *scène à faire* was the scene which contained heightened dramatic conflict and confusion – and some members of the audience would choose to arrive in the theatre only in time to see this one scene. A number of stock character types are conventionally deployed in the well-made play. These include the *raisonneur*, usually a respectable professional man such as a doctor, lawyer or clergyman, whose function it is to restore harmony and re-establish the social *status quo* at the end of the play. Another important character type is the 'confidant', in whom the central character can confide and so reveal necessary information to the audience.

Further reading

Editions of Wilde's work

The Oxford University Press Collected Wilde is in preparation, but until its publication readers must choose between two now rather old Collected Editions of his work, or individual works and anthologies as follows:

Oscar Wilde. The Collected Edition, edited by Robert Ross in 1908, is still the most comprehensive edition of Wilde's work in uniform format. But it is not annotated and in terms of modern scholarship it contains inaccuracies which in part reflect Ross's sensitivity towards Wilde's surviving friends and family. Vyvyan Holland's edition of his father's *Complete Works* was published by Collins in 1948, with a third edition (by Merlin Holland) in 1994.

Anthologies

There are two useful paperback anthologies of his work:

Oscar Wilde, ed. Isobel Murray in the Oxford Authors series (Oxford: Oxford University Press, 1989) offers a carefully annotated selection of Wilde's work which represents the range of his achievement. It does not include 'The Soul of Man Under Socialism' nor *A Woman of No Importance* but it does print three of Wilde's *Poems in Prose* and his late aphorisms.

Oscar Wilde. Plays, Prose Writings and Poems, ed. Anthony Fothergill (London: Everyman, 1996) contains all four social comedies and 'The Soul of man Under Socialism', but excludes *The Picture of Dorian Gray*.

Poems

Selected Poems, ed. Malcolm Hicks (Manchester: Carcanet, 1992).

Plays

The New Mermaid editions of individual plays have excellent annotations:

Lady Windermere's Fan, ed. Ian Small (London: New Mermaids, 1993).
A Woman of No Importance, ed. Ian Small (London: New Mermaids, 1993).
An Ideal Husband, ed. Russell Jackson (London: New Mermaids, 1993).
The Importance of Being Earnest, ed. Russell Jackson (London: New Mermaids, 1980).
The Importance of Being Earnest. The First Production, ed. Joseph Donohue with Ruth Berggren (Gerrards Cross: Colin Smythe, 1995) prints the text of the 1895 production, with rich illustrations and encyclopedic notes.

For a scholarly edition of the early play, *Vera*, students should consult *Oscar Wilde's 'Vera; or, The Nihilist'*, ed. Frances Miriam Reed (Lewiston: Edwin Mellen Press, 1989).

Paperback anthologies of his plays include *The Importance of Being Earnest and Other Plays*, ed. Peter Raby (Oxford: Oxford University Press, 1995) in the World's Classics series.

Prose

The Picture of Dorian Gray, ed. Isobel Murray (Oxford: Oxford University Press, 1974).
The Picture of Dorian Gray, ed. Donald Lawler (Norton Critical Edition, 1988).
Complete Shorter Fiction, ed. Isobel Murray (Oxford: Oxford University Press, 1979).
Complete Short Fiction, ed. Ian Small (Penguin, 1994).

Journalism and Critical Essays

The Artist as Critic: Critical Writings of Oscar Wilde, ed. Richard Ellmann (New York: Random House, 1969) provides a comprehensive and usefully annotated anthology of Wilde's journalism, together with the critical essays from *Intentions*.

Aristotle at Afternoon Tea. The Rare Oscar Wilde (London; Fourth Estate, 1991), edited and introduced by John Wyse Jackson, collects Wilde's journalism from the *Pall Mall Gazette* and elsewhere. It includes his 'Literary and Other Notes' from the *Woman's World*.

Letters

Rupert Hart-Davis' edition, *The Letters of Oscar Wilde* (London; Rupert Hart-Davis Ltd., 1962) is a monumental collection, richly annotated. It contains the first uncensored printing of 'De Profundis', Wilde's

1897 letter to Lord Alfred Douglas from Reading Gaol. *More Letters of Oscar Wilde*, ed. Rupert Hart-Davis (London: John Murray, 1985) helps to complete the picture.

Biographies

Richard Ellmann's *Oscar Wilde* (London: Hamish Hamilton, 1987) is an indispensable and extraordinarily detailed account of Wilde's life. It is, however, coloured by Ellmann's view of Wilde's character and his fate. Wilde is presented as the tragic hero of his own drama whose fatal flaw was his homosexual infatuation with Lord Alfred Douglas. *Oscar Wilde: A Biography* (London: Eyre Methuen, 1976) by H. Montgomery Hyde offers an alternative, if less detailed, reading. Hyde also edited documents of cross-examination relating to *The Trials of Oscar Wilde* (New York: Dover, 1973). Jonathan Goodman's *The Oscar Wilde File* (London: Allison & Busby, 1988) updates this with a collection of documents from the newspaper reception of Wilde's trials. E. H. Mikhail has edited two volumes of accounts by Wilde's friends and acquaintances about their encounters with him: *Oscar Wilde: Interviews and Recollections* (London: Macmillan, 1979). A pleasing pictorial biography is given by Juliet Gardner's *Oscar Wilde. A Life in Letters, Writings and Wit* (London: Collins & Brown, 1995). Wilde's son, Vyvyan Holland, published a biographical account of his father, *Son of Oscar Wilde* (London: R. Hart-Davis, 1954). *An Oscar Wilde Chronology* by Norman Page (London: Macmillan, 1991) offers detailed information in tabular form. A biography of Constance Wilde by Anne Clark Amor, *Mrs Oscar Wilde. A Woman of Some Importance* (London: Sidgwick & Jackson, 1983) describes the domestic context of Wilde's life, while *Mother of Oscar Wilde. The Life of Jane Francesca Wilde* by Joy Melville (London: John Murray, 1994) extends our knowledge of Wilde's family life. *The Importance of Being Irish*, by Davis Coakley, with Foreword by Merlin Holland (Dublin: Town House, 1994) describes the Irish context of Wilde's family and life.

Tomb

Michael Pennington, *An Angel for a Martyr: Jacob Epstein's Tomb for Oscar Wilde* (London: Whiteknights Press, 1987) tells the mysterious story of how money for Wilde's monument was anonymously donated, and of Epstein's tribulations in the creation of his sculpture.

Bibliography

Stuart Mason [C. S. Millard], *Bibliography of Oscar Wilde* (London: T. Werner Laurie, 1914; rpt. 1967) gives a comprehensive account of Wilde's publications, and prints many facsimile illustrations and book designs.

General Critical Studies

Karl Beckson, *Oscar Wilde. The Critical Heritage* (London: Routledge & Kegan Paul, 1970). An indispensable collection of reviews which Wilde's works received on first appearance, and a series of articles about his fluctuating posthumous reputation.

Reginia Gagnier, *Idylls of the Marketplace: Oscar Wilde and the Victorian Public* (London: Scolar, 1987). An immensely scholarly study which places Wilde's work in the commercial and artistic culture of the late Victorian period.

Regina Gagnier, ed. *Critical Essays on Oscar Wilde* (New York: G. K. Hall, 1991). An anthology of recent critical responses.

Christopher Nassaar, *Into The Demon Universe: A Literary Exploration of Oscar Wilde* (New Haven: Yale University Press, 1974). An incisive analysis of the range of Wilde's work, from the fairy tales to *The Ballad of Reading Gaol*.

Peter Raby, *Oscar Wilde* (Cambridge: Cambridge University Press, 1988). An informative guide to Wilde's work, emphasising the achievement of the drama.

C. George Sandulescu, ed. *Rediscovering Oscar Wilde* (Gerrards Cross, Colin Smythe, 1994) contains the papers given at a conference held on Wilde in Monaco in May 1993, and covers a broad range of aspects of his work.

Sexuality

Jonathan Dollimore, *Sexual Dissidence: Augustine to Wilde, Freud to Foucault* (Oxford: Clarendon Press, 1991); Alan Sinfield, *The Wilde Century. Effeminacy, Oscar Wilde and the Queer Moment* (London: Cassell, 1994); Camille Paglia devotes two chapters to Wilde in *Sexual Personae: Art and Decadence from Nefertiti to Emily Dickinson* (London: Yale University Press, 1990)

Theatre

Harold Bloom, ed. *The Importance of Being Earnest. Modern Critical Interpretations* (New York: Chelsea House Publishers, 1988). A useful anthology of key articles.

Reference section

Sos Eltis, *Revising Wilde. Society and Subversion in the Plays of Oscar Wilde* (Oxford: Clarendon Press, 1996). An examination of the evolution of the plays from their multiform manuscript states to performance scripts, emphasising both Wilde's indebtedness to others and his innovative political vision.

Joel H. Kaplan and Sheila Stowell, *Theatre and Fashion. Oscar Wilde to the Suffragettes* (Cambridge: Cambridge University Press, 1994). The first chapter gives a fascinating account of the reciprocal relationship between costume on and off stage for the first productions of Wilde's plays.

Margery Morgan, *File on Wilde* (London: Methuen, 1990) lists performance details of the plays and quotes from newspaper reviews.

Kerry Powell, *Oscar Wilde and the Theatre of the 1890s* (Cambridge: Cambridge University Press, 1990) situates the plays in the context of late Victorian theatre, showing how Wilde borrowed extensively from the popular successes of the day while forging original twists to old tales.

William Tydeman and Steven Price, *Wilde. Salome. Plays in Production* (Cambridge: Cambridge University Press, 1996) offers an international performance history of *Salome*.

Katharine Worth, *Oscar Wilde* (London: Macmillan, 1983): a clear account of the plays which pays special attention to performance dynamics and Victorian culture.

The periodical *Modern Drama* dedicated Volume 37.1 (1994), ed. Joel Kaplan, to essays on Wilde's theatre, and is an indispensable resource of recent, wide-ranging investigation.

Nineteenth-century theatre

Michael R. Booth, *Theatre in the Victorian Age* (Cambridge: Cambridge University press, 1991).

Frantisek Deak, *Symbolist Theatre. The Formation of an Avant-Garde* (Baltimore and London; Johns Hopkins University Press, 1993). Helpful background for *Salome*, this gives an account of the development of symbolist theatre, particularly through the experimental work of small French theatres in the 1880s and 1890s.

Anthony Jenkins, *The Making of Victorian Drama* (Cambridge: Cambridge University Press, 1991).

242

George Taylor, *Players and Performance in the Victorian Theatre* (Manchester: Manchester University Press, 1989).

Nineteenth-century culture

Linda Dowling, *Hellenism and Homosexuality in Victorian Oxford* (Ithaca and London: Cornell University Press, 1994).

Sally Ledger and Scott McCracken, eds *Cultural Politics at the Fin de Siècle* (Cambridge: Cambridge University Press, 1995).

John Stokes, *Resistible Theatres* (London: Paul Elek, 1972); *In The Nineties* (London: Harvester Wheatsheaf, 1989); *Oscar Wilde. Myths, Miracles, and Imitations* (Cambridge: Cambridge University Press, 1996). These offer fascinating insight into the political, artistic and cultural context in which Wilde worked.

Index

Women Crossing Boundaries